PLATO GOES TO CHINA

Plato Goes to China

THE GREEK CLASSICS AND
CHINESE NATIONALISM

SHADI BARTSCH

PRINCETON UNIVERSITY PRESS
PRINCETON & OXFORD

Published by Princeton University Press
41 William Street, Princeton, New Jersey 08540
99 Banbury Road, Oxford OX2 6JX

press.princeton.edu

ISBN 9780691229591
ISBN (e-book) 9780691229614

British Library Cataloging-in-Publication Data is available

Editorial: Rob Tempio and Chloe Coy
Production Editorial: Mark Bellis
Jacket Design: Karl Spurzem
Production: Erin Suydam
Publicity: Alyssa Sanford and Carmen Jimenez
Copyeditor: Michelle Garceau Hawkins

Jacket images from top to bottom: Bust of Xi Jinping by GeeGuit /
TurboSquid. Classic statue of Plato by vangelis aragiannis / Shutterstock
images. Socrates, marble, first century, Eric Gaba / Wikimedia Commons.
Statue of Confucius at Confucian Temple in Shanghai, Phillip Lange /
Shutterstock images.

This book has been composed in Arno

Printed on acid-free paper. ∞

Printed in the United States of America

10 9 8 7 6 5 4 3 2 1

For my mother, Lila Sepehri Bartsch

Isfahan, Iran 1939–Reston, Virginia 2021

πολλῶν δ᾽ ἀνθρώπων ἴδεν ἄστεα καὶ νόον ἔγνω

she saw the cities of many and knew their minds

CONTENTS

PREFACE

THIS BOOK REPRESENTS a revision and expansion of the four Martin Lectures I delivered at Oberlin College in 2018. Long before that, however, I had had the idea of trying to see the texts of my field—the Greek and Latin texts of classical antiquity— from a perspective outside, not inside, the main cultures of Western Europe and the United States. The impetus for the study was to learn in what ways the Chinese and their culture are *different* readers of these foundational texts that lie behind western concepts of individuals, citizens, politics, rationality, and even morality. Because these norms were shaped in part by the ideals of classical antiquity (especially via its impact on the Renaissance and the Enlightenment), they had always made "made sense" to me as categories for thought, even when I disagreed with their contents. I wanted to break out of this hall of mirrors, to see how the categories and assumptions of this tradition were *not* universal. What would an entirely different civilization with its own traditions—namely, China—make of the Greek classics?

Immediately, I ran into my first problem: what the Chinese wrote about western antiquity, they largely wrote (at least in those days, about a decade ago) in Chinese. The prolegomenon to the project was therefore learning Mandarin, a language I found incredibly difficult despite my experience with Indo-European languages. On top of that challenge, at the time I started the project, the Mandarin words for figures like Socrates had not yet fully crystallized into one particular set of characters (*hanzi*), making research still more difficult. Moreover, my period of investigation (roughly 1890 to 2020) contained a dazzling array of major Chinese thinkers about the classical tradition whose opinions not only changed with their particular times, but sometimes even within a lifetime. I had taken on a Herculean task that in no way would I be able to fully complete.[1]

All the same, several amazing findings awaited me. The first was just how important the Greek classics have been in China, where they are often read as directly relevant to the Chinese politics, government, culture, and ethics of the present day. The second was that many Chinese thinkers have relied on these ancient texts to support broad generalizations about an imaginary "West." The last revelation was that from 1989 onwards (after the "incident" at Tiananmen Square), a conceptual revolution took place among a group of Chinese intellectuals, public thinkers, and even government officials as to how they read these classical texts. In other words, there was a before and an after to the study I had undertaken, not just a series of minor alterations. This about-face in reception (it did not include the dissidents in exile and mainland scholars not interested in political statements) was remarkably decisive in that its core mission—the application of these texts to support Chinese socialist and Confucian ideals—has been going on in much the same vein over the past thirty years. Let me be clear: I am not *criticizing* what some westerners might see as an "appropriation" of Greek political and philosophical thought, but rather, contemplating, sometimes with surprise, the various Chinese readings of antiquity I have come across in doing research for this book. A critique is not the right response: we must understand that new (even global, if you will) interpretations of old texts are embedded in cultures and locales that see ideas and texts differently from the original audience (which itself was never monolithic). This means that my investigation into the transformation of parts of classical antiquity, "does not ask primarily whether a given reference to a *reference culture* is correct or incorrect" (as the new field of "transformation theory" carefully articulates).[2] The point is, what *is* the reading?[3] And what can we learn from it about its readers, and about ourselves too?

A few comments about my procedures in the face of the mountains of information may be helpful. First, this study of Chinese responses to classical Greek thought, while it dips into the granular, is broad in scope. I do not cite readings produced by "institutional Greco-Roman classicists" at Chinese universities because their engagement is mostly with other classical scholars outside China and with the extant body of critical literature on classical antiquity.[4] The Chinese scholars I do investigate promote public and ideological responses to classical texts and are widely influential and well represented in the public arena. Second, I have tried to make sure my claims are representative of a broad readership by paying attention to citation indices on Chinese databases, by reading many different kinds of publications, and by looking to blog sites and social media as well. Finally, while I am sensitive to the difficulty of comparisons between vastly different cultures, I do not attempt to add to the discussion about the inadequacy of the binary categories "West" and "East" to stand for the complicated nexus of countries and cultures that is the world today.[5] Still, since I will be using these nouns around the specific topic of China and western antiquity, I hope that the reader will tolerate recourse to this terminology as the simplest way to refer to my topic.[6] As a small nod to the problem, I do not capitalize west and east.

In seeking to write a book that led me far outside my usual subject matter (it remains to be seen if I've done so à la Icarus), I have leaned on many scholars. Mentioning their names here is small recompense for their help. First, profound thanks to my amiable colleague Haun Saussy, who has answered many, many queries and always with a smile. I am grateful to the great Sir G.E.R. Lloyd for his scholarship and support. He has written many a recommendation on my behalf! Wentao Zhai at Harvard University reviewed the whole manuscript when it was done and saved me from many embarrassing mistakes. He also offered me a perspective well-informed in both Chinese and American culture. My gratitude to many other interlocutors, including Nicholas Koss, Yiqun Zhou, Zhang Longxi, Huang Yang, Jinyu Liu, Weihua Leng, Jue Hou, Hansong Li, Kaicheng Fang, Neville Morley, Daniel A. Bell, Leopold Leeb, Wu Jiaxun, and John Kirby. I received indispensable assistance from my graduate student researcher, Jiayi Zhu, and much help from a pair of plucky and hard-working undergraduates: Connie Chen and Henry Zhao. I even had the good luck to encounter three high-school students who volunteered to work as research interns: Erik Wang, Tony Zhou, and Mido Sang. May they thrive!

I am glad to have had the help of Princeton University Press's internal reviewers, one of whom, James Hankins at Harvard University, offered great insight. I interviewed Gan Yang (one of the figures in this book) many years ago at the start of this project and I am grateful for his kindness at that time. The Martin Lectures at Oberlin College provided the chance to think through the book's final shape, and I thank the Classics Department there for their hospitality, as well as my audience members on those occasions—many of them Chinese—for their thoughtful and challenging questions. I also thank the History and Theory workshop at Oslo, the commentators on Academia

.edu, and academic audiences at the University of Chicago, Harvard University, and the University of Chicago Center in Beijing. Finally, many thanks to my efficient and hard-working copyeditor, Michelle Hawkins. This was no easy manuscript to deal with.

Let me also voice a few notes of humility. This little book, I hope, merely opens the door to different studies of the interpretation of western antiquity in China. It has had to be narrow in scope: I do not consider ancient *literary* works, such as Greek drama and other forms of poetry. Nor would I claim there's a single point of view, or one standard interpretive technique, with which Chinese readers, then or now, approach the western classics—though I do claim there are trends. In the end, there are different sorts of interpreters of these texts, but the scholars who are most relevant to this project publish in newspapers, speak on television, debate each other publicly, and create an audience and a following. As I've noted, a few of them have flip-flopped from their views in the 1980s to new pro-government perspectives, transmitting these opinions via their changed interpretations of the classics. For all these reasons, both the academics and their writings are a fascinating object of study.[7] As Fredrik Fällman puts it, the topics that are "discussed in Chinese *academia* reflect the state and the trends of the country as much as reports on economy and politics."[8]

In closing, although I spent much of my childhood in Asia, I have also attended European schools and American universities, and I know that I am largely a creature of the latter intellectual and cultural traditions. Despite my ten years studying Mandarin (including at two universities in Beijing and Taiwan), my many visits to different parts of China, and my immersion in the Chinese twentieth century, I will never be culturally Chinese or understand the myriad ways in which their complex present is informed by their equally complex past.[9] This book is an effort by a British-American classicist who grew up outside the United States to see through the eyes of yet another culture. Let me apologize in advance: I will make mistakes; I will over-emphasize some things and underemphasize others; I will offer incorrect assumptions; I will end up generalizing when I should not do so; and, undoubtedly, I will cite a webpage that has since ceased to exit. Pitfalls await and I have already irked some of the scholars I write about.[10]

Earlier versions of Chapters 3 and 4 have appeared in previous articles. I thank the University of Chicago Press and Wiley-Blackwell for permission to use revised versions of that material. Very often, I found access to Chinese articles to be easier online, where they were often reproduced, but without page numbers. Finally, unless otherwise indicated, all translations from Mandarin are ineluctably mine.

Shadi Bartsch
Chicago, November 2021

EDITIONS AND TRANSLATIONS

Confucius, *Analects*

The Analects of Confucius 論語. Translated by A. Charles Muller. Available at http://www.acmuller.net/con-dao/analects.html.

Plato, *Republic*

Plato's Republic. (1992). Translated by G.M.A. Grube, revised by C.D.C. Reeve. Indianapolis, IN: Hackett Publishing Company.

Aristotle, *Politics*

Politica (1941). In *The Basic Works of Aristotle.* Edited by Richard McKeon, translated by Benjamin Jowett, 1127–1316. New York, NY: Random House.

Thucydides, *The Peloponnesian War*

Strassler, Robert B., ed., *The Landmark Thucydides.* (1996). Translated by Richard Crawley. New York, NY: Simon and Schuster.

PLATO GOES TO CHINA

The Ancient Greeks in Modern China

All under heaven there is no place but the King's land; and within the borders of all the land, there is nobody but the King's subject.

—BEISHAN, THE *SHI-JING*[1]

I. Why the Ancient Greeks?

There are, of course, no ancient Greeks in modern China—nor anywhere else these days. But the ancient Greeks live on in China through their works. Over the past century, the philosophical and political texts of western antiquity, especially those of classical Athens, have sparked the interest of Chinese intellectuals, journalists, reformers, and nationalists. Given that China was closed to the West for most of the Ming and Qing dynasties, this interest is barely a hundred and fifty years old. It was not until the second half of the nineteenth century that Chinese reformers and intellectuals started to turn to western texts on political theory and philosophy to help them reimagine future possibilities for a Chinese nation. And, as this book illustrates, they found it appropriate to turn, not only to modern texts, but also to works from western antiquity—works by figures such as Plato, Aristotle, Thucydides, and, to a lesser extent, the Romans Cicero and Vergil. These age-old thinkers took their place among Kant, Rawls, Montesquieu, Rousseau, and others.[2]

The Chinese turn to western texts for social and political guidance and inspiration first occurred during the years of crisis and revolution leading up to and following the fall of the Qing dynasty in 1911. More recently, there has been a second wave, one that coincides with the surge in Chinese confidence and nationalism.[3] But these two "turns" could not be more different. In the last decades of the Qing dynasty and the early days of the short-lived new republic, the classics of western antiquity were considered relevant to the scientific and political development of China out of a system much like serfdom. Articles by prominent intellectuals such as Liang Qichao helped to disseminate the political ideas of Greek antiquity that grounded the challenge to the dynasty (Confucius, himself an ancient wise man, was generally criticized as an abettor of the hierarchical dynastic system). Public reformers even believed that the content of these texts, and the traditions that had developed from them, contributed to the west's enviable scientific trajectory, a notion widely explored in journal essays and newspaper articles.[4]

In the China of today, there has been a sea-change. Once again, the western classics are a topic of conversation and debate, but the outlook is different. On the one hand, an academic field of western classics exists and has found institutional representation in many major universities, even if specific departments of western classics are still rare. This new development is thanks to the work of scholars who have worked hard to include the topic in undergraduate education.[5] On the other hand, in particular contexts classical texts have been galvanized into supporting ideas that uphold China's extant government—a fact partially made possible by their inclusion in the nationalistic topic of "studies in Chinese civilization" (国学 *guoxue*). Used in this way, these texts meet two receptions that produce the same result, criticism of the west and support for China. Either they are excoriated for the *bad* values they represent, in which case the west is seen as having inherited precisely those values; or they are praised for the *good* values they represent, in which case they are shown to be in harmony with contemporary (and also ancient) Chinese political and ethical theory. Socrates may be claimed to be a copy of Confucius; Aristotle may be read as a slave-monger; Thucydides was wise, and so was Plato. Originally considered relevant to China's problems of modernization, the western classics are now invoked in discussions that are deeply critical of the United States and Europe.

These classical western texts, and those of China's own classical tradition, have become newly important as China and the United States jostle for the position of moral superiority—a struggle in which they can claim to represent "harmony" or "democracy," to criticize each other for human rights abuses and racism, or to point mutually to past atrocities. Part of this situation is normal enough: nationalists will often look to their own intellectual (and ethical) traditions to ground moral claims, especially in China, where a nearly unbroken tradition of Confucian philosophy is very much alive in the present day. But as the interest in the western classics shows, China is now in the unusual position of also turning to *other* intellectual traditions to ground its political ideology, uniting multiple traditions into a single pro-Chinese government argument reproduced by intellectuals, public thinkers, bloggers, and journalists alike. This is striking. Imagine if texts from Chinese classics became a topic of public debate in the United States because they were deemed relevant to the government, and the *Book of Rites* helped to inform the American political scene.[6] Imagine if the *Book of Poetry* (the Democrats claimed) endorsed the Democrats! No one would care. So, the Chinese development is all the more curious because, in the western culture at whose origin these classics (partly) lie, there is a growing sense that the works of classical antiquity have little to say and may not even deserve a place in the educational system. As universities in the United States are closing down their classics departments—judging them useless, the province of the elite, or worse still, purveyors of imperialism—the Chinese are reading about Plato in Party editorials.[7]

Why would the Chinese privilege the texts of a foreign antiquity to cast light upon their own present? The reasons are embedded in Chinese culture as well as in the changing circumstances of the country's political situation. For one, the Chinese deeply respect their own classics. The texts of the Confucian traditions (and, to a lesser extent, the Daoist and Buddhist traditions) have always shaped Chinese culture and thought.[8] Although Confucius and his teachings were denounced and suppressed by Mao after his rise to power in 1949, that era is over. With the help of the government, different manifestations of Confucian traditions have rebounded as influential forces in contemporary Chinese society. Some modern thinkers (the "Neo-Confucians," the New Confucians, and the "political Confucians") are even suggesting that only a return to Confucian values will rescue the modern Chinese state from its current malaise as it floats somewhere between socialism with Chinese characteristics, a major force among market economies, and a political player on the world stage whose main rival is felt to be the United States.

Today in China, it is normal for ancient Chinese philosophy to be cited in nationalist rhetoric, and at the highest levels.[9] Confucius's legacy has been deemed so important that President Xi Jinping regularly quotes him in speeches. In 2015, 135 of Xi's quotations from classical Chinese philosophy were even published in a book titled *Xi Jinping's Classical Allusions* (习近平用典 *Xi Jinping Yong Dian*) by the main Communist Party newspaper, *The People's Daily* (人民日报 *Renmin Ribao*).[10] Most of Xi's quotes come from such Confucian classics as the *Analects* of Confucius, *The Book of Rites* (*Li Ji*), Mencius, Xunzi, and *The Book of History* (*Shujing*), and they often invoke moral exhortations or examples of a benign monarch governing the country.[11] For example, one citation Xi included from the *Analects* reads, "When a prince's personal conduct is correct, his government is effective without the issuing of orders. If his personal conduct is not correct, he may issue orders, but they will not be followed."[12] Presumably, this is meant to reassure the Chinese that however much power Xi may hold, the "prince's" authority is fundamentally moral, not authoritarian.[13]

In the west, I think it may be said that politicians do not hold up classical antiquity as a badge of national pride or urge its various ethical teachings on the public. Certainly, in the city where I live, Chicago, I have never heard the mayor urge us to contemplate the virtues of Seneca's *On Anger*. If the western nations do have Greek and Roman philosophy lurking deep in their political and ethical marrow, it's not the topic of much conversation in politics. Antiquity had its brief moment of glory at the birth of the United States, during the colonists' struggle for independence. At that time the Founding Fathers looked to ancient Greece and Rome for both guidance and warnings; James Madison famously eschewed the model of Athenian direct democracy and was wary of "the mob" because he viewed it as too easily swayed by passion, a phenomenon antithetical to rational leadership.[14]

In contrast, Chinese interest in western antiquity is comparatively widespread. Looking to the continued vitality of ancient thought in their own culture, Chinese scholars have assumed, and continue to assume, that the study of western antiquity is a valuable source of information about the contemporary west. Some take that assumption further and view modern westerners as the direct product of Greco-Roman antiquity. On these grounds, studying the ancients would be a way to understand what is at the core of the west via the west's genealogical tie to some ur-essence, as it were. This view seems more or less pervasive: even at the high school level, Chinese textbooks proclaim that that western civilization descended straight from the glory days of ancient Athens.[15] The standard history textbook I consulted, appropriately named *Normal High School Curriculum Standardized Experimental Textbook* (普通高中课程标准实验教科书 *Putong gaozhong kecheng biaozhun shiyan jiaokeshu*), identifies ancient Athens as the source of modern western democracy. It's not a new phenomenon, but a sentiment as old as the writings of several reformers at the end of the Qing period.[16] Liang Qichao (1873–1929) stressed the point in his 1902 article "On Ancient Greek Scholarship" (论希腊古代学术 *Lun Xila Gudai Xueshu*), where he identified ancient Greece (especially Athens) as the source of contemporary western civilization. In short, this belief that the west is as fundamentally shaped by its classical antiquity as the Chinese are by theirs has guided Chinese engagement with the west from the end of the nineteenth century to the present day.

The value of Greco-Roman antiquity is not only intellectual and cultural, but also political. For some Chinese thinkers, learning about antiquity has become a project aimed at outdoing the west on its own terms, the "key" to absorbing and overcoming the strengths of the west.[17] The editorial statement of *The Chinese Journal of Classical Studies* (古典研究 *Gudian Yanjiu*) lays this out clearly. Founded in 2010 by Liu Xiaofeng, a leading public thinker, professor at Renmin University, and conservative who has written on Christianity, Leo Strauss, and Plato, and much more, the journal first notes that its mission is to "interpret the perennial classics of Chinese, western, Hebrew and Arabic civilizations on the basis of concrete texts from a cross-cultural and interdisciplinary perspective."[18] It then proclaims its *raison d'être*—to use these classics to invest in China's future.

> Chinese civilization has a surefooted and temperate educational tradition. However, under the impact of the modern culture of western civilization, this tradition has already been shattered to pieces. For over 100 years, scholars of our country have faced the yet unfulfilled historical mission to command a profound understanding of western civilization and then to restore the spirit of China's traditional civilization . . . If we do not understand the classical civilization of the west, we will probably be unable to have a comprehensive and profound grasp of modern western civilization, and if we do not have a thorough understanding of the whole pattern of western civilization, we will also not be able to fully and deeply understand and grasp the spiritual situation of Chinese civilization and its future destiny.[19]

Here the ultimate reason for the study of ancient western texts (and, to some degree, Hebrew ones) is to benefit China itself: to give China a cutting edge and vision of her future by understanding the alien world that is the west.[20]

II. What's in It for the West?

Although I have explained why the Chinese might look to Greek antiquity, I have yet to suggest why the west might want to pay attention to the Chinese engagement with the west's "classical canon." Is there something to be learned by and for the west from looking at the Chinese engagement with classical antiquity—and with texts that many westerners themselves feel have little relevance to everyday life in modernity?[21] Apart from scholarly interest in the context of comparative reception studies, is there a point to observing Chinese thinkers reading Plato or Aristotle? My answer is an emphatic yes. For one, the west can now see the Chinese watching the west. I don't mean as a sort of espionage. On the contrary, looking at how Chinese scholars read the west's classics provides the west with an opportunity to see itself in another culture's mirror. We can see our axiomatic assumptions reflected back at us in a way that can make them newly strange: assumptions like philosophy is based upon rationally deductive principles; or that democracy is the best form of government; or that the category of the citizen is or should be a universal one; or that the independent Cartesian ego is the foundation of selfhood; and so forth. Many such assumptions are seen by the Chinese as not self-evident, but rather as coming straight from classical western culture. From our perspective, these categories can feel natural because only rarely have we paused to ask if there is something unenlighteningly circular about interpreting the texts of classical antiquity with normative assumptions that partly grew out of that very same classical antiquity. The encounter with China shows us that such values are not universal; they are merely ours (and not even consistently so). For this reason, a study of the Chinese reception of these texts has the capacity to enable us to understand our own assumptions.

But there is more, exploring the changing history of the Chinese reception of Plato, Aristotle, Thucydides, and others is a way of understanding what is happening inside China itself. The suppression of the democratic principles prized most by the west—which proved largely unsuccessful in Iraq and during the Arab Spring—bolstered the Chinese view that the attack on western values at Tiananmen Square was good policy in the end. Over the past three decades, the Chinese government has become quicker to assert the superiority of their own civilization over the west, particularly the superiority of the Confucian tradition to the western ("rationalist") tradition. As a result, the history of how the Chinese have been reading western texts offers a uniquely illuminating vantage point for observing China's transformation in its cultural and political self-confidence as it rises to the status of a competitor with the US on the world stage.

Turning to western texts to support Chinese claims of civilizational superiority requires a complicated balancing act on the part of the Chinese intellectuals. A central paradox which begs to be answered is: if western classics seem to support a political system more Chinese than western, why are we, the west as the heirs of that tradition, not closer to the Chinese ourselves? The Chinese explanation rests on a perceived turning point in the west since the Enlightenment. After that period of learning, (they say) the west fell away from classical values of virtue and civic responsibility. This is of course a trajectory that relies on broad brushstrokes and a certain disregard for the complexities of history and philosophy. Christianity, for example, is treated as playing a minimal role in shaping the modern west, while the eastern belief systems of Daoism and Buddhism are also shortchanged in order to back the superiority of the new Confucian-themed society of twenty-second-century socialist China.[22]

The Chinese scholars in this group pointedly disregard the Renaissance theory and practice of virtue ethics in politics, perhaps because it looks too similar to Confucian thought or, perhaps because it was not very successful.[23]

III. From "Master Li" to Chairman Xi

To recognize the magnitude of the shift the Chinese people experienced with the fall of the Qing, we must remind ourselves that, until the late nineteenth century, the Chinese elite believed themselves to represent not only the geographically central "Middle Kingdom," but also a culture superior to that of all other nations, in which they accordingly took little interest.[24] The so-called "Mandate of Heaven" ensured that the emperor held his position by divine *fiat*; wars and changes of dynasty simply meant that the Mandate had passed to a new emperor "of all the lands under heaven" (*tianxia*). This belief in China's cultural superiority crumpled over the second half of the nineteenth century, as the Chinese experienced military defeat at the hands of the British and French in the Opium Wars of 1839–42 and 1856–60 as well as the colonization of major coastal cities such as Shanghai and Hong Kong. Subsequent attempts at internal reform influenced by contact with the west contributed to the overthrow of the Qing dynasty in 1911—and a new void in the leadership of the country.

Crucially for us, the first decades after the fall of the Qing were rich in debate about what a post-dynastic China should look like. The overthrow of the Russian Empire in 1917 and the subsequent humiliation of China by the European powers who crafted the Versailles Treaty led many Chinese reformers and thinkers to look beyond China for new ideas about citizenship, government, and national development. The sense that the country could learn from the western powers was influential in producing the "May 4th Movement" of 1919, in which students and reformers called for democratic values, a commitment to science, and an end to the old patriarchal culture.[25] The reformers of the Qing dynasty at the turn of the twentieth century seized on western political theory for answers—going all the way back to Aristotle's *Politics*, which was cited for the argument that human beings were unfulfilled unless they were citizens of a state and political actors.[26] As mentioned previously, some thinkers even traced the triumph of democracy and science in the west—the reformers' twin desiderata—to causes as old as the culture of classical Athens.

However, the ascendance of the Chinese Communist Party (CCP) greatly changed this intellectual climate. In 1949, after decades of struggle between rival warlords, Mao and the CCP took power, and interest in classical political texts waned accordingly. It was not until the famous economic reforms set in motion by Deng Xiaoping in late 1978 (改革开放 *gaige kaifang* "reform and opening up"—and "it doesn't matter if the cat is black or white") that liberal democratic tendencies once again crept into the public domain and would-be reformers agitated for political reform and greater freedom of the press. The subsequent government clampdown once again influenced the reading of classics of political and philosophical antiquity. Yet the classics came back—with a difference. Those two great moments—the May 4th Movement and the current interest in western antiquity—are the topic of this book, along with an earlier encounter of two worlds during the Jesuit mission to China.

The chapters follow an arc in time from the mid-sixteenth century, when the Jesuits first brought classical texts to China, to the events of the tumultuous twentieth century, and on to the present day. Chapter 1, "Jesuits and Visionaries," revisits the

Jesuit mission to China (especially in the person of Matteo Ricci, or "Li Madou"), the May 4th Movement of the early twentieth century, and the years leading up to June 4, 1989. We start with the Jesuits because they so well illustrate how one might use classical texts to further one's own agenda—a context in which it's westerners who are cast as the appropriators of antiquity. The rest of the book explores approaches to the classics that reflect trends in contemporary China. Many of the scholars I discuss share a belief in the validity of "ancient values," both Confucian and Platonic, but feel disdain for the United States. Others take to task the political texts that have traditionally underpinned such basic ideas as citizenship, rule of law, democratic voting, and citizen government.

Chapter 2 addresses examples of reception that are hostile to Aristotle's *Politics* and Athenian democracy. Some authors recast the "free" Athenian citizen as a slave to his polis, while in other hands democracy is rebranded as a "superstition" (the Mandarin word is 迷信 *mixin*, roughly "confused faith.") For some, the *real* democracy is China. Tracing an example of pro-China interpretation, Chapter 3 examines the reception of a famous section of Plato's *Republic*: the picture of the "beautiful city" painted by Socrates (ironically? earnestly? allegorically?) for his interlocutors. This proposed city-state—Kallipolis— deeply disturbs modern scholars of Plato for its eugenic vision of an ideal society in which people are ranked in three castes.[27] To perpetrate this hierarchy, a "Noble Lie" is needed to explain it as a natural phenomenon traceable back to mother Earth herself. The Lie will be believed by generations that come after the philosophical mastermind that crafted it, both underpinning an ideology that largely blocks movement between classes and categorizing this society as "just." Chinese ideological reactions to Kallipolis are fascinating, not least because it's impossible to tell if writers who endorse the necessity of a Noble Lie in politics are actually engaging in an exposé of their government!

Chapter 4 focuses on another debate with roots in Plato and Aristotle: what role does rationality play in human thriving? The study of rationality as a comparative cultural phenomenon is a topic of serious scholarly debate in some contexts (the difficulty of defining the term "rationality" being part of the problem).[28] However, some Chinese intellectuals are simply manipulating the term as a means of showing the moral vacuum at the heart of the west. Western rationality, they say, promotes technology at the cost of ethics. It operates outside of, not within, any moral framework, and, as such, it is free to be entirely instrumental in its operation: the most efficient way of getting something done is the best way. This western "instrumental" rationality is often traced to Kant, but also back to Plato—after all, Plato, with his desire for a rational city ruled by the most rational men, is easily implicated here. Interestingly, the Chinese condemn the west using a western critique, taking much of their terminology and their perspective from the German socialist Max Weber. Following other European thinkers, some Chinese scholars are just about willing to claim that Plato caused the Holocaust.

Chapter 5 turns to the wild popularity (only just now abating) of the conservative political thinker Leo Strauss among Chinese thinkers and asks how and why this phenomenon came to be. Part of the answer has to do with Strauss's own views on the value of classical texts, which give these texts a political and philosophical importance essentially in aeternum (a very Chinese way of thinking about tradition) while denigrating the present moment in western civilization. Equally importantly, Strauss elevated the philosopher's role to a speaker of riddling truths critical of the status quo (hence making him politically relevant). Furthermore, he provided a model of how to interpret philosophical texts in support of one's own political and ethical beliefs. And finally, Strauss too was concerned about the limits of reason: as Leora Batnitzky puts it, Strauss was concerned with "the philosophical, theological, and political consequences of what he took to be modern philosophy's overinflated claims for the self-sufficiency of reason."[29] The statement of this problem, for Strauss, could be found in philosophers such as Plato, Maimonides, and Spinoza (as long as one searched for esoteric messages hidden from the general public).

Chapter 6 focuses on the florescence of Confucian-based nationalism in China over the past twenty years—a far cry from the disdain for Confucian texts in the earlier days of the CCP, when Mao condemned the old sage and his teachings. Confucianism now underpins the new nationalism by offering it an intellectual and ethical history; some public voices have gone so far as to link Confucianism to concerns about ecology and sustainability. Hu Jintao's stress on the Confucian value of harmony (*hexie*), now with Xi Jinping's added emphasis on "a harmonious society of the future," allows the government to lay claim to a new domestic and foreign policy deeply in contrast to western "aggression." Seeking to represent these Confucian values as universals, intellectuals turn to readings of Confucius that claim deep parallels to the themes of Plato's *Republic*, especially given that "harmony" and "justice" are collapsed into one concept. The theme of musical harmony and its relationship to the emotions also seems to offer a superficial parallel. Plato and Confucius, then, will lead us forward in a new (China-dominated) world order. But of the two, Confucius is still shown to be superior in his thought. In three recent conferences about Socrates and Confucius, the Chinese argued Confucian harmony improves on Socratic antagonism, and the latter's repudiation of tradition is singled out for criticism—and likewise, the modern west's "repudiation" of the hierarchical, supposedly merit-based *Kallipolis* that lies at the foundation of its own tradition of political thought. [30]

Given the potential value of classical texts in Chinese ideology and their service in the cause of Chinese nationalism, there is conflict in Chinese academic circles about what one *should* do with these texts. This battle pits together some of the loudest public intellectuals against essentially apolitical professors. [31] In a 2015 interview, ten foreign-trained Chinese classicists— including such senior figures as Huang Yang (Greek history, Fudan University), Nie Minli (Greek philosophy, Renmin University), and Liu Jinyu (Roman history, DePauw University)— made explicit their desire for the study of these classical texts to be formally institutionalized in university departments, with strict language training and the study of western historiography as well. [32] The Chinese classicists voiced a desire to collaborate and be in dialogue with contemporary western classicists. And they spoke also of their distance from the other, more prominent figures who have been open about their pro-Chinese agenda, such as Gan Yang and Liu Xiaofeng. [33] This latter group seeks to create a different sort of classical studies that (1) takes Chinese tradition into account alongside the western one, and (2) is directly relevant to contemporary Chinese politics. Gan and Liu are also the very visible leaders of the Chinese Comparative Classical Studies Association, *Zhongguo Bijiao Gudianxue Xuehui* (founded in 2009 by the collaborative effort of six universities), which has openly echoed the sentiment of the editorial pages of the journal *Gudian Yanjiu*—ultimately the study of the western classics must be for the greater good of China. [34]

As indicated earlier, the intention of this study is not to criticize the readings or appropriations (however we define that) of western classical texts by the subjects of this book.[35] Instead, my interest is in how ideologies shape readings (a point not without relevance for the debates now prevalent in the US about the value of the classics, and whether they have anything to say to anyone but a defunct elite). The texts that shaped much western philosophy and political thought can function as a mirror to the changing mood of China *and* the US on the global stage, past, present, and possibly future. One benefit of understanding this will be, hopefully, that we will be able to move on from the more facile political narratives and virtue-claims produced by thinkers and theorists in both countries.

1

Jesuits and Visionaries

We believe that only Mr. Science and Mr. Democracy can bring salvation from all the darkness in China, be it political, moral, intellectual, or spiritual.

—CHEN DUXIU 陈独秀

AS WE TRAIN our eyes on the vast complexity of modern China, we must pause at the brink of the late twentieth century to turn back to a period four hundred years earlier: the arrival of the Jesuit mission in China. Long before the "unequal treaties" that followed the Opium Wars of the nineteenth century, when China finally had to open up to trade with the west, an earlier band of determined, courageous, and perhaps foolhardy Jesuits from Portugal, Spain, and Italy had set sail for that unknown land. They brought with them the tenets of Catholicism, selected non-Christian texts, and some of the wonders of western science. Those who survived the voyage eventually settled in Macau, from where they worked to gain the Wanli Emperor's attention.[1] In 1601, Matteo Ricci, an Italian Jesuit from Rome, was finally invited to enter the Forbidden City in Beijing; the emperor wanted his input on astronomy and calendrical science.[2] By then, Ricci and the others had learned how to read classical Chinese and speak Mandarin. They had also learned that it was in their interest to dress like Confucian scholars rather than like lowly Buddhists, and had changed their self-presentation accordingly. At court, the Jesuits now had access to the elite circles of the court scholars. The priests engaged with Confucian philosophers in discussions in which they tried to advance their own perspective as Catholics. And they also sent news of China back to the west, such that one can speak of a small efflorescence of European interest in this strange reflection of their monarchies.[3]

In the long run, things did not go well for the poor Jesuits. With the turbulent dynastic change from Ming to Qing, the tide of imperial thought turned against them and many were exiled or killed, their plea to the pope unheard.[4] A few managed to quickly adapt to the new political system. According to one anecdote, the German Jesuit Johann Adam Schall von Bell (1591–1666) and others hung a placard on their home which read: "This is the residence of apolitical scholars who also know a lot about cannon making," a claim that is said to have saved Schall von Bell's life.[5] He was lucky in the longer run as well: gaining access to the newly installed Shunzhi Emperor, Schall von Bell became a trusted councilor and bureaucrat, contributing to the continuity of the Jesuit mission until his (not so lucky) death sentence in 1664. By that time, both in numbers and in spirit, the Jesuits—already at war within themselves—had come to the end of their influence in the Chinese court.[6]

I. Missionaries with Greek Characteristics

At the start of the Jesuit mission, the foreigners from afar quickly found out that it was the scientific texts and instruments they had brought with them that were greeted the most enthusiastically by the emperor and his court: treatises such as Euclid's *Elements*; a collection of ancient and modern scientific texts on hydraulics, cartography, the calendar, botany, and astronomy; as well as western clocks and musical instruments. Matteo Ricci (Li Madou), with his vast learning and linguist skills, soon adapted himself to the culture of Wanli's court, where he shared his knowledge, thereby winning favor for the Jesuit mission itself.[7] The scientific materials turned out to be a good backup for the Jesuits' proselytizing: such texts offered evidence that Europe was correct in its Christian worldview. How else could one explain the European mastery of astronomy, watch-making, mapping, and more? As the Jesuit Alvarez Semedo (1586–1658) put it, "[our convert Leo Li Zhizhao] was learning in tandem both the placement of the kingdoms of the world and the Laws of the Kingdom of Jesus Christ."[8] In 1605, the Jesuits even acquired some property on which they quickly built a church: the first religious, European-style building in China.

But the Jesuits faced a roadblock. The Chinese elite were not particularly interested in the tenets of Catholicism. The Chinese scholars considered themselves wiser than a bunch of barbarians, and were backed by centuries of tradition.[9] Slowly, the missionaries learned what they had to do. They had already become virtual Mandarins, putting on the garb of Confucian scholars (and not of lowly Buddhists) and learning Confucian teaching in order to engage the Chinese scholars at court in what the latter would consider intelligent conversation. Then, the Jesuits learned to borrow Confucian terminology and concepts to "translate" what they were saying into issues and categories that sounded familiar to the court. And of course, the Jesuits had to self-censor. Ricci at least understood that some of the basic doctrinal elements of Catholicism were likely to discourage conversion because they seemed too fantastical for their Chinese audience—for example, Jesus's virgin birth and his "low-class" death by crucifixion. So many Jesuits downplayed or omitted this part of the catechism.[10] Finally, the Jesuits learned they had to bend their own rules by allowing their converts to continue ritual practices such ancestor-worship, which the friars explained to the Vatican as a social and political activity rather than a religious observation.[11]

The Jesuits took an even further step that was striking in its boldness. Ricci, Alfonsus Vagnone, and Alessandro Vaglinano developed a method to make Christianity more palatable to the Confucians: they passed it through the sieve of the pre-Christian west, and specifically through Aristotle and the Stoic teachings of the Greek ex-slave Epictetus (c.50–c.135 CE). The Jesuits—well-trained themselves in how to use classical philosophy in Christian theology—saw that the non-monotheistic ethical systems common to the Greek philosophers were closer to Confucian tradition than Christianity and, therefore, more useful to the Jesuits' long-term purpose. They thus "transmitted" Greek philosophy to the Chinese while tacitly representing it as Christianity.[12] In the process, they carefully avoided parts of Stoic philosophy that were not Confucian, and also parts of Stoic philosophy that clashed with Christianity. Alien to the Confucians, the Stoic emphasis on the place of rationality in the will was not stressed; alien to the Christians, the Stoic absence of an afterlife dropped out of their teaching.[13] But, as Ricci saw, there were also real points of contact between Stoicism and Confucian thought—points which, if handled carefully, could suggest that the two traditions held some beliefs in common. Even if the story of a poor and humble son of God and the miracles he wrought had no parallels in Confucianism, teachings about self-control, benign providence, deceptive goods, and appropriate actions towards others were familiar to the Chinese court.[14] As Christofer Spalatin points out, "Following the model of Jesuit humanistic education of the Renaissance which used the pagan moral philosophy of Stoicism as a propaedeutic for Christianity, Ricci attempted to use the pagan moral philosophy of Confucianism as a preparation for the fullness of Christianity."[15]

Ricci proved himself remarkably proficient at presenting Stoicism as a sort of Christianity. He recognized that it was flexible enough to be poured into a Confucian mold while also sharing some of the moral (if not metaphysical) injunctions of Christianity. So Ricci literally adopted the teachings of Epictetus— particularly his *Handbook*, or *Encheiridion*—for Chinese use. If the Stoic's four books of philosophical discourses had already been adapted and used in Jesuit education, it would not have represented much of a stretch for Ricci to recycle Epictetus's basic teachings: the importance of understanding the difference between what was in our power (thought, impulse, belief) and what was not (riches, power, health); the recognition that emotions were based on false judgments; and the view that man, nature, and the (benevolent) universe were rational and co-extensive.[16] Epictetus encouraged benevolence to others and self-examination and self-critique for ourselves. He emphasized that people should look beyond external appearances of what was "good" and understand what their actual value really boiled down to (automatically liking a pretty girl was not a good response, while having a difficult experience offered a chance to build up your emotional resilience).

In 1605, Ricci published a moral handbook entitled "Twenty-Five Paragraphs" (二十五言, *Ershiwu Yan* that was a modified and shortened version of Epictetus's *Handbook*. It was probably his most popular work of "Christian doctrine," although Ricci acknowledged in the introduction that he "spoke well of virtue a little Stoically."[17] There was not much transparency about the place of these "pagan" contributions in his proselytizing.[18] Perhaps Ricci did not find it necessary: in the sixteenth century the Roman Stoic Seneca was still believed to have been a Christian convert and his letters to St. Paul genuine; so Stoics could well have been proto-Christians.[19] And as mentioned previously, a Jesuit education incorporated classical texts; Jesuits followed the doctrines of Saint Thomas in theology and those of Aristotle in logic, natural philosophy, ethics, and metaphysics.[20] In deciding on this "accommodation" to Confucianism, Ricci relied on his belief that Stoicism and Confucianism were similarly valuable ethical systems that also shared a connection in their mutual ignorance of Jesus Christ.[21] As Goodman and Grafton note, "The Jesuits in particular were probably Europe's leading specialists in forcing texts to send messages and serve purposes that their authors had never intended."[22] Ricci's "edits" did not mean to pull the wool over Chinese eyes; as one who had knowledge of Christ, Ricci was simply carrying out the necessary "interpretive operations" to render antiquity fit for both China and Christendom.

With an eye to accommodation, Ricci's "Twenty-Five Paragraphs" of course left out any Greco-Roman material that would be too jarring to either Christian or Confucian belief-systems. He did, however, add material that would appeal to his readers. He changed Epictetus's use of plural gods to a single God, altered the examples taken from Greek mythology to figures familiar in Chinese legend, and eliminated material that might have offended the Chinese, such as analogies to gladiatorial combats and explicit comments about sexual relationships.[23] As was done by Christian authors in the Middle Ages, and very likely by his own teachers at the Jesuit Collegio

Romano, Ricci changed all the ancient designations of the deity or deities used by Epictetus (Zeus, Apollo, Destiny, and so on) into the singular Christian term for God, whom he presented in his Chinese translation as *Tianzhu* (天主, *Lord of Heaven*). In section 13 of "Twenty-Five Paragraphs," Ricci even managed to insert the five basic Confucian values into his text: *Ren* (humanity), *Yi* (righteousness), *Li* (propriety), *Zhi* (wisdom), and *Xin* (fidelity). As Yu Liu remarks of this sleight of hand, "Ricci retained the basic meaning of Epictetus but put everything most deftly into the philosophical and cultural lingo of China. [For example,] while false piety was still about blaming divinity for the failure of the desire to get or avoid what was not in one's power to get or avoid, true piety became the exercise of the five cardinal virtues of Confucianism."[24] The Jesuits also delved into the writings of the Roman Stoic Seneca, several Jesuit texts even laying out a version of the ten commandments that derived from Seneca's views rather than the original![25]

How discerning Ricci was in appealing to Confucian beliefs can also be seen in his *The True Meaning of the Lord of Heaven* (天主实义, *Tianzhu Shiyi*) a dialogue in which a Confucian and a Christian talk about ethics and metaphysics, with both being critical of Buddhism and Daoism.[26] Ricci's Christian mouthpiece fuses aspects of Catholicism with the neo-Confucianism practiced at the time by pointing out, for example, that Christianity included the Confucian notions of righteousness (*yi*) and humanity (*ren*). The unpalatable is left out; although Ricci discussed the Immaculate Conception of Jesus, he carefully avoided speaking of the crucifixion. Most significantly, Ricci's Christian claims that the Chinese *already* had a Christian god of sorts. Ricci's learned Christian uses the Chinese term "Lord of Heaven," avoiding the more common Confucian usage

Shangdi 上帝, a sort of anthropomorphized heaven.[27] As Po-chia Hsia writes:

> Ricci aimed at demonstrating, usual natural reason and invoking Confucian textual authority, the existence of an omnipotent God, creator of heaven and earth, called the Lord of Heaven, *Tianzhu*, in the discourse of the Jesuits, but named God on High, *Shangdi*, or simply heaven, *Tian*, in the ancient [Chinese] Classics.[28]

More technically, Ricci's answer to the Confucian query as to who made God himself employed the Aristotelian principle of essence versus accident to argue for the existence of an unmoved mover. This harmonized with the neo-Confucian belief in a self-generated universe—a particularly rationalist and secular form of Confucianism represented by the writings of the neo-Confucian Zhu Xi (1130–1200). Fascinatingly, Ricci chose *Tianzhu* (literally, sky-god) because it was akin (via Japanese borrowing) to the Greek Zeus, the European sky-god, though it originally meant "master" in Chinese. Notwithstanding his equation of the two gods, the devout Ricci probably did not believe that the Confucians had an actual deity that correlated to the Christian one. Ricci was in the business, after all, of creating converts.[29] Ricci even claimed that the Chinese *intended* to be Christians, and that this would have happened if not for want of a compass. The tradition was that the Han emperor Mingdi dreamt of a flying golden deity and sent envoys to India who returned with the *Sutra in Forty-Two Sections*, introducing Buddhism to China. According to Ricci, however, the emperor originally had intended to send his emissaries to the Holy Land, but they lost their bearings and brought back the teachings of Buddha from India instead![30]

For his "adjustments"—in fact for his entire practice of accommodating his audience by merging theology with Aristotelian and Stoic philosophy and a soupçon of Confucianism—Ricci has been both praised and blamed in discussions of this mission.[31] David E. Mungello calls Ricci's policy "a brilliant insight which not only accorded with contemporary reality, but also melded with what little was known of high Chinese antiquity and appealed to the Chinese reverence of antiquity."[32] Another prominent scholar, Jacques Gernet, condemns the procedure as an act of knowing seduction.[33] The jury is divided. But if, as may be likely, few Chinese were actually convinced by Ricci's hybrid offerings but rather wished to show respect for his learning, Ricci's efforts may have been neither brilliant nor seductive, but merely in service of opportunities for friendship and respect. When his arguments did persuade, most converts saw them as minor variations on what the Confucians already knew.[34]

Epictetus did not hog the Christians' pedagogy; Aristotle too played a role, both because the Jesuits had read Thomas Aquinas's Aristotle-influenced *Summa Theologia*, and because Aristotle appeared in his own right in a work of the Jesuit Julius Aleni (1582–1649) entitled, *Introduction of Western Culture and Education* (西学凡 *Xixue Fan*). In this work, Aristotle—alongside Confucius—is represented as one of the ancient sages and great teachers of philosophy—he taught Alexander the Great himself![35] In classical Mandarin, the Jesuits transliterated Aristotle with the characters *Yalisiduo* (亞理斯多), which may have been chosen because they convey something like "a great principle for Asia," or, more likely (since the Chinese had not accepted yet the Jesuit name for Asia) simply meant "vast reasoning."[36] In a geographical work in which he identified Greece as the origin of western culture, Aleni described Aristotle as a famous scholar of antiquity who studied matter and principles, but in this text his name is transliterated differently as 亞利斯多 (roughly, *great benefit*).[37] Either way, Aristotle's name was carefully chosen to show his intrinsic value to the Chinese.

Aristotle's political thought, however, was of little use to the missionaries, since citizens and democracies did not map well onto Chinese dynastic traditions, nor onto the idea that the emperor ruled "by the mandate of heaven." All we can say of his influence here is that the Rev. P. Alphonsus Vagnone (1566–1640) composed two volumes on western political theory in which Aristotle made a brief appearance (*Xixue Zhiping* 西学治平). Like Aleni, however, Vagnone tended to stress the elements of Aristotle's thought that would appear familiar to Chinese Confucians.[38] He emphasized, for example, the importance of virtuous kings, claiming that monarchy was formed to protect "the better sort of people against the multitude" and "virtuous kings should administer their countries' laws and should not abuse their power."[39] As in Ricci's work, Vagnone treated classical philosophy as a sort of corollary to traditional Chinese thought because it had an ethical system without the benefit of revelation. Again, accommodation was carefully observed, so that the Chinese would value the "barbarians'" thought. To the same end, a 1623 map of the known world designed by Aleni—the *Zhifang Waiji* (职方外纪)—carefully set China at the center of the map, and the world.[40]

Over the course of 1637–39 Vagnone also published sections of his *Western Study of Personal Cultivation* (修身西学 *Xiushen Xixue*), which he co-wrote with several Chinese scholars. Once again Greek philosophy plays the role we might have expected of Christianity. In appealing to the Confucian concept of the virtuous man as a parallel to the good Christian, Vagnone carefully avoided claiming that Heaven was a reward for virtuous behavior because, as Thierry Meynard remarks, "since the times of Confucius, the Chinese looked at the idea of profit (*li*) as morally unacceptable and opposed to the notion of justice (*yi*)."[41] Instead, Vagnone concentrated on the eudaimonic and Confucian concept of contentment as a reward in *this* life. Although Ricci had already described the afterlife in *The True Meaning of the Lord of Heaven,* Vagnone addressed the challenges of rewarding virtue by putting a shocked Chinese scholar in the dialogue to ask, "Since a scholar-gentleman (*junzi*) does not do good in order to obtain profit or avoid harm in this world, how could he consider profit or harm in the life to come?"[42]

Plato too made an appearance among the Jesuits. Ricci admired the Confucian learning that was needed to pass the governmental exam system, which he linked to the Platonic notion of philosophers becoming, if not kings, at least advisers to kings.[43] Ricci even suggested that China was close to instantiating the ideals of Plato's *Republic.* In Ricci's own words:

> it raises admiration that these people who have never traded with Europe have achieved as much by themselves as we did in contact with the whole world; and I just want His Highness to assess this by evaluating their government, to which they put all their efforts and see in it so much light, leaving behind all the other nations; and if, to nature, God might want to add our divine holy Catholic faith, it seems that what Plato speculated on in his Republic, China put into practice.[44]

Still later, other Jesuits, especially French ones, used Platonic ideas in their teachings based on the idea of *prisca thelogia,* that is, the idea that the pagan ancients—whether Greek or Chinese— had had contact with ancient Jewish leaders like Noah and Moses, from whose learning they drew up their own truths. As no lesser a figure than Gottfried Wilhelm Leibniz wrote to the Jesuit missionary Joachim Bouvet:

> I praise the prudence of that great man Matteo Ricci in following the example of the Fathers of the Church, who interpreted Plato and the other philosophers in a Christian sense. . . . I have always been inclined to believe that the ancient Chinese . . . were far from idolatry. . . . And I find it strange that there should be such an outcry against your colleagues who have written that the ancient Chinese had true religion.[45]

For the Jesuits it would seem, just about all ancient thinkers were proto-Christians, including the Pythagoreans and the authors of the Orphic texts.[46]

The Jesuit missionaries' use of Greek antiquity is an example of adopting the classics to an unlikely context—even at the cost of doctrinal theology or the integrity of the text itself. Already in this first encounter between China and the western canon, to read the western classics was to transform them to other ends. Perhaps this should not surprise us. Classical western texts have held a wide range of meanings for thousands of years and have been adapted to different ideologies and audiences as times changed—not always with interpretive self-consciousness around the process. In the Middle Ages, Vergil's *Aeneid* was read as the story of a Christian everyman, which seems positively laughable to us today. This is a salutary reminder that, while western readings may seem "natural" or "true" to the west, those readings actually are shaped invisibly by the cultural, political, and historical context in which the texts are received. The well-being of many an academic department rests on the fact that interpretations (and for that matter, scientific truths) change over time.

II. Aristotle and a New Nation

The Jesuits were not to return to China in significant numbers until 1842. Meanwhile, the Chinese of the Middle Kingdom continued to see themselves as a culture superior to that of other nations. As the Emperor Qianlong wrote to George III with some acerbity in 1792:

> Our Celestial Empire possesses all things in prolific abundance and lacks no product within its own borders. There was therefore no need to import the manufactures of outside barbarians in exchange for our own produce . . . Moreover, our dynasty, swaying the myriad races of the globe, extends the same benevolence towards all. Your England is not the only nation trading at Canton . . . I do not overlook your excusable ignorance of the usages of our Celestial Empire.[47]

In short, we don't need your goods or your belief systems. As noted at the start of this chapter, it was not until the brutal outcomes of the Opium Wars of 1839–42 and 1856–60 that the Chinese came to a new understanding of their situation vis-à-vis the west. The Chinese defeat at the hands of the British and French forced them to concede Hong Kong to the UK, legalize the opium trade, and open specified ports to the west—shattering the myth of Chinese exceptionalism. It was a blow only worsened by the Chinese loss in the First Sino-Japanese War of 1895. In between came the Taiping Rebellion and revolts in the Uyghur country. The ruling Manchu dynasty had little popular legitimacy among the Han and the country was breaking apart.

In this context of social upheaval swelling calls for new policies—many coming from foreign-educated Chinese intellectuals who had returned to China—finally spurred the

Guangxu Emperor's attempt at appeasement via the Hundred Days' Reform of 1898.[48] When the reform effort collapsed through the actions of the rather fearsome Empress Dowager Cixi (who put the emperor himself under house arrest), many of the most vocal protestors were forced to flee to Japan in exile—where they waited, and wrote. In 1908, bowing to increasing pressure, Cixi herself promised that the dynasty would adopt a constitutional monarchy. In response, over 5,000 local councils were formed across China to provide a previously absent link between the common people and the court.[49] But these measures did not appease those revolutionaries who wanted the dynasty's complete overthrow. Among them was Sun Yat-sen, who had spearheaded several failed rebellions already and finally succeeded in the Xinhai Revolution of 1911.[50] The child emperor Pu-yi was unseated, and the dynastic system was terminated in 1912.[51]

China's young intellectuals and reformers clamored for a new, republican China with radically different values. They were by no means in agreement with each other—their ranks included traditionalists as well as radicals, anarchists and socialists, people who called for compromises with extant cultural and political values as well as those who called for new starts. The need for some kind of change was felt by all. But the nature of their demands was shaped, fundamentally, by western political theories. These intellectuals looked to Montesquieu, Rousseau, Dewey, and others for their ideas.[52] They also looked to Aristotle's *Politics* and other Greek philosophical and political writings.[53] Not all these texts existed in Chinese translation—some were accessible only through Japanese versions—but they compelled the attention of many who were interested in alternatives to the dynastic system. As Alexander Beecroft writes, "Reformers . . . sought to find explanations of the decline in China's prestige relative to the west in a failure of traditional Chinese values and explored the Greco-Roman tradition as the source of the (presumably more effective) values of the west."[54]

Many of the late Qing intellectuals met these texts while studying abroad in the US, Britain, France, Germany, and especially Japan, which was culturally similar to China but further along the path to industrialization. Ensconced in their Japanese safehold and away from their homeland, several of the most prominent intellectual expats had already been publishing their thoughts on the need for reform before the fall of the Qing, often pointing to China's technological weakness as a sign that the old ideas (and traditions) were a hindrance to scientific progress. Among them was the hugely influential essayist and intellectual Liang Qichao 梁啓超 (1873–1929), who had fled China for Japan (together with his teacher, Kang Youwei) after his role in the failed Hundred Days' Reform.[55] In Japan, Liang was free to write and think. The result was an astonishing output of articles on Greco-Roman antiquity: from December 1898 to 1903, Liang published some thirty pieces on Greek and Roman history and politics.[56] The essays did not languish in Japan. Liang's reach was magnified by his use of print media, and his ideas reached many on the Chinese mainland. His journal entitled *The New Citizen* (新民丛报 *Xinmin Congbao*), first published in 1902, enjoyed a circulation of nearly 10,000.[57]

Over a period of years that began with his authorship of the first Chinese article on Aristotle's *Politics*, "The Political Theory of Aristotle" (亚里士多德之政治学说 *Yalishiduode Zhi Zhengzhi Xueshuo*), published in *The New Citizen* in 1898, Liang intrepidly introduced concepts from classical political philosophy to his audience of reformers keen to rethink China's dynastic legacy. Liang was convinced that Aristotle was the best representative of Greek thought and therefore worth bringing to the Chinese:

> Greek thought was best represented by Athens; and Athenian knowledge was concentrated in the writings of Aristotle. Therefore, Master Aristotle[58] is truly the singular representative of ancient civilization. The fact that "politics"[59] could become its own discipline and develop as such to attain its soaring heights today, must be credited to Aristotle as well.[60]

Liang was particularly struck by the terminology with which Aristotle, in the *Politics*, described the nature of the citizen and his relationship to the city-state. Citizenship and participation in the city-state (the polis) is what makes us fully human: man is "an animal of the polis" (a *politikon zoon*) by nature, and only by fulfilling this nature can he (and I use he advisedly) fulfill his potential, which includes understanding and applying such moral concepts such as justice.[61] In this sense, the individual human is secondary to the city-state, for he cannot become fully human without it. As Aristotle wrote:

> Further, the state [that is, the polis] is by nature clearly prior to the family and to the individual, since the whole is of necessity prior to the part; for example, if the whole body be destroyed, there will be no foot or hand. . . . The proof that the state is a creation of nature and prior to the individual is that the individual, when isolated, it not self-sufficing; and therefore he is like a part in relation to the whole. But he who is unable to live in society, or has no need because he is sufficient for himself, must be either a beast or a god: he is no part of a state.[62]

These ideas—of the natural citizen and of the natural state—are familiar in the west; they stand near the beginning of our tradition of political thought. China had no parallels to such ideas. The transformative influence of these Aristotelian ideas underlies much of what Liang would come to write, and their impact was dramatic. Both in the essay on Aristotle and in one of his most famous essays in the collection *Xinmin Shuo*— *Discourse on the New Citizen*, 新民说—Liang adapted the meaning of the extant Chinese word 国民 (*guomin*) to mean, not as "subjects of a country" as had been previously done, but rather as "citizens of a nation," creating a parallel to the "citizen" of Aristotle's *Politics*.[63]

For many Chinese, "the citizen" was a completely new idea. Although theorists of western politics from Aristotle and Cicero to Machiavelli had all emphasized the importance of political participation, the traditional Confucians (who had not encountered these texts) considered personal moral development and familial duty as far more important human responsibilities. In commending Aristotle's idea of the citizen, Liang was going against the grain of thousands of years of tradition, both with the idea of the citizen and with the further explanation that the citizen had the right and even the duty to participate in the state's legislative, executive, and judicial processes and to occupy any state position without restriction.[64]

Unsurprisingly, Liang was particularly concerned with just how Chinese "subjects" (for which the traditional term was *chen* 臣, used by officials to their superiors) were to be transformed into "citizens" with rights and responsibilities, and how the erstwhile empire might become a nation-state.[65] This would be no easy task. Traditionally, according to the historian Sima Qian (ca. 145–86 BCE), "Wherever there is a sign of human presence, all are subjects of the emperor."[66] One catalyst, Liang hoped, would be his own writing. He would transform *chen* (subjects) into *guomin* (citizens).[67] His new coinage "made *guomin* a phrase that completely escaped from its original Chinese linguistic situation, and became something deeply influenced by western political theories."[68] *Guomin* came to stand for the key idea behind the fledgling nationalist movement that desperately wanted to rid China of its dynasties and to introduce a constitutional republic, or some other non-dynastic government.[69]

That said, Liang did balk at one aspect of Aristotle's political theory. As he was quick to argue, the only respect in which Aristotle could *not* be applied to China at the present moment of transformation was Aristotle's critique of democracy as the tainted parallel to a republic:

> I consider Aristotle's classification of six types of polities to be inapplicable [to the present]. I believe that the matter of justice and injustice should be raised before the discussion is complete. Only a democracy can be truly just; no other type of polity deserves the name. Why? Because a nation is essentially a body formed by the people. The people are to the nation what blood is to the human body; if blood becomes congested and repressed, then the whole body can have no stability. This is why sovereignty must lie with the people. This matter is obvious and I do not need to say more about it.[70]

No matter if Aristotle, like Thucydides, focused on the idea that democracy entailed the ultimately destructive right to "living as you want," or if this sort of freedom was also criticized by Isocrates and Plato, who argued that it undermined the rule of law and turned pleasure into the common goal.[71] For Liang, Aristotle had simply made a mistake here that needed to be corrected. Monarchy, then, was obviously out—and so, a fortiori, the dynastic system was out too. Dismissing Aristotle's claim that all three polities can be just, Liang wrote, "it is not theoretically untenable, yet if you take a look at history you will find that there may not be one corresponding case of such justice among a billion."[72]

Guomin was not the only concept up Liang's elegant sleeve. In his essay on the *Politics* and in subsequent writings in the collection *Discourse on the New Citizen*, Liang introduced China to further concepts that were as un-Chinese as "citizen" itself.[73] As the historian Timothy Cheek eloquently writes, "The tools that intellectuals of Liang Qichao's generation had at hand were predominantly words—old words, new words, confusing words, inspiring words."[74] These were words like republic (共和国 *gongheguo*), democracy (民主 *minzhu*), society (社会 *shehui*), science (科学 *kexue*), rights (权利 *quanli*), and economy (经济 *jingji*), almost all of them taken from Japanese translations of the original terms—and all of them western concepts, many dating back to classical antiquity.

But even with a new set of linguistic tools, Liang faced an uphill battle. Most Chinese had no concept of a potential relationship between the nation and its citizens; to the extent that any relationship existed, they conceived of themselves as the obedient children of the emperor. This was from the Confucian framework which focused on the family and its hierarchies and described the state as the family writ large.[75] As Liang wrote in frustration in "On the Origin of China's Weakness" (中国积弱溯源论 *Zhongguo ji ruo suyuan lun*):

> The biggest problem of the Chinese people is that we do not know what kind of thing a nation is and accordingly confuse the nation and the court, mistakenly believing that the nation is the property of the court . . . One family owns the nation and all the rest of the people are subjects (of the family). This is why, although there are forty million "fellow people"

(同胞 *tongbao*) in China, there are actually only dozens of human beings (*ren*).[76]

To fight back against the model of the emperor as the paternal "owner" of the people, Liang turned the dynastic concept inside out: now the people owned the state, rather than the emperor owning everything under the heavens:

> *Guomin* refers to the ideal which sees the state as the common property of all her citizens; the state is the collective accumulation of citizens, without whom there is no state. When all the citizens of a state manage the affairs of a state, write the laws of a state, protect the interests of a state, and defend the safety of a state, then the citizens shall never stumble, the state shall never fall, and we shall henceforth call ourselves *guomin*.[77]

Here was traditional Confucianism, set on its head.

In another blow to tradition that was influenced by his reading of Aristotle, Liang argued that the traditional family and its larger unit, the tribe or clan, were impediments to nationhood and citizenship—as they had been perceived to be by ancient Greek reformers.[78] Humans were supposed to form nation-groups, not family or clan groups. In Liang's view, "Of the animals best at grouping themselves (as the saying of the western scholar Aristotle goes), people are the foremost—is this not what makes us so far above the animals?" In "On Grouping" (说群 *Shuo Qun*) Liang argued that the west had nations, which contributed to its strength; it had transcended local bonds of loyalty (and fostered) loyalty towards the abstraction of the nation.[79] Liang thus helped to conceptualize a paradigmatic shift in the self-understanding of China itself: it was to be a *guojia* (国家 "nation-state"). In the words of Peter Zarrow, it became "a realm of public associations reasonably free from state domination . . . [that] combine[d] self-interest . . . with a disinterested concern for the nation."[80] Liang also acquainted himself with Roman law, which he saw as the origin of modern civilization because it was rights-based, not duty-based—again a new argument in his historical context, since the Chinese had not been trained by Confucian philosophy to think in terms of rights."[81]

There were other perceived failings in Chinese culture compared to the Greek city-states. As Yiqun Zhou notes, Liang's extensive opus included many invidious remarks spelling out China's shortcomings: the underdevelopment of logical reasoning, the lack of research in science, the absence of a climate of debate, the excessive reverence for (Confucian) tradition and authority, and more.[82] Enlightenment rationality, Liang wrote, was a necessary condition for scientific advancement, and that advancement had in turn depended on the rediscovery of Greek thought in the Renaissance—but China had no such fallback.[83] Liang even claimed that Socrates made a major contribution to improving the status of rational knowledge in his endless debates with Athenian citizens (never mind if the Athenians put him to death for this contribution).

Liang's perspective on the origins of western politics, the nature of citizenship, and China's failings would be hugely influential during the May 4th Movement in 1919 as well as during the "New Culture Movement" that followed the fall of the dynasty.[84] Through Liang, Aristotle played a role in the emergence of the first (short-lived) Chinese Republic, which technically lasted from 1912 to 1949, at which point the government of the Republic relocated to Taiwan after their defeat by the communists.[85] Liang's concepts and categories rendered possible the reimagining of a country dominated for thousands of years by a dynastic system.

Of course, Liang was not alone. The famous translator Yan Fu (1854–1921)—in some accounts the man who, above all others, made accessible to the Chinese the west's political and economic theories—was simultaneously sprinkling comments drawn from Aristotle's *Politics* throughout his translations of John S. Mills, Adam Smith, Herbert Spencer, and others. Like Liang, Yan Fu claimed that Aristotle really preferred democracy to all other forms of government, no matter what the *Politics* actually said. As Yan Fu added to a translation of Edward Jenks's *A History of Politics* (社会通诠 *Shehui Tongquan*, more literally, "A Full Account of Society"):

> It was the Greek philosophers who studied the division of ancient constitutions first. And among the Hellenic political books only Aristotle's *Politics* was admired most by late generations. It divided the constitutional system of the Ecumene into three parts: Monarchy, Aristocracy, and Democracy. But the system of democracy is the main and the best one in the ancient Greek constitutions. All the Europeans who study politics regarded Aristotle as their pioneer . . . and regarded his division the basis of further studying and development.[86]

Yan Fu deliberately misread the *Politics* so that he could employ Aristotle's authority to argue in favor of democracy as the best form of government for a future Chinese republic—even though Aristotle identified democracy as a pernicious form of government in which the poor held control and used their power for themselves, for example, by taxing the rich very heavily.[87]

Similarly, Li Dazhao 李大钊, a fervent nationalist, fan of Liang's, and communist-to-be, contextualized democracy in the history of western political thought, rewriting that thought in the process. Whether influenced by Liang or directly by Aristotle, Li cited the latter's six types of political regime and argued against Aristotle (once again!) that democracy was not necessarily one of the three "bad" systems. According to Li, the nature of democracy's existence in the modern world did not reproduce the characteristics of ancient democracy and, therefore, did not face the danger of disintegrating into a tyranny of the people (*baomin zhengzhi*, literally "rule of the violent masses").[88] Once again Aristotle was made to lend his support to a political system he had denounced in the *Politics* so that Li and other Chinese intellectuals could call on his authority to support their political ideals. So much authority was given to the *Politics*, or perhaps to the authority of its author, that its arguments were only secondary![89]

Ironically enough, at the very time of the May 4th Movement, Liang was becoming disillusioned with the west. A post-World War I visit to several European capitals left him critical about western morals and the damage wrought by technology. But the over 3,000 students from thirteen universities in Beijing who protested the terms of the Versailles Treaty in 1919 had drunk deep at his well. The leaders of the May 4th Movement wanted more democratic government and more civic participation. Even more than Liang, they were critical of traditional Chinese values and culture, holding them responsible for the political and scientific weaknesses of the nation and its humiliating treatment after the war. Fervent nationalists, the May 4th leaders were eager to see the sort of modernization that Japan had enjoyed. And they called for at least a selective adoption of western science and democracy—both seen as the product of reason.[90] A striking example of this appeared as late as 1986, when the chemist Jin Guantao, a member of the pre-Tiananmen Futurologist School, and his wife Liu Qingfeng not only argued that Confucian culture created an internal restraint on logical thinking, but also stressed the classical syllogism as the foundation of deductive rationality. In their view, the formal logic that characterized Aristotelian thought was the foundation of mathematical logic and hence of science itself.[91]

The influential philosopher Feng Youlan (馮友, 1895–1990) traced western "logical superiority" as far back as the classical tradition. He praised the use of reason in classical western philosophy and criticized Chinese philosophy for being weak in metaphysics, epistemology, and logic.[92] Chinese philosophy, Feng complained, paid more attention to daily life than to abstract principles. With the exception of the School of Names, few philosophers "intentionally took the processes and methods of thinking and debating as objects of study."[93] Feng even tried to take matters into his own hands. According to Jiyuan Yu, "Feng's own philosophical system, contained in the six-volumes published between 1936 and 1948, especially the New Principle Learning (Xin Lixue 新理学), is to employ the method of logical analysis to reexamine traditional Chinese philosophical terms and theses, with an aim to render a solid metaphysical foundation to Chinese philosophy of life."[94]

One of the May 4th reformers, Chen Duxiu 陈独秀, deserves attention here too. Chen edited a journal entitled New Youth (新青年 Xin qingnian, also entitled La Jeuness) that provided a forum for debate on the causes of China's present weaknesses.[95] Contributors often supported the adoption of a western culture in which human rights, democracy, and science were paramount. They also emphasized an un-Confucian stress on the individual, not the family or society, as the focus of attention, and on creative thinking rather than orthodoxy. Chen himself argued that, in order to build a new Chinese nation, "the basic task is to import the foundation of western society, that is, the new belief in equality and human rights. We must be thoroughly aware of the incompatibility between Confucianism and the new belief, the new society, and the new state."[96] During the New Culture Movement, Chen called for "Mr. Confucius" to be replaced by "Mr. Science" and "Mr. Democracy." In an essay published in January 1919 in *New Youth*, Chen wrote that, "only these two gentlemen can save China from the political, moral, academic and intellectual darkness in which it finds itself."[97] Liang's influence is clear throughout: as Chen stated in 1916, "Only when we read of Liang Qichao did we suddenly realize that foreign political principles, religions, and learning had much to offer."[98]

The ultimate effect of reformers such as Li Dazhao and Liang Qichao on the unfolding of the Chinese twentieth century is difficult to gauge.[99] As their thinking ceased to be broadly influential, the possibility for the realization of their views likewise vanished, lost with the seizure of power by warlords such as Yuan Shikai and, eventually, with the ascendency of the communist Mao Zedong and the CCP.[100] Yet none other than Mao himself provides testimony to the pull that the reformers had in the first decades of the new century. The young Mao admired Liang, and in his teenage years quoted Liang approvingly to the effect that, "When the country is legitimately founded, it is a constitutional nation: the constitution is made by the people and the crown is appointed by the people."[101] Of course this would not reflect the later Mao, nor was his nation-building the sort that Liang had in mind.[102] Already in his talks at Yan'an in 1941, Mao was criticizing the intellectuals who "cited the Greeks whenever they spoke."[103] In his 1941 essay "Reform our Studies" Mao wrote:

> Many party members are still in a fog about Chinese history, whether of the last hundred years or of ancient times. There are many Marxist-Leninist scholars who cannot open their

mouths without citing ancient Greece; but as for their own ancestors—sorry, they have been forgotten.[104]

Mao commented on ancient philosophy in his work on dialectical materialism, in which, perhaps unsurprisingly, he condemned Plato as an idealist and reactionary for his argument that only the Forms had any real existence.

III. To Tiananmen Square, But Not Back

One man clung to the specter of classical Athens in Mao's China, and paid dearly for it. A dedicated communist, Gu Zhun 顾准 (1915–1974) became an economic adviser to the CCP after they had captured Shanghai, one of the few "special" cities where western capitalism was permitted to continue. As Christopher Leighton explains, the new CCP was anxious about how to control and reform China's financial heart:

> For help, they turned to Gu Zhun (1915–1974), an accounting wunderkind, native Shanghainese, and veteran member of the Chinese Communist Party (CCP). Over the next three years, he oversaw and overhauled the city's financial structure from various perches in government, sometimes concurrently heading as many as three municipal bureaus.[105]

But Gu Zhun fell afoul of party ideology when his policies, as expressed in his own "Tax Newsletter," did not line up with communist ideals. His 1957 article "On Commercial Production and the Theory of Value under Socialism" insisted that the market, rather than a central plan, should be the basis for productive decisions. That argument got him exiled to the countryside, and, eventually, sent to jail. He would be sprung free and jailed (or "re-educated") more than once, but the famine and cannibalism he saw in Xinyang, Henan Province, where some 200,000 people died, led to his unflinching rejection of the Great Leap Forward 大跃进. As Gu Zhun wrote defiantly in his prison diaries, "I too believed in the same ideology [communism]. However, when people change revolutionary idealism to conservative and reactionary autocracy in the name of revolution, I will unambiguously choose realism and pluralism as my guides and fight this autocracy to the end."[106]

Gu Zhun turned to the ancient Greek city-state system to answer questions about the problems inherent in socialist economics.[107] One of his most influential essays—*On the Institution of the City-State in Greece* (希腊城邦制度 *Xila chengbang zhidu*)—was probably written in the last year of his life, 1974, though not was published until 1982. In it, Gu made radical claims about the history of Chinese and Greek civilization and trade, much to the detriment of China.[108] He argued that important traits of the Greek city-states—such as democracy, citizenship, rights, and the law code—not only distinguished their culture from the rest of the world at the time, but also made possible other developments that led to the preeminence of the west long after Ancient Greece ceased to exist. Gu wrote, "The common feature [among China, Egypt, Israel, and India] was that we all had a God-granted ruler, a tyrant. He possessed absolute power, and all people were subject to his will . . . The king had to be spiritually superior as well; that is, the king's power had to be claimed as inherited from God."[109] This was the belief that had held back the east.

Aristotle, once again, was not far away. On autocracies, Gu Zhun quoted the Greek's *Politics* approvingly: "The Asian barbarians are more slavish than the European barbarians, so they often endure autocracy instead of rebellion."[110] He also used Aristotle to define the city-state and citizenship itself, citing the

Politics to the effect that "He who has the power to take part in the deliberative or judicial administration of any state is said by us to be a citizen of that state; and, speaking generally, a state is a body of citizens sufficing for the purposes of life."[111] Finally, Gu repeated Aristotle's view of the primacy of the city-state over the individual:

> Since the city-state is a citizen group that "takes turns to rule," the city-state is certainly higher than each of its individual citizens and higher than all its rulers. This is the "democratic collectivism" of the city-state—one with the highest sovereignty of citizens . . . At the same time, since the city state is self-sufficient, it must also have various laws to guarantee this self-sufficiency. That is to say, the city-state must have laws on citizenship, citizenship rights and obligations.[112]

Hence Gu Zhun's praise of Athens.

There was one more factor that Gu Zhun felt was central to the prosperity of the Greek city-states, and hence, eventually, of the west. It was the geographic position of Greece and her many islands, which was particularly conducive to fostering a sea-based civilization; this location allowed for economic development that in turn fostered democracy.[113] Other factors influenced by a maritime civilization included colonization, trade, cultural exchange, and the weakening of blood ties. In Gu's pithy (and dramatic) phrasing, "Capitalism was the fruit of Greek-Roman civilization. The Indian, Chinese, Arabian and Orthodox traditions could not breed capitalism. This is not accidental."[114] In his view, non-maritime civilizations had an affinity for authoritarianism and tended towards political and economic stagnation.[115]

Published in 1982, *On the Institution of the City-State in Greece* provided a prescient view of a famous, and fateful, Chinese TV

documentary called *River Elegy* (河殇 *Heshang*) that echoed Gu
Zhun's fundamental ideas and was a catalyst for the events of
June 4, 1989.[116] The screenwriters explained their work as a
mass audience-directed version of scholarly ideas already in the
air, though none professed to have studied Gu Zhun in particular.[117] *River Elegy* was broadcast in six parts by China Central
Television (中国中央电视台 CCTV) in 1988, during the period
of maximum openness and freedom of the press. The authors
of the script repeated the May 4th Movement's calls for
"Mr. Science" and "Mr. Democracy" and called for China to
break out of the confines of the Great Wall.[118] They praised
Yan Fu for understanding western values, noting that "From his
extensive observation of the west, Yan Fu discovered that the
great achievements of European culture lay in developing the
potential of the individual, thereby providing a sort of social
contract."[119] And they informed the Chinese people that the
path to national greatness lay in rejuvenation through the
spirit of science and democracy, the secret of the west's
success—which they held, in turn, to have come from its seafaring and trade. As the voice-over to part six, entitled "Blueness," intoned:

> Confucian culture may indeed possess all sorts of ancient
> and perfect "gems" of wisdom, yet over these past few thou-
> sand years it has been able to create neither a national spirit
> of initiative, nor a legal order for the state. . . . History has
> proven that to attempt to modernize using the style of con-
> trol of a "land-based" culture [will not] infuse the whole na-
> tion with a strong, civilizing vitality.[120]

Alas, "Confucian culture had gradually attained a position of
sole dominance in this land."[121] It was time to turn away from
it and towards openness, democracy, and the sea.

To shore up this message with unmistakable imagery, the producers of the series drew a clear distinction, expressed in color metaphors, between cultures of the earth and cultures of the sea, between yellow cultures and blue cultures. In the documentary the "yellow" of the Yellow River is arrayed against the "blue" of the ocean and the sky; and while yellow is linked to feudalism, stagnation, and closure, blue represents trade, exploration, expansion, and progress. The voice-over repeats: "This stretch of dirt-yellow land cannot teach us the true spirit of science. The unruly Yellow River cannot teach us a true democratic consciousness."[122] Understanding the strength of "blueness" only came via the Chinese confrontation with the west during the Opium Wars, but, despite the efforts of the reformers, China had not changed. Athens, meanwhile, is set at the center of western culture and western power: "Long ago, in ancient Greece, the democratic ideology of Athens arose contemporaneously with the growth of Athens as a sea power, and so it was sea-power that led to a democratic revolution."[123]

As Chen Xiaomei notes with some acidity, "Such an image of an 'annexed' Athens as the 'cultural capital' of Europe is most typically underscored in *Heshang*'s glorifications of the rise of Hellenism, the conquest of Alexander the Great, the discovery of the New World, and the triumph of colonialism and imperialism."[124] Even that proud Chinese symbol, the Great Wall, was reinterpreted as a wall that shut China *in* rather than one that kept the barbarians out. The message of the documentary was that in order to survive, China had to learn from the "blue" civilizations, establishing inter alia a market-based economy.[125] The country (according to the series) had not learned what Adam Smith had said about China in *The Wealth of Nations*, where he declared that Chinese culture "suffered from stagnation as a result of neglecting overseas trade." In short "all of the negative aspects of Chinese culture are finally traced to Confucian ideology, whose monolithic social system resists plurality and change."[126]

Eyewitness David Moser, a student at Peking University at the time, described online the reaction to this documentary:

> During the week the show was broadcast it became clear that the documentary had hit academic circles like an atomic bomb. The series's content—a sweeping, brutally painful critique of the deep structure of Chinese culture—was the topic of conversation among many of the Peking University grad students I was hanging out with. They had seen nothing like it. "At last," they would say to me, "a TV show that tells the truth" . . . Seen by more than 200 million viewers, the miniseries also galvanized the general population. The *People's Daily* [the official newspaper of the Central Committee of the CCP] actually published transcripts of "River Elegy," and references to the themes of the documentary began popping up everywhere in the local newsstands.[127]

In this unique moment of history, as Xu Jilin writes, "pressures generated by a combination of relative economic laxity and dated ideological control led to a situation in which intellectuals began to call for an accommodation between the ideas propounded by the Marxist humanists and neo-enlightenment thought."[128]

There was good reason for the pro-democracy students and workers to think that the 1980s might bring the fulfilment of their dreams. After Mao Zedong's death in 1976, Deng Xiaoping had gradually moved the country away from Maoist principles, initiating the so-called "reform and opening-up of China" (改革开放 *gaige kaifang*) and implementing market-economy reforms. In 1981, the CCP formally announced during the Sixth

Plenary Session of the Central Committee that the Cultural Revolution was "responsible for the most severe setback and the heaviest losses suffered by the Party, the country, and the people since the founding of the People's Republic."[129] At the same time, Deng introduced "socialism with Chinese characteristics" and opened China to foreign investment and the global market. He was the *Time* Person of the Year twice, in 1978 and 1985. Encouraged by the new leadership, in the 1980s students and workers returned to many of the demands of the original New Culture Movement. They called for freedom of the press, democratic reform, and the rule of law. They were angry at corruption within the Party, the unfair distribution of economic incentives, inflation, restrictions on political participation, and the limited and nepotistic job market. They wanted change.

And change there was, though not what they had hoped for. The death of a top Party official sympathetic to the movement, Hu Yaobang (胡耀邦), in April of 1989 led to calls for a revival of his legacy, and thousands of students began to gather at Tiananmen Square to make public their demands.[130] Provoked by *River Elegy* and their own democratic idealism, the students clamored for reform. At Tiananmen and elsewhere in Beijing, students were accompanied by poor suburban workers who wanted better living conditions. Initially, the government attempted to appease the protesters through concessions, but the students were obdurate, not even vacating the square for a state visit by Gorbachev. Ultimately, Deng Xiaoping and other hardliners of the Party leadership turned to force to suppress the movement. Martial law was declared on May 19 and military convoys entered Beijing on the evening of June 3. Under strict orders to clear Tiananmen Square by dawn, the army mowed down all protesters in their path, killing hundreds and possibly thousands of civilians.[131]

Following the crackdown, the leaders of the protests and the most conspicuous pro-democracy activists were exiled or imprisoned; those charged with violent crimes were executed.[132] The government produced a propaganda campaign against *River Elegy*, denouncing it as a dangerous example of "spiritual pollution" that blindly advocated total westernization and boosted "national nihilism." One of the screen writers for the series, Su Xiaokang, was included among China's seven mostwanted dissident intellectuals; he and his coauthor Wang Luxiang now both live in exile. The tragic, and perhaps inevitable, irony was that it was Deng Xiaoping's own policy of reform and openness to the west that had created the opportunity for such protest in the first place.[133]

Silence descended upon students, protestors, intellectuals, and professors. By the time their voices—and their comments on the texts of classical antiquity—began to be heard a decade after the massacre, there had been a dramatic shift in what prominent intellectuals, including some at major universities, had to say. No more would reform-minded twentieth-century Chinese readers of western classical texts turn to the Greek classics as a source for the values—and successes—of modern western civilization. No more would they look to the ancient world, in particular to Athenian democracy, as a model for these values or as a way of introducing the concepts of individualism, citizenship, and liberty to China.[134] And no more would they tweak Aristotle in support of their own hopes for democracy. An era of looking to the western classics that had lasted for a century was over.

2

Classics after the Crackdown

To weaken popular democratic superstition, and to appreciate classical Chinese genius, has been the purpose of presenting the history of ancient Greece here.

—PAN WEI 潘维

OVER THE EIGHTEEN months following the incident at Tiananmen Square, as the CCP purged itself of members who had shown support for the protests (including General Secretary Zhao Ziyang) and subjected thousands of Party cadres to "Party discipline," some public voices stepped back altogether from scholarship that supported democracy, remolding themselves as social activists.[1] Many other voices from the pre-Tiananmen era, in contrast, retained their ideologies but became increasingly disestablished and could no longer publish in the national Chinese media. Others who were seriously involved in the student movements and had escaped a jail sentence moved to the United States or other western countries. Others still turned to academia proper, burying themselves in the equivalent of ivory walls, where for a long time the CCP granted more intellectual freedom than in the public arena.[2] Still other voices began to be heard that were never implicated in the democratic movement at all—for example, the Shanghai-based historian Xiao Gongqin (蕭功秦) who emerged staunchly in favor of authoritarianism in 1989, or the Confucian scholar Tu Weiming (杜維明) who, like others, saw a "Confucian ethic" behind the economic boom in the non-Communist cultures of East Asia.

In 1992, a group of intellectuals published a widely read article, "Realistic Responses and Strategic Choices for China after the Disintegration of the Soviet Union," which advised the government to look to traditional Chinese culture as a source of ideology rather than to the failed specter of European Marxism. The article became a bastion of today's Neo-Conservatives and political Confucians. By the late 1990s, broad intellectual trends—some of them again turning to the western classics—were once again visible and influential. The scholars involved, however, were no democratic idealists. As Zhao Suisheng observes "One truly remarkable phenomenon in the post-Cold War upsurge of Chinese nationalism is that Chinese intellectuals became one of the driving forces. Many well-educated people . . . have given voice to and even become articulators for a rising nationalist discourse."[3]

It seems even the May 4th Movement has been appropriated to speak for the CCP these days. In a 2019 article in the *China Media Project*, David Bandursky demonstrated the complete "takeover" of the actual ideals of that movement by a new way of framing what the protest was about. As Bandursky writes, in Xi Jinping's speeches, exhortations to "make full use of the spirit of May Fourth" now mean that the youth must take "as their task the great rejuvenation of the Chinese people, not failing the hopes of the Party, the expectations of the people, and the great trust placed in them by all people of Chinese ethnicity." Mr. Science and Mr. Democracy, the two stalwarts of the original movement—and of the 1989 movement—are nowhere to be seen. A Hong Kong journalist who complained of this in the *Apple Daily* came in for heavy criticism in a newspaper controlled by the Central Government's Liaison Office, the *Ta Kung Pao*: "This is a distortion of history, and a major insult to the spirit of the May Fourth Movement," the article claimed. It continued, "One of the slogans of the May Fourth Movement that year was a call for 'Mr. Democracy' and 'Mr. Science,' meaning for democracy and science. But why did the youth call for and demand 'Mr. Democracy' and 'Mr. Science'? What was their goal? Was it not so that the nation could prosper and grow strong, for love of their country?" For the *Ta Kung Pao* "loving the country, loving the Party and loving socialism are identical, and they are the only true patriotism."[4]

This is a nationalist discourse, but not a democratic one. Intellectuals still invoke classical western texts but read them in ways that run counter to the reformist ideas of the May 4th Movement and the 1980s—even if some of these intellectuals were themselves the authors of reformist writing during the 1980s. Often returning from stints at western universities, they use terminology and critical approaches picked up there, but to support a very different political stance. Among these are the Chinese Straussians represented in the pages of *The Chinese Journal of Classical Studies* mentioned previously: there is an Experimental Class for Classical Studies in Renmin University set up in 2009 and led by Liu Xiaofeng, the former editor of the journal. And there are others, not Straussians, who read the classical texts as relevant political documents for the present but do not extol their values anymore. Such scholars echo the negative governmental views on values such as democracy and human rights—made clear in 2012–13 by a confidential document simply known as "Document 9," which was circulated within the Party by the General Office of the Communist Party of China. The document warned of the danger of western values, including of media freedom, democracy, and independence of the courts. Teaching on any such topics was forbidden. Above all, the Chinese leadership denounced "western forces hostile to China and dissidents within the country" for "constantly infiltrating the ideological sphere."[5]

There are now two schools of "classicists" in contemporary China. One school reflects the desire of foreign-trained students of the Greek and Latin languages to study western antiquity in the manner of western classics departments. This academic interest is reflected in the creation of the Peking University Centre for Western Classical Studies, founded in 2011 by Professor Huang Yang. There is a nucleus of classics faculty in the History and Philosophy Departments of Fudan University, Shanghai Normal University, and Tianjin University who are deeply invested in classical scholarship.[6] Classics as a topic of apolitical academic study is flourishing in many universities, and some of these students are traveling outside of China for further training.

The second school is represented by a group of scholars wishing to make the classical past relevant for contemporary socialist-Confucian China—relevant in the sense that the classical past is seen as supporting the values of the Chinese government. These voices are responding to changes in domestic and foreign policy over the past two decades that have increased the distance between China and the US. Even as the pro-democracy protesters were gearing up for what would be their final and fatal act in 1989, the First National Symposium on Modernization Theories held in Beijing in November 1988 redefined authoritarianism as "enlightened autocracy" and argued that the economic miracle of the four "little dragons" in

East Asia was due to Confucianism, not in spite of it.[7] And among many Chinese, there is a sense of hostility that has been fed by recent events convincing many that their country was the target of systematic discrimination. A flood of bestsellers attacking the west, and particularly the United States, appeared in the 1990s, providing the context in which conservative pro-government intellectuals could make their views felt. They supported the official version of state nationalism "by arguing that a centralized power structure must be strengthened in order to maintain social stability and economic development."[8] And as Zhao Suisheng has documented, the Party's official position was influential in persuading the Chinese people that "western bullies" were behind the failure of the Chinese bid for the 2000 Olympics, and that the United States was a "black hand" driving the independence movements in Tibet.[9] In all of this, Greek antiquity has been used to show that American democracy is wrong, wrong, wrong.

I. Thucydides Warns the West

An op-ed piece that appeared in *The New York Times* in February 2012 had much to say about the future of the United States. Penned by the Chinese exceptionalist and venture capitalist Eric X. Li, the op-ed argued that the American government would do well to take a good look at classical Athens and the fate of *that* democracy before trumpeting the universal value of American democracy.[10] Setting up a direct parallel between Athens and modern America, Li argued that:

> In the history of human governance, spanning thousands of years, there have been two major experiments in democracy. The first was Athens, which lasted a century and a half; the

second is the modern west. If one defines democracy as one citizen one vote, American democracy is only 92 years old. In practice it is only 47 years old, if one begins counting after the Voting Rights Act of 1965—far more ephemeral than all but a handful of China's dynasties. Why, then, do so many boldly claim they have discovered the ideal political system for all mankind and that its success is forever assured?[11]

To be sure, the comparison Li made might raise some eyebrows. In targeting American democracy, why did Li (like the enthusiastic proposers of reform from the previous century) focus on classical Athens, when few of its institutions are relevant to modern American democracy? Unlike both China and the US, Athens was a direct democracy in which officials (apart from military and financial leaders) were chosen by lottery. After Pericles's citizenship legislation of 451 BCE, both parents of a citizen had to be Athenian, changing the meaning of democracy as we understand it into a closed system into which entry was admitted only by blood. And classical Athens boasted 30,000 citizens at its height, while the US has 330 million—the Athenian way of doing politics via direct democratic vote would not be remotely scalable. Athenian women were not citizens; juries could consist of up to 501 members; and the chief magistrate, the archon eponymous, held power for one year and was accountable to a review process when he stepped down.[12]

Why then compare the US to Athens? One might argue, as Li pointed out, that, as the first democracy, Athens can land a huge ideological punch, in contrast to the uneasy feelings of the Founding Fathers about the precedent she provided. But the answer seems to be that Li decided to use the materials critical of Athenian democracy that were *already* abundant in antiquity.

He did so for the same reasons that Aristotle was turned into a pro-democracy advocate during the May 4th Movement: to rely on the authoritative stature of these texts as (a) ancient and (b) the so-called source of modern western civilization. Li could look to Plato's implicit critiques of the ignorant masses and Thucydides's candid assessment of the problem with Athens in *History of the Peloponnesian War* to support his condemnation of democracy, which was as old as democratic Athens itself. Even Americans who idealize ancient Athens must do so in the face of these ancient critiques:

> The modern desire to look to Athens for lessons or encouragement for modern thought, government, or society must confront this strange paradox: the people that gave rise to and practiced ancient democracy left us almost nothing but criticism of this form of regime (on a philosophical or theoretical level). And what is more, the actual history of Athens in the period of its democratic government is marked by numerous failures, mistakes, and misdeeds—most infamously, the execution of Socrates—that would seem to discredit the ubiquitous modern idea that democracy leads to good government.[13]

Contemporary Chinese intellectuals such as Peking University's Pan Wei and Pan Yue of the Central Academy of Socialism in Beijing would agree: Thucydides's criticism and the extreme picture painted of the ideal city-state in Plato's *Republic* react precisely to the "failures, mistakes, and misdeeds" of the Athenian democracy.[14]

To be sure, this is the *post*-Tiananmen Thucydides. Before that date, the historian seems to have been relatively unknown except among academic readerships, who saw in him telling precursors of material socialism rather than warnings about democracy. Li Changlin 李长林 suggested that:

> the naive materialist view of history in the background [in the Peloponnesian War] is generally expressed in three aspects: striving to separate human history from the state of the unity of God and man, focusing on the discussion of the causal relationship between historical events, and trying to explain the causes of historical development in terms of economic relations.[15]

Zhang Guangzhi 张广智 praised Thucydides in the context of praising "the brilliant wisdom of outstanding people" during fourth-century Greece. Thucydides was "a famous representative of historiography at that time whose 'History of the Peloponnesian War' relied on simple materialism and realism. As for the naive materialist view of history shown in the works of Thucydides, there seems to be no monograph in our history."[16] Other pre-1989 authors praised the historian for his economic focus or compared him to the ancient Chinese historian Sima Qian. Thucydides, before 1989, seemed to have little to say to the Chinese government.

By contrast, Li was all but quoting Thucydides when he claimed that modern America is plagued by what ailed its political and intellectual ancestor. To use Li's words about the present US, "elected representatives have no minds of their own and respond only to the whims of public opinion as they seek re-election."[17] It is a critique developed at length in the *Peloponnesian War*, where Thucydides, long before Li, argued that one factor contributing to the deterioration of the Athenian democracy was the fatal inability of its citizens to make wise choices in leadership because of their need to flatter or benefit the masses.[18] In Thucydides's view, only the general Pericles, both far-sighted and strong-willed, was able to keep the masses in hand, because he was governed neither by self-interest nor fear.

> Pericles indeed, by his rank, ability, and known integrity, was enabled to exercise an independent control over the multitude—in short, to lead them instead of being led by them; for as he never sought power by improper means, he was never compelled to flatter them, but, on the contrary, enjoyed so high an estimation that he could afford to anger them by contradiction.[19]

But after Pericles's death, the Athenian people succumbed to one demagogue after the other, following the lead of any politician who promised them personal benefit, and unwilling to make the sacrifices or show the self-restraint that would keep Athens on the winning side of the Peloponnesian War.[20]

Li dramatically suggested that the life span of Athenian democracy suggests that "History does not bode well for the American way. Indeed, faith-based ideological hubris may soon drive democracy over the cliff."[21] Americans, like the citizens of the Athenian polis (and like the general Pericles himself in his famous funeral oration for the fallen war dead), have elevated democracy to the status of an absolute good and even a form of religion. In Li's words, "The modern west sees democracy and human rights as the pinnacle of human development. It is a belief premised on an absolute faith."[22] Just as Athens saw itself as a model for other states, most Americans believe that their political system could be (as Pericles put it) "the school of Hellas."[23] This self-regard renders American voters incapable of making choices that are not preconditioned by their "religious belief" that democracy is the best form of government.[24]

Li's criticism of US democracy by appeal to a voice from classical texts reflects the intellectual pastime of many a political commentator across China. Lin Qifu and Dong Cunsheng of the Department of Political Science at Jilin University argue in the *Journal of the Fujian Provincial Committee Party School* that reflecting on the limitations of Athenian democracy can offer insight into the problems of "modern democratic politics" since the ancient Greek city-state is "similar" to contemporary democracy.[25] The authors suggest that, perhaps because the men of ancient Athens merged Plato's views on morality and the Forms with Aristotle's comments on citizenship and ethics, the ancients were brainwashed into believing that it was their duty to constantly strive for the highest and most transcendent forms of moral excellence. As such, democracy actually limited citizens' freedom, denying them independent thought. Moreover, the shared belief that the polis trumped the individual limited heterogeneity and individualism and over-emphasized consensus:

> Citizens are not independent in the individual sense because the person is only a part of the city-state community . . . The basis for being "human" is to evince the qualities and virtues of the city-state citizen community. The people here are simplified to symbolize the homogeneity of the citizen groups. The measure used is whether and to what extent they can satisfy the overall interests of the city-state and the common good.[26]

Here is Aristotle's citizen, but turned on his head. Precisely because the city-state precedes the citizen as the most essential unit of democracy, the citizen is censored in his behavior and beliefs, which cannot be in his interests as an individual, but only in the interests of the city-state. This restriction limits the

emergence of new ideas, and in any case eminence of any sort
is perceived as a threat to the greater unit. Hence the existence
of ostracism, the Athenian institution for exiling prominent
citizens. In a reverse echo of Liang Qichao's view of Chinese
nationals, instead we read, "Aristotle's free citizens are exactly
the opposite: they are slaves."[27]

Like others, Lin and Dong looked to Thucydides for further
critique of the west. In their view, the very medium of democratic
politics contributes to the corruption of the individual, because
democratic leaders look to rhetoric, sophistry, and emotion as
means of manipulating public debate. As represented in
Thucydides's account of the Mytilenean debate, citizens will
vote collectively in a moment of passion and impulsiveness and
regret their decision the very next day: that is, "the power of
speech in the heyday of Athenian democracy is often no longer
used in the maintenance of common ethical life, but as a means
for people to pursue narrow or personal utilitarian goals. And
the people themselves may not be aware of the corruption of
the city-state."[28] In Lin and Dong's characterization of ancient
Athens, greed for power and wealth is rampant, moral values
have disappeared, self-interest runs rampant, the losers of fac-
tional struggles are exiled, and the mindless mass holds power.
Finally, since the juries were made up of 201–501 citizens, the
civilian masses essentially monitor and limit themselves, a morally pernicious circle. Not all of this is parallel to modern democracy, but in Liu and Dong's article, all of this Thucydidean
account is used to condemn it.

On top of these problems, say Lin and Dong, the Athenian
democracy "fostered collective judgment" and thus "restricted
and eroded personal thinking, independence of speech, and
creativity." This is the opposite of the usual view that the dexter-
ity needed to support one's argument generally hones critical

thinking. Instead, Athens's reliance on rhetoric was a further assault on the good of the state and the individual:

> Individuals must be willing and able to be responsible for their actions. Does such an individual exist in Athenian democracy? . . . . It seems that only a clear and stable consensus on justice can make Athens's democracy assume responsibility. However, unfortunately, the Athenians' concept of justice lacks a clear and stable character. ,,. There are no external constraints for responsibility, no clear guidelines for the principles of justice, and Athens's citizens collectively think they can do everything. . . . They are more concerned with how to employ rhetoric in the debate, using sophistry and other means of expressing emotions in a way that makes others believe in their own opinions. . . . Emotions tend to be more dominant than reason . . . Citizens are provoked to act in the service of unsatisfied greed for external material interests.[29]

Democracy makes a cult out of individual freedom, but is unfree to the extent that it demands political participation of every citizen.

Aristotle does not fare well in these recent discussions either. We may recall the reverence he was treated with in the writings of Liang Qichao and others who influenced the May 4th Movement. In the 1980s Aristotle retained his status as the father of western political philosophy, the man who had made citizenship a condition for being fully human. While not quite the guiding light he had been in the post-Qing period, Aristotle still commanded scholarly attention for his influence on the west and his pioneering thought. At the end of the Cultural Revolution, scholars were cautious about where they stood with regard to his views, but by the mid-1980s it was safe for Wu Shuchen to opine that Aristotle's theory of the rule of law was a shining peak in the history of western political and legal thought.[30] In 1981, Xu Datong argued that Aristotle's *Politics* determined the understanding of political science in the west and, in 1982, Wang Junlin described the ancient philosopher as praiseworthy for seeing that a republic was the most authentic, stable, and victorious government system.[31]

Aristotle's glory has dimmed indeed. Where reformist thinkers once saw the blinking lights of the word democracy, now they see the darker faces of slavery and exclusionism.[32] Much of the critique has been leveled against Aristotle's claim in the *Politics* that slavery is a natural state (perhaps an unnuanced view of Aristotle's complexity). Slavery is actually, Chinese scholars say fairly enough, the dirty underbelly of a prosperous democracy.[33] The fact that Aristotle calls non-Greeks barbarians is singled out as narrow-minded (a bit odd given the old Chinese tradition of treating all non-Chinese as barbarians). Liu Chenguang 刘晨光 (currently a professor at Shanghai Teacher's University) argues in one of his *Four Treatises on Greece* (希腊四论 *Xila Si Lun*) that Aristotle is simply irrelevant to the Chinese-speaking world. Since Aristotle theorized about governments in the context of a particular time and place, he should not be taken to be speaking for different cultures and different peoples (even if he collected different constitutions). Moreover, since Aristotle was at pains to justify the institution of slavery and considered non-Greek cultures barbarous, why would one want to universalize his views in the first place? Even Aristotle's accounts of the truly virtuous man are muddled; Liu uses inconsistencies between the *Ethics* and the *Politics* to show that Aristotle was not so great a philosopher after all.[34] Aristotle showed the same weakness as much western political thinking: both make the fundamental error of one size fits all, a particularly western blindness long annoying to the modern Chinese.[35] Aristotle, in short, is an inconsistent, localizing racist, and there's no cause to read the Stagirite's work at all.

II. China's Model Democracy

Lin and Dong are not particularly preeminent among the best known post-Tiananmen intellectuals, and one might argue that publishing in a Party journal necessitates this sort of rhetoric about ancient democracy and its ills. But there are other scholars who are much better known—Pan Wei, Bai Tongdong, Gan Yang, Liu Xiaofeng, Cui Zhiyuan, Wang Hui, to name a few— and who, while not sharing the same perspectives, have developed related arguments that look back to classical antiquity (both Chinese and western) to support the view that the Chinese form of government is better than a western-style democracy.[36] Relatedly, there are also journals with a wider readership than the *Journal of the Fujian Provincial Committee Party School*. In 2017 one such publication—*Qiushi* (*Seeking Truth*), the Chinese Communist Party's theory-oriented periodical— published an editorial that took a different tack in its approach to democracy. Condemning ancient Athenian democracy for its abuses of human rights, the *Qiushi* editorial linked such abuse to the institution of slavery in the US. An appreciation of the shared flaws of both groups, the authors argued, will demonstrate that China is the largest democratic country in the world.[37] Unfortunately, the authors complained, the west isn't willing to share the term "democracy," but rather hogs it greedily to its metaphorical chest and polices other countries that fail to be democratic in the same way:

> The west has no right to monopolize the standard for the "democratic state." The essence of contemporary western political discourse is that it is trying to establish western democracy as the only "legitimate" form of democracy. Westerners deliberately refuse to apply the democratic form to contemporary China despite its own democratic pluralism.... Socialist democracy with Chinese characteristics is the broadest, most authentic, and most effective democracy that upholds people's fundamental interests and constantly shows its authenticity, effectiveness, and superiority.[38]

Though the CCP describes China's government as a meritocracy, the official view is that democracy is inherent within that meritocracy, due in part to the 1988 decision to allow citizens to vote for local officials.[39] Popular elections are held locally for representatives to the lowest of the five legislative parties, each of which elects delegates for the National People's Congress—which meets once a month to "rubber-stamp" the decisions of the Party leadership. Thus, Fang Ning, a researcher at the Institute of Political Science in the Chinese Academy of Social Sciences, writes that the People's Congress System (NPC) is the embodiment of China's democratic politics, which is not the same as the western version, but an adaptation for the Chinese condition. In his words, "Democracy is all human beings' goal, but different nations have different paths of democratic development and adopt different forms of democracy. The system of democracy is chosen by humans based on objective historical condition."[40] At the Party level too, there are calls for the United States to give up its dubious right to define what democracy truly is. "There is no fixed model of democracy; it manifests itself in many forms," the Chinese State Council argues in a 2021 position paper entitled "China: Democracy That Works."[41] In speeches, in articles, and on state television, Party officials praise Chinese-style democracy, especially its efficiency in crises (where, they say, American-style democracy can only muddle along).[42]

The authors of the *Qiushi* piece dismiss western democracy as a political flash in the pan.

> Both history and reality have proved that western democracy is only a temporary historical form of democracy under current historical conditions, and that it has largely been alienated as money politics and populist politics. It is not suitable for other cultural backgrounds and historical development conditions in non-western countries.[43]

In this understanding, democracy's connection to classical Athens is not a commendable fact, but rather part of a shameful legacy: the Athenian democracy relied on slave labor, denied women the vote, and dehumanized non-citizens. And the apple has not fallen far from the tree: the US had slaves until 1865 and women were not allowed to vote until 1920. At present, the Americans are slouching towards an aristocracy or a plutocracy: the Kennedy family, the Bush family, and the Clinton family are prominent (political) families; presidents can win the popular vote but still lose an election; lobbyists have too much power; and, as the authors put it, "contemporary western democracy is only a phased evolution of the capitalist political system under the economic and technological conditions of the 21st century. Its essence is still the political arrangement for safeguarding the interests of the bourgeoisie and monopoly capital." The authors thus manage to have their moon cake and eat it too, denouncing democracy while announcing that China is in fact the world's most democratic country—just not in the corrupt Athenian model.[44]

Another variation of the "Chinese democracy" model suggests that the Greek city-state was not a political formation particular to a specific place and time, but rather a universal stage in the development of all civilizations. This is a difficult claim to evaluate, because what exactly is included in the definition of a "city-state" (the coined Mandarin word is 城邦 chengbang, literally, wall-state) can be as little as the presence of old city walls (in terms of archeological discoveries) or as a tripartite division of citizens, elders, and leaders. Although Gu Zhun's posthumous work on the Greek city-state maintained that there was no such system in the ancient east, western scholars are criticized for calling the city-state unique to classical antiquity while charging China and other countries of the ancient east with "Oriental despotism." In fact (the argument goes) China, Mesopotamia, Egypt, and many other ancient civilizations were fundamentally based on the city-state. This claim is most associated with the historian Lin Zhichun 林志纯 (also known as Ri Zhi 日知), who in 1989 published a hefty edited volume entitled *The Study of the History of Ancient City-States* (古代城邦史研究 *Gudai Chengbangshi Yanjiu*). The book's first four chapters address his theorization of the city-state, while the following essays focus on particular case-studies in North Africa, India, west Asia, and the Americas. The book concludes that the political form of the city-state has gone through four stages, starting out as a primitive democracy—and eventually evolving into empire. In this schema, western democracy would be a sort of reversion to a less evolved form of government. A number of Chinese historians have followed in Lin's footsteps, positing the existence of city-states in China up to the Warring States period.[45] As Xin Fan remarks, the implication of the argument by Lin

Zhichun and his colleagues is that "ancient democracy was not a monopoly of western civilization and that civilizations in the East and West shared the same nature and followed similar trajectories in historical development."[46]

Athens, then, has been coopted to various ends since the 1990s. There is the ancient critique of Athens as fodder for the contemporary critique of the United States. There is the condemnation of ancient Athens as a place marked by the absence of liberty because of the constraints of citizenship. Then there is the excoriation of Athenian politics as a mere site of rhetorical grandstanding. We have seen both classical Athens and the United States condemned for the complicit source of their wealth in the enslavement of other human beings. And finally, taking the value of the city-state as a positive rather than as a negative, some scholars have suggested that the Chinese had the city-state first. But perhaps the most surprising post-Tiananmen development around western antiquity is the wholesale rejection of "Western Civilization" by scholars who argue that the west's ancient civilizations were built mostly—or even entirely—on the discoveries (as well as sufferings) of others. These are scholars who represent a radicalized Martin Bernal in Chinese, if you will, in arguing that what made western antiquity great was what it took from non-western cultures.

In its most extreme form, this is the position of the conservative, pro-government Chinese author He Xin 何新, who has written two books arguing that Renaissance scholars faked the existence of classical Greece and Rome and instead themselves wrote most of the classical texts we have.[47] Even the archeological findings, He insists, are forged. Western academia deliberately created this false Greece and a false history of its reception in order to seize the intellectual heritage of Asians. As He puts it on his blog site, "One of the important methods by which western academia created a false history of Greece is by stealing the developed ancient civilizations and philosophies in Asia Minor, disguising them as European civilizations on the Greek peninsula."[48] He Xin continues:

> Exposing the pseudo-history of Greeks and Romans pokes a big hole in the myth of western civilization. I believe that the Chinese . . . will eventually discover that the entire world history currently compiled by the west is actually forged based on the values of modern times in the west. The false history of Greece and Rome that I have revealed is just the tip of the iceberg.

This is a startling claim, to put it mildly. But why would Renaissance scholars go to all the trouble of inventing these pseudo-history?[49] In He's view, the scholars were embarrassed at not having a distinguished cultural lineage of their own. He concedes that there were some ancient figures that actually existed, but not as we have learned of them. Aristotle was legitimately ancient, but he's not really Aristotle, because "Aristotelian" texts are "probably imposters from the works of many different periods and different authors in ancient Asia Minor. . . . Since the time of the Holy Roman Empire, western Caucasians have always claimed that Greece and Rome are their ancestors. But as Voltaire famously said, 'This empire is neither sacred, nor Roman, nor an empire!'"[50]

To be fair, He Xin has presented more defensible observations. For example, he argues that so-called "western culture" is wrong to claim descent from ancient Greece and Rome, for the story of that relationship is much more complex. Homer, for example, was from Asia Minor, and Alexander from Macedonia. Many of the greatest philosophers (Plato aside) were not Athenians. The civilizations of Crete and Mycenae have been appropriated as "Greek." Not all white people are descended from Greeks and Romans. Moreover, Greece was not a unified country at the time in question. As such, the west's ontologizing claims to "classical culture" are problematic, and (He stresses) this bears repeating more often and in more contexts. The main difference here from the three volumes of Martin Bernal's *Black Athena: The Afroasiatic Roots of Classical Civilization*, is the attribution of the culture of the classical Greeks to "Asians" alone, without the influences of the cultures of ancient Egypt and North Africa.[51]

What does He Xin think he is accomplishing in writing about the "forged past" of western culture? According to his own website, He Xin worked as a researcher for the Institute of Literature of the Chinese Academy of Social Sciences and was then transferred to the National Committee of the Chinese People's Political Consultative Conference. He also translated the Swiss historian Jacob Burckhardt's *The Civilization of the Renaissance in Italy* into Mandarin. He is hardly an uneducated madman. His autobiographical comments suggest that his whole effort to erase classical antiquity stems from a desire to win the approval of the current regime. He claims that he advocates neo-conservatism and was considered "the standard-bearer" of said view in the late 1980s. On his blog, He Xin claims to have written to Deng Xiaoping urging him to suppress "political heresy," and even advocated for a foreign policy that looked first to national interests. He, then, is trying to show his support for Xi Jinping's China by pitting its dynastic glory against the (fake) ancient history of the west. Hence the ending to his comments:

The white foreigners themselves have no ancient history that they can be proud of: their origins are barbaric.[52] Ashamed,

they created a fake Greek and Roman history to be their past.
The so-called "Renaissance" is actually a movement of white
people (Latins, Germans, Anglo-Saxons) systematically
forging western civilization. . . . Chinese civilization declined
in the past three hundred years as it became a colony of Don-
ghu [東胡, eastern barbarians], Manchuria, Qing Dynasty,
but the ancient civilization of Great China since the Han,
Tang, Song, and Ming Dynasties is extremely glorious. The
Chinese should reshape their cultural self-confidence, self-
esteem and pride![53]

It is revealing, to go back to some of the points made in the introduction to this volume, that a Chinese scholar would consider it a defense of his country to claim that Greco-Roman
antiquity was a forgery. It seems unlikely that a US scholar,
however hostile to China, would claim that the glories of
Chinese civilization were a figment of the Chinese imagination.
On the Chinese side, however, He Xin's views provoked real
debate—at least for a while.[54]

One well-respected scholar who took a few steps in He Xin's
direction but has avoided the provocation of saying that ancient
Greece is a fiction is the aforementioned Pan Wei 潘维, a
widely published professor at Peking University. Apart from his
appointment at the School of International Studies at Peking
University, Pan Wei is also the Director of the Center for China
and World Studies. As such, his perspective has some claim to
be one with a global reach—not to mention that he received his
PhD in Political Science at the University of California, Berkeley. In 2003 Pan Wei published a book entitled *The Rule of Law
and "Democracy Superstition,"* the gist of which is repeated in a
very long publication entitled "Ancient Greece and Democracy," published in 2006 on Aisixiang, an online thinktank of

sorts.[55] This online history of Greece is the source for the epithet that began this chapter: "To weaken popular democratic superstition, and to appreciate classical Chinese genius, has been the purpose of presenting the history of ancient Greece."

But just how does Pan Wei weaken "democratic superstition" (meaning a false belief in democracy) by writing a history of Greece?[56] It's all in the interpretation. Pan writes a serious history of antiquity backed up by well-known western scholarship, but interprets this history in new ways, stepping in with editorial comments to make sure his readers understand antiquity "properly."[57]

To open with, Pan notes/complains that, in western historiography, "Most scholars today belong to the 'democratic faction,' who regard democracy as a 'universal value.' Thus, criticizing democracy is naturally regarded as 'heresy.'"[58] Most western scholars *are* of the "democratic faction," and so what they criticize tends to be classical failures to live up to modern democratic ideals. But criticizing democracy is certainly not heresy in China, so Pan weaves the history of ancient Athens together with interpretations deeply critical of that democracy's stupidity and criminality, and in the process casts blame, not praise, on the "better" modern versions of democracy. For example, Pan argues that Socrates's "fierce criticism of the democratic system led the citizens of Athens to vote to execute him." Aha— so much for the free speech that is so valued by the west! Against this view, many scholars have pointed out that Plato's *Apology*, in which Socrates defends himself, casts his trial as essentially apolitical: his crime is "corrupting the young" and "not offering reverence to the city's gods, but introducing new ones." On the other hand, Pan Wei's interpretation is similar to that of the journalist I.F. Stone, which relies on the reported content of a lost text by Polycrates. In his 1988 book *The Trial of Socrates,* Stone argued that Socrates was very much enmeshed with the city's aristocracy (he taught many of them) and their non-democratic values.[59] According to both scholars, the original democratic government killed a supporter of oligarchy: who has a bad record on human rights now? There go two of the central claims of pro-democratic advocates.

Pan Wei also carefully detaches the institution of (bad) democracy from the (good) glory days of Athens, that is, the fifth century BCE. Disparaging the common idea that democracy and its practices stimulated great works of political theory, drama, and philosophy, Pan argues that any "flourishing of thought" was not due to Greek genius, nor to a system that encouraged creativity and rhetoric in public life, but rather to non-Athenian influences.

> It is superficial to attribute the achievements of ancient Greece to Athens, and it is even more absurd to attribute all of the achievements of ancient Greece to the democratic system of Athens, just as the modern world civilization is attributed solely to the United States, and the achievements of the United States are entirely attributed to the democratic system. The broken-armed Venus did not belong to Athens. Many Greek scientific and cultural achievements were made before the establishment of the Athenian democracy or after the decline, and most of them were not produced in Athens.

Again, Athens is used to discredit modern US democracy. Pan is clear that democracy definitely does not spur genius:

> The main scientific achievements of ancient Greece were obtained after the decline of Athenian democracy. The rise of Rome does not depend on democracy. The establishment of the Spanish Empire in modern times was not the result of democracy. The British Empire established by Queen Elizabeth

was not a democratic country, but it gave birth to Shakespeare
and Newton.

To support his views on antiquity, Pan Wei must ignore a
few problems. For example, when he strives to attach a critique
of British (and North American?) colonialism to ancient
Greek colonization, he omits the fact that Athenian colonization was very limited and that, in the context of colonization,
Athens is not the right city for the usual analogy between
democratic Athens and the western empires.[60] Our attention
to this discrepancy is diverted by an amusing tableau. Pan envi-
sions happy British colonizers singing Shakespeare (singing?)
as they set off to the New World to realize their imperialist
intentions:

> Just as the ancient Greeks colonized under the inspiration of
> Homer's epic, the early British colonists sang Shakespeare's
> poems to open up North America: "This happy breed of men,
> this little world,/ This precious stone set in the silver sea."[61]

Shakespeare's John of Gaunt, most oddly, must bear the burden
of proof in this analogy, even if it's unclear what exactly is being
proven by the quotation: that both Athens and the British were
maritime civilizations? (Greece is not an island, of course).
Most likely the citation is meant as a critique of the English love
of their "blessed plot" and "teeming womb of royal kings," such
royal kings being renowned for their unpleasant deeds far from
home. One does wonder if the Chinese dynasties had some
teeming wombs of royal kings themselves, given all those
concubines.

Consider another recent public-oriented essay, this one by
the respected intellectual Pan Yue 潘岳, whom we have already
met as the executive vice president of the Central Academy of

Socialism in Beijing. Pan Yue's 2020 piece "A Serious Misunderstanding of the 'Roots' of Civilization is the Biggest Issue in Today's Dispute Between China and The West" was reprinted and uploaded to the internet almost immediately after publication.[62] As Pan Yue begins, we see the familiar understanding of western culture as springing from antiquity as if from a father. Since "modern civilizations contain the spiritual genes of classical civilizations," Europe, the US, and ancient Greek and Roman civilizations are put in the same box and treated as having similar values. The Greeks, of course, laid the foundation:

> Ancient Greece contributed to freedom, democracy, and humanism in politics, and became the main spiritual source of the European Renaissance and Enlightenment. Only by understanding the classical civilization of Greece can we understand the inner world of modern civilization in Europe and America.

Fortunately for the Chinese, the classical civilization of ancient Greece is their "friend" (a new perspective) even if the modern west that sprang from it is not. "[Samuel] Huntington said that we need to define the enemy in order to know ourselves. This is the custom of the West. The Chinese people know themselves by defining friends. Classical Greek civilization is a friend." The sword of Damocles falls and cleaves off China and with it Classical Greece, those two great *pengyoumen* (friends), leaving behind the modern west, where people think aggressively and not peacefully. Like the Greeks, the Chinese had freedom of thought in their tradition: "The contending of a hundred schools of thought is the first peak of freedom in Chinese history, and it is also a grand scene admired by Western intellectuals."

For Pan Yue, Chinese historical unity is in sharp contrast to the multiple Greek city-states. The former left its boundaries open, laying the foundation of the multi-ethic integration of later generations (apparently the Uyghurs did not get the memo) while the Greeks always called other people "barbarians." Historically, Greek city-states fought each other until their collapse, while the Great Unified Han Dynasty started the long and harmonious dynastic period. China, hundred schools or not, always aimed at the establishment of a unified order.[63] Pan Yue points out that calls for pan-Greek Hellenism were rejected by the city-states, with Isocrates a lone voice arguing in favor. "The Greek city-state was a single-celled organism that could be reproduced indefinitely but could never unite to form a powerful nation-state. Instead, the Greeks colonized others to exploit their land and resources, wanting to take over even Persia and Asia." What's more, according to Pan Yue, "this line of thinking became the embryonic form of Western colonial imperialism in later generations."

Meanwhile, Pan Yue points out, Aristotle, Plato's best student, could not inherit his teacher's academy because he lacked Athenian citizenship—ironically enough, thanks to Pericles's insistence on Athenian blood for citizenship. Undaunted, Aristotle went off to Macedonia to be tutor to Alexander the Great, and we all know what *he* was good at. Even Alexander's "successes" were due to Aristotle: "This method of western imperialism, violent conquest and the spread of civilization, was invented by Aristotle."[64] It's time for us to ask the question, says Pan: freedom or order first? "Which one is more worth pursuing, the stability brought about by long-term peace or the innovation brought about by chaos and freedom?" Ending on a note of compromise, he points out that the goal for both countries should be "introspection, tolerance, and a harmonious coexistence."[65]

Pan Yue's essay has received much attention from fellow Chinese intellectuals, partly because of its revisionary view of the

Confucian philosopher Xunzi, who held that human nature is evil, but partly, I suspect, because everything it says about the west will ring familiar and therefore "true" to his Chinese readers. These simplifications run through many Chinese views of the west, impacting their understanding of what the west *is*, and what the Chinese place in the world *should be*. Of course the representation of Chinese unity and long-term peace isn't a particularly nuanced view of China or the rest of the world. As Daniel A. Bell points out, Aristotle's defense of slavery is morally abominable to the modern west as well, not just to the Chinese culture.[66] Plato and Aristotle do not say much about *ren*, benevolence, true (and odd enough), but other western traditions did have a rough parallel to the idea, Christianity being the foremost with its compassion for the weak and the oppressed—a point which receives very short shrift in Pan Yue's essay. It's handier to ignore this in order to produce a one-sided west with no heritage of human charity.

Some scholars do invoke Christianity, as Pan Yue does not—but only to assign blame for the modern west there and not with the Greeks. Now it is not the polis that is seen as lurking behind modern democracy, nor the fact that we have ignored Thucydides's warnings, nor that Aristotle was a bad theorist (if he existed and could be considered Greek). What westerners have inherited, instead, is bad *character*: or rather, a belief that human nature is bad, which inevitably leads to a political system that has to be vigilant and policing rather than trusting and benign, in the Confucian mode. This is another "big idea" about the west. According to Wang Huaiyu, western political theorists assumed human nature is evil because of the influence of Augustine's view of original sin, that is, the sin of Adam and Eve against God that was punished by exile from Eden (and, strange but true, by man's inability to control his erections).[67] In Augustine's thought, this original sin has polluted every human being since: we are born with a burden of evil. From here, argues Wang, derives the west's belief in the need for restrictive government and policing tactics throughout European history.

The Chinese, by contrast (according to Wang), were influenced by the view of Mencius (372–289 BCE) that people are born good, not bad. (Unsurprisingly, it would not be convenient to bring up the opposing view of the philosopher Xunzi here, though it is true that Mencius seems to have had broader influence). Wang writes:

> The doctrine of human nature in ancient China was Mencius's theory of human nature. Mencius during the Warring States Period believed that human nature is good, and that everyone is born with the "four good ends:" kindness, righteousness, courtesy, and wisdom . . . Some people cannot become good people without cultivating and expanding these "good practices." Some people strive to cultivate and expand their good deeds and they can become good people. . . . Since the monarch treats the people with kindness just as a father loves his children, the people should control themselves with kindness, righteousness, courtesy, and wisdom, and obey the monarch's rule just as children obey their father. Chinese monarchy is characterized by monarchs and fathers and sons. The inner unity of filial piety and loyal minister is obedience.[68]

Alas, no Chinese government has ever followed the precepts of Mencius and the first Ming emperor even wanted to ban him. Nevertheless, the Chinese people (themselves good) could also put their trust in the goodness of their benign ruler (although such trust, as Wang concedes, often failed them), a salutary situation all round. Meanwhile, the west's suspicion of potentially

corrupt leaders has led them down the wrong path of developing democracy. Yes, a belief in man's core evilness (and not social contract theory or the like) lies behind western politics:

> Due to the different foundations of the theories of human
> nature, a very different political doctrine took shape. Chi-
> nese political doctrine requires trust, loyalty, and the wor-
> ship of rulers; western political doctrine requires suspicion,
> vigilance, and supervision of rulers. The former becomes the
> ideological basis of the autocratic system, and the latter be-
> comes the ideological basis of the democratic system.[69]

For good measure, Wang throws in Martin Luther, Calvin,
Feuerbach, and St. Paul as fellow skeptics of human goodness.[70]
Wang's unusual speculation provides an excellent example of
how, in these discussions, we can see that (a) the Chinese tend
to find the source of a culture in the influence of the past; (b)
different arguments about different sources all lead to a similar
statement about Chinese superiority; and (c) what is published
even in academic journals can sound very alien to western
scholars of antiquity.[71]

In this case and several others, we must acknowledge that
non-Chinese readers are faced with a bit of a conundrum.[72] Is
Wang serious that Christianity made the west suspicious of
human nature and led to democracy? Wang's argument seems
to turn on itself at the end, producing a sort of political *ouробо-
ros* in which the qualities he criticized in the west turn out to be
also Chinese:

> [In the west] if the rulers are not carefully watched, they will
> yield to greed, or try for more power; and if the people end
> up worshiping them, democracy will evolve into dictator-
> ship. Heroes are hostile to democracy, and they are a threat

to a democratic society. Therefore, a democratic society must always guard against heroes and beware of heroes expanding their power indefinitely and dismantling democracy . . . [As for the CCP], it is necessary to safeguard the prestige of the party leaders and at the same time ensure that their activities are under the supervision of the party and the people . . . The development of socialist democracy . . . has led some officials on a no-return path to corruption even if originally the party's criteria for selecting cadres were moral. The root of the problem is the lack of oversight of power.[73]

This sounds like a self-protective way of pointing out that some contemporary Chinese officials are, well, corrupt at heart. Have we been reading these Chinese critiques of the west too simply? Are some of them, in fact, examples of esoteric texts meant for the few who know the deeper meaning? It is an interesting question with no obvious answer.

III. A Dissident Echoes the Past

This chapter, like the book it finds itself in, considers only intellectuals and public figures in mainland China. The reason for that should be obvious: the views of many scholars in Taiwan and Hong Kong (until the latter's relationship to the Chinese government changed) are not published in the context of Chinese anti-democratic pressure and reprisal against open criticism of the government. When scholars outside the mainland write about the western classics, they tended to assimilate Confucian thought with democracy rather than communism, suggesting that it is democracy and not modern Chinese policy that is more in harmony with ancient Confucian values.[74]

But what about Chinese exiles? Not surprisingly, perhaps, we find that much of what they have to say still reflects the interpretations and emphases of the May 4th Movement. For example, the treatment of Plato and Aristotle by Hu Ping 胡平, a well-known Chinese activist and human rights supporter who joined the Xidan Democracy Wall Movement in 1979, falls into that category. While still in China, Hu Ping wrote a famous (and secretly circulated) essay "On Freedom of Expression" that eventually appeared in the journal *Fertile Soil*. A decade later, in 1987, Hu Ping left China to pursue a PhD at Harvard University, and a year after that—just one year before Tiananmen Square—he moved to New York to work for an organization supporting the pro-democracy movement in China, the China Democratic Solidarity Alliance, where he was selected to be chairman. Unsurprisingly, the Chinese government promptly canceled his passport—and Hu Ping is still in New York. He is currently the Honorary Editor-in-Chief of the pro-democracy journal *Beijing Spring*, Executive Director of China Human Rights, and the Honorary Director of Independent Chinese PEN.

Hu's comments on Aristotle are worth comparing to the trends we have seen. Like Liang Qichao, Hu Ping praises Aristotle as the first to have a more complete and systematic discussion of the concept of citizenship as:

> people who have access to judicial affairs and governing bodies, or more broadly have the right to political participation. . . . This reflects a universal ideal of the ancient Greek city-state society. According to this ideal, political activity is the highest form of human activity, and only political activity gives life a complete meaning.[75]

Yes, slavery is a problem, and Hu does not seek to defend it. However, "if we only focus on the above-mentioned abstract criteria for citizenship, we must say that they are generally correct."

Apparently in response to critiques of Athenian citizenship that claim it denied the individual his freedom, Hu writes that "The beauty of Aristotle's view is that he values the development of the individual." Hu concedes that Aristotle's views were those of a particular time and place, but he still finds value in them:

> [Aristotle's] reflected the interests and aspirations of the so-called middle class, that is, the class of small and medium-sized slave owners and reflected the prejudices of the exploiters and their historical limitations. We must have a clear understanding of this, but if we analyze his views carefully, they do offer some enlightening insights ... Even if we are sure that big countries are not suitable for democracy, it does not mean that big countries are suitable for autocracy.

The views expressed in this chapter by mainland Chinese scholars illustrate the somewhat depressing fact that the classics tend to be appropriated by those in power to service their own ends (and this has been true in general, not only in China). Nie Minli 聂敏里, professor of ancient Greek philosophy at Renmin University, has made the point that "resorting to ancient classics, especially political ideals in ancient classics, is the most common strategy used by conservatism,[76] because traditions and classics ... always play important cultural functions in the history of various nations."[77] No matter which route the public-facing pundits (and their less visible academic followers) take through ancient classical history, politics, and philosophy, they all emerge safely on the other side with their own ideologies and perspectives about China intact and untarnished. This, of course, entails not looking too closely at the details of what they are reading, and many of their interpretations may seem hasty or incorrect from the point of view of western academia. But western academia is not the target audience: that would be the

Chinese people and the Chinese government. At the same time, these Chinese readings that seem radical to us offer hope for the much-battered field known as "classics" in the present day. If these texts deal with a body of work that, like Egyptian gold, can be repurposed to meet the values of its present-day readers in the west as well as the east, there will no longer be any reason to consider the classics "outdated" or representative of "dead white men." The classics can live in the west just as vibrantly as they do in China.

3

Thinking with Plato's "Noble Lie"

Perhaps lies (if they are good) are sometimes more useful and beneficial to the city and people than the truth? Socrates used the metaphor of gold, silver, copper and iron as a lie, but is this really a lie?

—CHEN YAN

WHILE CHAPTER 2 investigated the turn in classical studies in China that led to the use of ancient philosophical and political thought in order to criticize the west, this chapter turns to the most influential philosopher in that tradition—the Athenian Plato (429?–347 BCE). The strength of Plato's legacy provoked Alfred North Whitehead to quip, "The safest general characterization of the European philosophical tradition is that it consists of a series of footnotes to Plato."[1] Perhaps it is unsurprising, then, that Plato has garnered so much attention in China, especially in the case of the Chinese Straussians interested in producing "esoteric" readings of his dialogues, interpretations that are visible only to a chosen few.[2] The *Republic,* in particular, has won a broad audience; it is the most accessible, broad, and didactic of Plato's works, with implications for politics, philosophy, community, hierarchy, propaganda, marriage, the family, and much more. Accordingly, the *Republic* has generated more commentary in China than any other ancient (western) text. Interest in its message was largely responsible for the post-Tiananmen return of classics as an object of study—and also its institutionalization in universities. As Weng Leihua writes:

> The establishment of the discipline of western Classical Studies in China in the past two decades was largely kindled, promoted, and supported by the reading of Plato in contemporary mainland China since the 1990s. . . . [T]he name of Plato and many Platonic concepts have been referenced in many books, journal articles, online forum discussions, as well as commentary essays on popular culture. Plato has been serving as the backbone of discussions across disciplines, and his work has even reached general audiences to become part of popular culture.[3]

What do contemporary Chinese scholars make of the *Republic*, Plato's investigation into the nature of justice, the good citizen, and the ideal state? For the most part (unlike Plato's readers in the west), Chinese scholars approve of Plato's vision of a hierarchical, class-based society that depends on both genetics and merit—the best people, Plato argued, are usually born of the best parents.[4] Thus critics have used the *Republic* to suggest that Plato's hostility to democracy should have steered the misguided democratic states of the present world, especially the United States.[5] And yet this Chinese enthusiasm may strike us as peculiar, given the old-fashioned communist commitment to the equality of men. Though Plato held no such beliefs, maybe he, too, can be poured into a convenient container; the ideological dissonance here is not unusual, but rather the natural outcome of picking and choosing from classical texts. And as usual, there are cultural factors in play to ease any ideological discomfort. The revival of "Confucian philosophy" enables comparisons to Plato's *Republic*, and also familiarizes the supreme authority of Plato's philosopher-kings. As it turns out, the *Republic*'s description of a putatively ideal state is seen as sharing—or perhaps *does share*—many similarities with the ideology of the CCP today.

I. Justice, Big and Small

The topic of the *Republic* is the much-pondered nature of justice: how is it achieved within a person? And, as a corollary, how is it achieved within the city-state? As the dialogue between Socrates and several Athenian and non-Athenian interlocutors unfolds into a discussion of the first of these questions, Socrates introduces the idea that we can see the correct nature of individual justice by turning to justice "writ large"—that is, justice in a city-state—for guidance. This is an odd move on the philosopher's part. In fact, both the analogy of a person to a state, and the idea that there can be an internal justice in a person, are not popular ideas in western discussions of justice related to Plato. The western tradition tends to treat justice as something that emerges in the interaction between two or more individuals, or between state and citizen, or even between state and state.[6] But Socratic justice in the *Republic* is a self-contained system.[7] The analogy of justice in a person and justice in a state has led to one of the most famous and problematic of Platonic ideas—the nature of Kallipolis, the beautiful city-state.

In Socrates's exposition, justice in the state is the result of "doing one's own work and not meddling with what isn't one's own."[8] The philosopher-kings are best fit to rule; the guardians, to guard; and the ordinary rank of men, to deal with the mercantile and banausic aspects of life. In the same way, justice in the individual lies in the proper hierarchy of the elements Plato described as constituting the soul: the rational, the spirited, and the appetitive. These elements compete with each other for control of the individual, but justice can only be present when the rational element (*to logistikon*) rules over the other two, just as the logic-minded philosopher-kings of the ideal state must rule over the "spirited" warriors and the "appetitive" merchandise-grubbing *hoi polloi*.[9] The philosophers-kings *must* rule because they are the only ones who know what is best for the other two classes as well as for the society as a whole. Kallipolis will be led by those who have contemplated the abstract Form of the Good, the highest form of rational thought. As Socrates puts it, "It is better for everyone to be ruled by divine reason, preferably within himself and his own, otherwise imposed from without, so that as far as possible all will be alike and friends, governed by the same thing."[10] The non-rational citizens may not know that they are incompetent to rule themselves, which is part of the problem: if they were wise, if rationality ruled in their souls, they'd both see this truth and no longer be in need of rule from above. However, as it is, these citizens who cannot know what is in their own best interest need to be led to it, one way or another. Indeed, the characters in the dialogue who demonstrate the typical appetites that Socrates seeks to purge from the ideal city-state, suggest that "normal" Athenians would be loath to give up their luxuries—culinary, sexual, and other—to contemplate the Form (rather than the experience) of happiness or pleasure.[11]

Socrates's stress on the rule of the rational in his description of the soul and the city has shaped arguments about good government at least since the Enlightenment.[12] One of the reasons the Founding Fathers viewed Athenian direct democracy with suspicion is because they knew all too well that political actors (i.e., voters) do not always make choices in a rational way—at least if "rational" is defined as oriented toward the well-being and stability of the democracy itself rather than seeking individual advantage.[13] For Plato, this fact—possibly exemplified for him by the conduct and outcome of the Peloponnesian War, not to mention the trial and execution of his teacher Socrates in 399 BCE—would have seemed evident enough. A city-state ruled by philosopher-kings, whose rationality Plato predicated on their ability to see beyond the apparent but deceptive "goods" of this world, may even have had some appeal for an Athenian audience aware of the irrational and harmful decisions made by their own demagogues as well as the perils of a government in which offices were distributed largely by lot and policy matters were influenced by rhetorical fluency.[14]

But here we have a problem. If rational argument about the political good will not sway the non-philosopher classes, how are they to be kept in their place? What if it all went wrong? What if the warrior-guardians killed the philosophers to seize power? What if the philosopher-kings decided ruling was a chore? What if garbage men went on strike, or merchants used their wares as bribes? The problem is that chaos has not yet been ruled out of the eventual development even of the ideal city-state. And here we come to the crux of how to keep Kallipolis stable—there must be a "Noble Lie" to keep everyone doing their own thing. Never mind that elsewhere Socrates stressed the importance of truthfulness; in Kallipolis that must be suspended in the service of a greater good.[15]

II. A Not So Noble Lie

Let us first turn to the "Noble Lie" itself. The Lie is meant to offer a solution to the problem of how a just state can remain that way. Even the rationality-loving philosopher-kings would rather abdicate in order to contemplate the Forms (their natural preference, according to Socrates) than rule the flesh-ridden masses. So how does one make all the citizens of a state love their country and feel content with their lot in life? How does one create a bulwark against revolution, fence in desire, and perpetuate inequality among citizens but keep everyone happy? The answer lies in the use of a Noble Lie, a *gennaion pseudos*—a fable about the naturalness of the different classes of men.[16] Socrates argues that the citizens of the ideal city-state—including the philosopher-kings themselves, if possible—should be told this Noble Lie once they reach the age of eighteen. They must be told that they did not come from a human mother, but sprang fully grown from the earth, a mother they all hold in common. Yet the earth did not birth them all on equal terms. During their gestation in their earthly womb, some acquired a measure of gold in their souls, others silver, and still others iron and bronze. The nature of the "metal" in the individual souls then decides the person's future career and place in the city-state: gold for the philosopher-kings, silver for the warrior-guardians of the city, iron and bronze for the craftsmen and merchants and other members of the masses. It is the philosopher-kings of Kallipolis who conduct the evaluation of souls, and this must be timed to match their entrance to adulthood, because only then will the philosopher-kings have enough information, based on each person's schooling, to decide who has gold in their souls and who does not. At that time, the young adults are told to forget everything they thought was real before: their education, their parents, even their childhood, were merely part of a dream. They start to exist now—in their respective classes.[17]

The Lie teaches that the differences between the city's classes are neither conventional nor random, but rather natural, a natural order being much more difficult to contest than an openly constructed one. At the same time, the citizen's belief in a common "mother" provides filial ties to the other classes. The premise of the Lie seems to be that a bronze or iron citizen presumably would be happy with his or her station in life, as representing a natural fact in the same way that we accept differences of nature that are patently out of our control, such as being tall or short, who one's parents are, or where one is born. In Socrates's explanation, the Noble Lie would lead to stability and a well-run state largely free of crime and insurrection. And yet, even though Socrates claims that the Lie "would have a good effect, making them more inclined to care for the state and one another," it has rubbed many readers of the *Republic* the wrong way.[18] Not only does the Lie naturalize hierarchies and base justice on a mythological etiology, but it also involves a slightly sinister tinge of eugenics in that the state will tightly control who gets to breed with whom. In the mating festivals that Socrates proposes, goldens must sleep with goldens to ensure the highest probability of future philosopher-kings, and likewise silver with silver and bronze or iron with bronze or iron. And then their children—who will never know their parents, nor their parents know them—will be taken away and sent to school, and later evaluated. Among the guardians, infanticide will take care of the offspring of inferior parents.[19] And only on very rare occasions will superior parents produce inferior children, or vice versa, in which case the philosopher-kings will switch the child to the right class.

For Karl Popper in *The Open Society*, the Noble Lie was even worse than brainwashing; it exemplified Plato's racist mentality and offered an unacceptable justification of totalitarianism.[20] Writing in 1945, Popper, of course, had the recent horrors of the Nazi government in his rearview mirror. However, Popper did not lay the blame with Socrates. Instead, Popper attributed the ideas voiced here to Plato, claiming that Plato had reverted to aristocratic form later in life and thus betrayed Socrates's more humanitarian ideals—an argument difficult to prove one way or another. Popper was not the first to make this complaint. Thomas Jefferson had done the same in a letter to John Adams in 1814, "Socrates had reason indeed to complain of the misrepresentations of Plato; for in truth his dialogues are libels on Socrates."[21] Popper further complained that this definition of justice was unrealistic, and he criticized Plato's apparent lack of interest in the more normative problems of justice in the state, such as resolving civic disputes or the nature of jury selection. Others have made the same point many times since.

Nevertheless, some western philosophers have tried to "save" Plato by interpreting the Noble Lie in ways that stress, as it were, its nobility. The classicist Desmond Lee removes the unpleasant implication of lying altogether. In his edition of the *Republic*, Lee argues that "Noble Lie" is a mistranslation, and a better expression would be "magnificent myth." This myth "is simply meant to replace the national traditions which any community has, which are intended to express the kind of community it is, or wishes to be, its ideals, rather than to state matters of fact."[22] Lee's interpretation largely strips the Noble Lie of its fangs, rendering it a national tradition about who we want to be, like George Washington and the apple tree, or Mao Zedong digging a well for the people.[23] And it's difficult to conceive of an entire society believing in the Lie without an overarching figure who has set it going—and there seems to be no candidate for this figure other than Socrates himself, a reminder, perhaps, that we are in the land of the impossible. Interestingly, the question of the "primus inventor" is not cleared up in the *Republic*.

The more common scholarly tactic for dealing with the Noble Lie in the democracies of the west has not been to mitigate its force but rather to argue that the Lie actually works towards democratic ideals—or at least, non-authoritarian ideals—in one way or another. For example, the philosopher Catherine Rowett suggests that the Noble Lie deals a blow against aristocratic values and ideas about blood-based nobility. In her reckoning, the Noble Lie is designed to provide the city "with greater fairness and equality of opportunity, to prevent prejudice or privilege arising from noble birth or wealth or any other unfair advantages, and to facilitate social mobility."[24] This is a corollary to the fact that aristocratic status plays no visible role in Kallipolis, whereas even in democratic Athens, the census made distinctions according to wealth and not all classes were eligible for all offices. Rowett is therefore enthusiastic about the lack of hereditary peerage and she stresses mobility between classes. "A shoemaker's son must become a ruler if he is fit to be a ruler. He must not be left trying to make shoes. Nor must a ruler's son be asked to make political policy if he is better at cobbling."[25] Plato's Noble Lie, thus, becomes a statement of the "American Dream." But, in Plato's Kallipolis, it is clear that this would have been the exception and not the rule.

The political scientist Demetra Kasimis offers another way of "saving appearances." As she points out, Socrates is describing Kallipolis and the Noble Lie to a group of Athenian citizens, a metic (foreigner), and a slave—people who had lived through the chaos of the Peloponnesian War and who were also familiar with Athenian nationalist ideology. By brazenly describing the Lie, Kasimis argues, Socrates is not urging its value on his Athenian audience, but rather exposing it and warning them about the dangers of such lies, especially warning the audience about ideologies about the superiority of Athenian birth. In her view, the description of the Noble Lie lays bare the artifice by which "regimes, including Classical Athens, produce membership status as a 'natural' category. Plato presents the regulatory fiction that one's political 'kind' (*genos*) expresses one's pre-given status as an open secret."[26] Now the Lie reveals, rather than conceals, that the "natural" distinctions of an exclusionary citizenship politics are the effects of willful political power. "This narrative strategy," Kasimis writes, "takes on specific significance in the context of the blood-based membership politics of Athens, which had its own Noble Lie. Accordingly, Plato's text is shown to provoke insights into questions of democratic difference usually assumed beyond its purview. The *Republic* . . . [exposes] the workings of an essentialist politics it is typically thought to originate and prescribe."[27] In other words, for Kasimis, the myth of the metals is in a sense parallel to the founders' myth of autochthony used by the Athenians.[28] This is a fascinating idea. But it still remains difficult to know if the Noble Lie is to be seen as an improved version of the Athenians' consensual fictions or as a rebuke to them, just as it is difficult to understand why Socrates compares the Lie to a sort of medicine and hence characterizes it as beneficial.[29]

The Lie, then, affords much chance for complex interpretation. And yet, Chinese nationalist interpretations of it tend to be alarmingly straightforward.[30] Pan Wei, the scholar of Greek history whose interpretations of Athenian democracy were discussed in Chapter 2, considers Kallipolis (and perhaps even the Lie it is based on?) as a parallel to an ideal proto-Communist Confucian state, with the Confucian "sage king" playing the role of Plato's philosopher-king. In fact, in Pan Wei's interpretation, Plato was not the first to see the importance of a government run by philosophers; Confucius beat everyone to this observation. In Pan's words:

Plato's "Kallipolis" is obviously based on Sparta [Athens's great competitor, and a monarchy], and the ideal of eliminating private institutions has since become one of the western traditions. The modern international Communist movement is a modern version of this ideal. However, Confucius was born more than 120 years earlier than Plato. He put forward communist social ideals earlier than Plato, and they were more concise, clear and humane than Plato's ideas.[31]

The contemporary Chinese, it seems, are the Spartan-like denizens of this Confucian-communist-Platonic state. This clashes with the current ideological claim, in the context of the so-called "Thucydides Trap," that China is actually . . . Athens. But that is a topic for Chapters 6 and 7.

III. Hierarchy for the People

Perhaps we will not be surprised that in the 1980s, Chinese scholars who read the *Republic*'s proposal for a hierarchical society based on a foundational lie generally voiced consternation similar to that of scholars in the west. Song Fugang described "Chinese scholars" who criticize the three hereditary classes on the grounds that it is "an extremely absurd endorsement of destiny and blood lineage;" still others bemoaned the fact that "one's hereditary status in the *Republic* is lifelong; furthermore, it is inherited by generations to come."[32] Song himself disagreed with this criticism, not because he supported a hierarchy based on these principles, but because he felt (like Rowett) that Plato in fact paid great attention to the differences between generations and emphasized that any child who proved to have greater or lesser capacity than his parents should be promoted or demoted to the relevant metallic class. "Therefore," Song suggested, "it is more accurate to say that Plato focused on the changes of hereditary classes rather than the hereditary classes themselves."[33]

Xiao Fan, another pre-Tiananmen scholar, argued that Kallipolis was not a model for a communist state. Plato "cannot [be called proto-communist], because an ideology is necessarily created in reaction to another ideology, and there was no such thing as capitalism to react against when Plato wrote the *Republic*."[34] And although Marx wrote approvingly that "In Plato's ideal republic, the division of labor is said to be the formational principle of the state," Chen Guanghua disagreed. Plato, he said, wanted "to eliminate all subjective freedom," making it impossible for any normal person to be happy; moreover, his division of labor would not spur enthusiasm for production, "because there is no hope of obtaining property."[35] Hu Zhongping, criticized Plato in yet another way, pointing out "the impossibility of harmonious development (moral, intellectual, and physical) in Plato's ideal republic since it is based on clan and class, and incorrectly privileges the select few."[36]

Whatever the reasons, then—and it is interesting that they vary—scholars in general did not applaud the conditions of Kallipolis in the decade before the crackdown. However, in connection to the new Confucianism and the cult of personality surrounding Xi Jinping, the majority of recently published Chinese views on Plato's Noble Lie are in its favor. Far from thinking that the overarching lie on which Kallipolis is based is fundamentally wrong, or that a society founded on a rigid hierarchical structure is a restraint on human freedom and free will, in the past several decades most of the Chinese commentors on the *Republic*—both popular and academic—have argued that Socrates is merely stating the obvious when he describes the non-equal value of each citizen (thereby taking a Confucian rather than a Marxist line). If an ideology is needed to get people to swallow this truth, well, so be it.

So says Cheng Zhimin, director of the Center for Classical Studies at Southwest University of Political Science and Law. Given "the limited nature of most people's cognitive ability and judgment," Socrates must use a story as a drug for society.[37] "Not everyone can grasp the truth, and different treatments must be designed according to each person's nature and aptitude," Cheng argues. The Noble Lie must exist because human beings need the most brilliant people to be rulers, but the same reason they need them is why they don't appoint them. (Most) human beings are not smart enough to see what they should be doing. As for young people, the immediate recipients of the Noble Lie, Cheng notes that they are especially easily deceived.[38] Professor Zhang Lili agrees, noting the mistaken persistence of modern political philosophy on the issue of equality, stating rather baldly that equality is nonsense, hierarchy truth.[39] Luo Xinggang likewise endorses the hierarchical system produced by the Noble Lie as good for the state and for the human being, while Qing Lianbin argues that different skills demand different pay grades.[40] "In order to attract people to take these burdens, society must provide greater wealth, power, and prestige to people who play these roles. Thus, out of unequal distribution of resources, social stratification is inevitable." Articles to this effect appear in daily newspapers, such as the one by Wang Wenhu praising social stratification in Chongqing. Different social classes, he writes, have different abilities and responsibilities; if all classes could just cooperate and do their jobs, a better social and economic development would be achieved.[41]

Blogs pitch in too. Chen Yan, author of an online essay entitled "Thinking about the Noble Lie," opines that "Perhaps lies (if they are good) are sometimes more useful and beneficial to the city and its people than the truth. Socrates used the metaphor of gold, silver, copper and iron as a lie, but is this really a lie? People are different and they need an ideology to tie them together, and even some westerners agree."[42] Chen points out that "Tocqueville reiterated this point in the analysis of dogmatic beliefs in 'On American Democracy,'" and as such it is not a particularly alien idea. In Chen's words:

> Ideological beliefs are different due to different times. . . . If a society does not have an ideology, it will not be prosperous; it can even be said that a society without shared beliefs cannot exist at all. We can always see the importance of this question of talent in human development, as well as the importance of political structure in life. For example, a group of children who play will always choose a "head," or a child with leadership skills. Some children have demonstrated special talents since childhood, knowing that they have made little effort. Some can achieve certain results, and those whose qualifications are not very good cannot achieve such results no matter how hard they work; an extreme example is that the blind man can never be a painter. In political selection, this is also the case. The results of modern empirical science have proved to some extent Plato's true meaning. Perhaps through this "Noble Lie" of Socrates, Plato is telling us a truth that can't be avoided. Without the Noble Lie, we have a pessimistic situation that seems to be unacceptable.[43]

This means that politics should be based on an obvious meritocracy rather than on a universal vote. In fact, argues Chen, democracy itself is a sort of lie, but not a *Noble* Lie. Democracy rejects the idea of different classes and as such lacks the wherewithal to create a stable political situation for itself. In other words, the real lie is what *democracy* believes; Plato's Noble Lie is actually a truth, and, what is more, the Lie is necessary for the best society to thrive.

Li Yongcheng, a professor at the School of International Studies at Peking University, goes still further by linking the use of a Noble Lie to the United States in particular. In a piece entitled "Domestic Politics, Foreign Policy and American Diplomatic Lies—Some Issues Concerning the Development of Sino-US Relations," Li introduces Plato's Noble Lie as an early version of the well-known role of ideologies in shaping political beliefs and national cultures.[44] Li then goes on pinpoint the role of the Noble Lie in American domestic and foreign policy. Essentially, he claims, Americans are brainwashed by a lie spread by their government which they have swallowed wholesale: the idea that American democracy represents the best and most just existing government; that its respect for human rights exceeds that of many other countries; that the freedom of the individual is properly represented by the one person, one vote policy; and that America has a moral obligation to spread this particular form of democracy around the world. Pointing out that "According to a poll published by Gallup, at least 73% of Americans believe in 'American Exceptionalism' while roughly 70% of Americans feel that the United States is obliged to play the role of leader in world affairs," Li notes the effectiveness of this American Lie. This Lie can thus do its job, which is the concealment of ugly acts in American history and the erasure of the real problems with American democracy— including those of human rights, wealth disparity, and weak leadership.[45] The Noble Lie has morphed from a tool to maintain hierarchy to a tool to maintain democracy! In short: either the Noble Lie is (a) true, (b) active in China (where everyone somehow sees through it), and (c) to the benefit of the people and the state; or, the Noble Lie is (a) the evil tool of American democratic leaders, (b) active in the US, where the population buys it wholesale, and (c) deleterious to the people and the state.

And all of this goes back to the western ur-philosopher Plato. It is perhaps odd that no Chinese scholar has pointed out that many of the Founding Fathers loved the *Republic*. Edmund Burke said no less in his "Letter from Mr. Burke to a Member of the National Assembly:"

> Men are qualified for civil liberty in exact proportion to their disposition to put moral chains upon their own appetites . . . in proportion as they are more disposed to listen to the counsels of the wise and good, in preference to the flattery of knaves. Society cannot exist, unless a controlling power upon will and appetite be placed somewhere; and the less of it there is within, the more there must be without. It is ordained in the eternal constitution of things, that men of intemperate minds cannot be free. Their passions forge their fetters.[46]

John Adams likewise condemned the stupidity of the multitude. It was for this reason that senators were originally not elected by the people but by state legislatures, until the passage of the Seventeenth Amendment in 1913.[47] But to be fair, some of the American Founding Fathers hated the *Republic* passionately. In an 1814 letter written to John Adams, Jefferson positively ranted about the book, saying that:

> Having [recently had] more leisure . . . for reading, I amused myself with reading seriously Plato's *Republic*. I am wrong however in calling it amusement, for it was the heaviest task-work I ever went through. I had occasionally before taken up some of his other works, but scarcely ever had patience to go through a whole dialogue. While wading through the whimsies,

the puerilities, and unintelligible jargon of this work, I laid it down often to ask myself how it could have been that the world should have so long consented to give reputation to such nonsense as this?[48]

In fine, the Noble Lie speaks to the values of classical Chinese culture. Confucianism is not only hierarchical, but also discourages popular participation in politics because it is impossible for most, and inappropriate for many. When a student asked Confucius how he might best contribute to government, the answer was "Just be a good son."[49] In other words, play your role. Confucius also opined that the masses can be ordered to do something but can't be taught, while Laozi famously said the people should be made "stupid" (deceived). Xunzi liked to emphasize that social and political harmony requires rank, a normative fact that comes straight from *Shangdi* (God) himself.

> Where the classes of society are equally ranked, there is no proper arrangement of society; where authority is evenly distributed, there is no unity; and where everyone is of like status, none would be willing to serve the other. Just as there are Heaven and Earth, so too there is a distinction between above and below. . . . Two men of equal eminence cannot attend each other; two men of the same low status cannot command each other—such is the norm of Heaven.[50]

The basic idea of the Noble Lie is already inherent in the Confucian tradition.[51]

Another reason for Chinese support for some of the ideas of the *Republic* may have to do with the influence of the political philosopher Leo Strauss in China, the topic of Chapter 5. Briefly, Strauss's insistence on the value of the Greek classics and his apparently anti-democratic readings of many such texts in favor of traditional virtue ethics has rendered his work agreeable to many Chinese intellectuals.[52] Like Plato, Strauss raised the question of whether politicians could be both truthful and effective, by implication suggesting that Noble Lies do in fact play a role in creating political cohesion among citizens. In *The City and Man*, Strauss openly argued that a myth such as the one underpinning Kallipolis was a necessity for all governments.[53] In Daniel Dombrowski's words, "Strauss does not find the 'noble' lie problematic because he does not find the present-day demand for liberal freedom to be sound."[54]

But this is not the end of the story. If we take a step back from the Chinese interpretations of the Noble Lie, we might wonder, more cynically, if many such articles open up a place of doubt around, of all things, the communist state itself. If Chinese thinkers imply that a Noble Lie is necessary for the good government of the state, is this perspective not unacceptably out in the open, a condemnation, as it were, of socialism with Platonic characteristics and the whole machinery of the CCP? The point of the Noble Lie was that the citizens of the *Republic* would actually believe it, not disbelieve it but then carefully deem it necessary in their writings. Certainly, one cannot imagine the idealistic Communists of the early Mao years seeing their own ideology as a Noble Lie. Does this mean that to laud the Lie is to suggest that the ideology propagated by the CCP is transparent and evident to its citizens—and possibly not in their interest at all? Are we meant to understand that a Noble (or not-so-noble) Lie is operative in contemporary China, and that Chinese scholarly endorsements of the Noble Lie as a good is actually a secret way of saying that the emperor has no clothes? What do we make of the fact that Cheng Zhimin, Lin Qifu, Dong Cunsheng, and others see "through" the lie and as such are showing that the Chinese Noble Lie (say, about the best society being a socialist-Confucian one headed by a visionary figure) *has failed*? Or are they so high up that they are merely recommending it as the opiate of the masses? This interpretive spiral takes us to a place where religion is just replaced by another "myth" to keep the people in check. If that's right, surely Marx is writhing in his grave.

It's no surprise that the dissident view is less slippery. Hu Ping, for example, charges that the Noble Lie is exactly what the Chinese government propagates.[55] In his 2017 essay on Plato and Aristotle, Hu agrees that we need a division of labor and approves of class mobility between the three "castes" of the ideal polis. But then he introduces a critical turn in his apparently pro-hierarchy view. Just how does one set up such a polis? What measures must be introduced to do so?

> Plato proposed two methods. One is to fabricate a set of myths to convince the average person that the supreme ruler is made of a special high-grade material (gold), while the general producer is made of an ordinary material such as iron. The second is to adopt all coercive measures that can be taken, from controlling cultural education, carrying out inspections of books and newspapers, monopolizing public opinion tools, and carrying out whistle-blowing—what cruel and cunning means cannot be adopted? . . . The extreme and unjust inequality in rights between the ruler and the ruled is, for Plato, the perfect embodiment of justice. . . . Lying, reporting, and slaughtering all become the most moral things, as long as they are all from the hands of the king of philosophy, because the will and justice of the king of philosophy are originally the same thing.[56]

Needless to say, the Platonic city has no "public opinion tools" like television or the internet. But China does, of course. We have moved, very smoothly, from a state that Plato called just, to its actual embodiment in contemporary China, where it is manifestly unjust.

Hu Ping's rejection of Kallipolis is also his rejection of Xi Jinping's policies. Yes, different people are differently abled and ideally should do what they are best at. But for Hu, the method of maintaining this situation and the absolute power of the philosopher-king can only lead to corruption. Plato has safeguards in place against this, largely based in education; Hu, however, seems to suggest that China does not. Humans must not be forced into positions that they are told are the right ones for them; they must discover this on their own. Even well-intentioned monarchs will err. Perhaps with the specter of Mao hanging over his thoughts, Hu argues that the implementation of an all-powerful monarch is simply the first step on the path to corruption, loss of freedom of speech, and moral inversion ("justice is injustice"). But as long as the powers that be control the definition of justice, so it shall be. Under these circumstances, the "ideal" country prevents change in the name of perfection, cancels competition in the name of harmony, stifles freedom in the name of knowledge, and negates personality in the name of order.[57]

Echoing Hu's view, Qiang Zha, a Chinese expatriate writing for the western publication *Inside Higher Ed*, picks no bones about comparing Xi's position to that of the teller of the Noble Lie.[58] But Qiang Zha also claims that the Lie inheres not only in Chinese politics, but also in Chinese philosophy, where different sorts of noble lies may hold sway. The greatest, he says, is the reappropriated Confucian ideal of "harmony" (和谐 *hexie*; for more on this ideal, see Chapter 6). Hu delivers a blistering critique of Chinese government propaganda around this concept, which was adopted by Deng Xiaoping himself as an ideal supporting the rule of the CCP and much bruited by Hu Jintao.

Hu Ping writes:

> Many ancient thinkers advocated harmony (including Confucianism), and some scholars thought that it was a very beautiful concept and a good medicine to cure the ills of modern society. They did not seem to realize that, for example, in Plato, the concept of harmony was a complete derivative of the concept of justice. Using Plato's metaphor, the harmony of a society is like the harmony of a band, the premise is that everyone obeys a single conductor unconditionally. Whether it is Plato or Confucius, the harmony they advocate is "indisputable." It requires members of the society to give up their will to be independent and autonomous. Under the only correct arrangement of the benevolent and omniscient supreme ruler, each of you and each division will achieve a predetermined perfect state.[59]

The value of national harmony, in this reading, would be China's Noble Lie.[60]

Who appreciates these pro-Kallipolis readings of Plato's *Republic* in China? This is a complicated question. On the one hand, our notion that all Chinese scholars must be pro-democratic gains traction by examining the Chinese government's treatment of intellectuals and artists such as Ai Weiwei, the Nobel Prize winner Liu Xiaobo, or Wang Youcai, one of the student activists who lead the protests in 1989. But international polls of Chinese citizens seem to suggest that many Chinese are more negative about American-style democracy than about the contemporary Chinese system because democracy seems fundamentally unstable. Its weaknesses—that it allows little room for meritocratic considerations, incorrectly privileges the individual's interests rather than those of the state, is vulnerable to the tyranny of a particular group (say, the extremely wealthy), and takes itself to be the best form of government for everyone on earth—are thought to outweigh its positives. As Ken Moak recently wrote in the *Asia Times*, "In view of more than 80% popular support [of the Chinese government] according to US-based Pew and Gallup polls and China's ability to deliver on most of its promises (such as improving people's livelihoods), the vast majority of the country's population seem content with Beijing's governance architecture."[61] We may be skeptical of these numbers, which are certainly influenced by Chinese media and the state apparatus. But they offer a corrective to our assumptions that either the newly emergent Chinese middle class or the long-suffering intellectuals are secretly and collectively clamoring for democracy.

We are left with only questions. Is siding with Plato in China an act of support or of resistance in a country perceived as having values similar to Kallipolis? Or do the Chinese critiques of western discomfort with the Noble Lie represent a genuine point of view within that eighty-percent figure cited by Ken Moak? Are the Americans—or the Chinese—exoteric readers, imbibing the public message of the *Republic*, or esoteric readers, seeing the truth underneath? (For more on these Straussian terms, see Chapter 5.) Is the US caught up in a bad Noble Lie, or the Chinese in a good one? As the young nationalist Tang Jie says, "Because we are in such a system, we are always asking ourselves whether we are brainwashed . . . We are always eager to get other information from different channels. But when you are in a so-called free system you never think about whether you are brainwashed."[62] And therein lies the final paradox for this chapter: only the oppressed understand they are being brainwashed; the "free never see it."

4

Rationality and Its Discontents

Social action, like all action, . . . may be: (1) instrumentally
rational (*zweckrational*). . . . for the attainment of the actor's
own rationally pursued and calculated ends; or (2) value-
rational (*wertrational*), that is, determined by a conscious
belief in the value for its own sake of some ethical, aesthetic,
religious, or other form of behavior, independently of its
prospects of success.

—MAX WEBER

RATIONALITY IS BIG in China, particularly as a topic used to
denigrate the west. It has lost the high moral status it had in the
days of old, when the May 4th reformers clamored for the
methods of western science and traced logical thinking back to
the Greeks. Now rationality figures in the charge that western
society, given over as it is to its sciences and technologies, has
lost its soul. Endless articles point to the mechanized and
amoral character of the west, tracing the genealogy of its harmful and rationalist ways at least to Kant and sometimes all the
way back to Plato. According to this understanding, the central
idea of the philosophical tradition has been represented by

"Enlightenment rationality," thanks to which the development of science and technology has become unmoored from larger ethical issues, while advances in technology are treated as ipso facto goods. This overemphasis on rationality is the source of the mess the west finds itself in now. Unpredictable innovations in artificial intelligence, genetic interventions into the human genome, and world-changing technologies rattle on at a terrific pace against the increasingly uncomfortable backdrop of global warming, itself an example of runaway technology.

The message is sobering, but the connection to the Enlightenment and to western antiquity demands investigation. What is "western rationality," exactly? Is there, for example, a Chinese rationality one might oppose to it? Or is China on the side of the irrational? Does China not support advances in technology too? Are we more soulless over here than the Chinese over there? Surely one could not come up with a more nonsensical idea. And yet these generalizations have staying power. From the Chinese perspective, western rationality is geared to economics, efficiency, and profit, whereas eastern rationality has the ethical life as its goal. Western culture is crudely instrumentalist, seeking to derive use from everything, while the Chinese (like Kant, himself a model for enlightenment) say one must never use another human for one's own end. Per this reading, the Chinese rationality is this way because its ethical traditions (Confucianism, Buddhism, Daoism) were not much concerned with the concept of rationality, but instead focused on social values such as kindness to others and respect for social hierarchies; western rationality, in opposition, relies on Plato who was fixated on mathematics and the Forms and the principle of non-contradiction and deductive argument.

China was not always so anti-instrumentalist. At the time of the 1898 reforms, the Qing dynasty official Zhang Zhidong

張之洞 proposed in his *Exhortation to Study* (劝学篇 *quanxue pian*) that the Chinese should adopt foreign ideas only in as much as they were useful, while keeping such ideas at arm's length from China's culture and identity. This was summed up in his famous motto "Chinese Learning as Substance, Western Learning for Application" (中學為体, 西學為用 *zhongxue wei ti, xixue wei yong*).[1] In other words, use the ideas that are useful, but don't adopt their creators' values. And Cai Yuanpei, chancellor of the National University of Peking (NUP) in the 1920s, stressed scientific rationality as the heart of the modern research university, transforming the NUP "into a locus of research with mottos like 'not to the preservation of national quintessence but to its reevaluation by scientific methods,' . . . absolute academic freedom, free expression of all theories and viewpoints on rational ground."[2]

I. The Soul-less West

Today instrumentality has circled around once again, but this time no one is eager to lay claim to it. The discussion of rationality at the heart of many an article in Chinese academia has taken the form of a Weberian split inside the (already slippery) concept of rationality itself, with one side designated as wholesome, and the other as unpleasantly capitalist.[3] A quick appraisal of the massive Chinese research database CNKI reveals *thousands* of scholarly articles over the past two decades that refer to "value rationality" and "instrumental rationality."[4] The topics of these articles range the gamut from law, education, bureaucracy, ethics, the media, big data, poverty, taxes, medicine, and human resources to beyond: rationality, after all, can pop up in almost any field. However, the authors' approach is almost always to employ a binary framework of instrumental and value-driven forms of rationality. And invariably, China and the west are characterized as using value-driven and instrumental forms of rationality, respectively—in each case reaching back to canonical texts in their cultures.[5]

The conceptual pairing of "instrumental rationality" and "value rationality" does not come from China's own ethical tradition.[6] Instead it derives from the work of the German sociologist Max Weber, who, in his *Economy and Society: An Outline of Interpretive Sociology*, as we saw in the header to this chapter, outlined this distinction between different types of social action:

> Social action, like all action, ... may be: (1) instrumentally rational (*zweckrational*). ... for the attainment of the actor's own rationally pursued and calculated ends; or (2) value-rational (*wertrational*), that is, determined by a conscious belief in the value for its own sake of some ethical, aesthetic, religious, or other form of behavior, independently of its prospects of success.[7]

This is, of course, an oversimplification, even within Weber's own corpus. As Barry Hindess points out, "Weber's discussion of the secular growth of 'instrumental rationality' posits numerous sources of variation ... [that] depend on the environmental conditions of possibility of certain kinds of rational calculation and action."[8] But it is Weber's disquiet about rationality and logical procedure as a means that concerns us here. Weber felt that the west had started to move too close to *zweckrational* (instrumental) action. This was the effect of the combined forces of technology, capitalism, and bureaucratization, which had turned life into an "iron cage," an economic machine in which the human is merely a cog.[9] "The fate of our times," Weber wrote, "is characterised by rationalisation and intellectualisation and, above all, by the 'disenchantment of the world.'"[10] Weber felt that we

today by cognitive neuroscience, econometrics, and analytic philosophy of the mind.[16]

Just so, British philosopher Jonathan Glover argued in his "moral history" of humanity that the Enlightenment view of human psychology looks increasingly "thin and mechanical," and that "Enlightenment hopes of social progress through the spread of humanitarianism and the scientific outlook" now appear naïve.[17] Glover attributed many of the atrocities of the twentieth century to technological advances and, beyond that, to the influence of the Enlightenment. Even if Stalin himself had little interest in the Enlightenment, he and his heirs were willy-nilly "in thrall to the Enlightenment."[18]

In their classic *Dialectic of Enlightenment,* the philosophers Max Horkheimer and Theodor W. Adorno showed their Weberian influence by characterizing Enlightenment logic as an unyielding tool of domination that is closely tied to the scientific method and the advance of technology.[19] Modern technologically oriented rationality deserved particular condemnation, according to Horkheimer and Adorno, because it marked the change of reason into a metaphysical good that resembled the very superstitions (i.e., religion) out of which Enlightenment reason had supposedly lifted mankind. Philosophy itself had become an instrument of technocracy—and the instrumental notion that efficiency must be the endpoint contributed to the horrors of the Nazi's annihilation of Europe's Jewish communities, and other groups. Another Weberian, the sociologist Zygmunt Bauman, has also used National Socialism as the punctuation mark for his argument about instrumental and value forms of rationality.[20] In his 1989 book *Modernity and the Holocaust,* Bauman argued that modernity provided the "necessary conditions" for the Holocaust to occur, because the principles of rationality and efficiency typical of the modern era were Hitler's helpmates in contributing to the scale of the Holocaust.[21] Which Enlightenment thinker is "responsible" for this deadly form of enlightened rationality? The Enlightenment, after all, saw a slew of ideas on the nature of man and his world.[22] Descartes, Spinoza, Leibniz, and Kant held the universe to be thoroughly rationally intelligible (Leibniz even proposed that all human ideas could be expressed in such a way that they could be handled mathematically!). Hobbes's arguments center on individualist rights and contracts. Hume held that reason operated together with sentiment in almost all moral determinations and conclusions.[23] The *Encyclopédie* of Diderot and D'Alembert is dedicated to three empiricists, Francis Bacon, Isaac Newton, and John Locke, the last of whom finds the source of all our ideas in the senses; so does the Abbé de Condillac in his "Treatise on Sensations."[24] In fact, many modern scholars have argued that issues such as human rights and the political ideals of liberty and freedom were more central to the Enlightenment than deductive rationality.[25] And, of course, many Chinese intellectuals are not part of this mainland trend, and recognize that there is no one "Enlightenment." The Taiwanese neo-Confucianist Tu Weiming (a professor now at Peking University) has commented that "a realistic appraisal of the Enlightenment mentality reveals many faces of the modern west incongruous with the image of 'the Age of Reason.'"[26] Meanwhile, the Hong Kong comparativist Zhang Longxi has noted of the neo-conservative group that follows this line of thought:

> its relationship with the west is a preposterous and contradictory one, for on the one hand it claims to represent the interest of China as a Third World country against the hegemony of the west, while on the other it relies heavily on

theories au courant in the west, those of postmodernism and postcolonialism in particular, and imitates the latest fashions in western theoretical discourse for conceptualization and methodology, even for sentence structure and vocabulary or jargon.[27]

In short, instead of upholding the tenets of postcolonial criticism (the Chinese are supposed to protest historical interference), these scholars are complicit in the structures of power they are supposed to expose and undermine.[28]

Among the less nuanced versions of the Enlightenment, most of the fingers seem to be pointed at Immanuel Kant as the guilty party who set the rationality train on its disastrous tracks. In his famous essay "An Answer to the Question: What is Enlightenment?" Kant defined enlightenment as requiring "nothing but *freedom*—and the most innocent of all that may be called 'freedom:' freedom to make public use of one's reason in all matters." Kant's Enlightenment was thus literally defined as acting on the dictates of an autonomous reason.[29] As Axel Honneth puts it, "Enlightening thought claims to liberate the thinker from the spell of handed-down traditions by subjecting to rational, universally reconstructable examination that which had previously been valid solely by being socially binding."[30] This is the message the Chinese critics of the Enlightenment have taken away. And the blogger Lao Ji 老几 avows in his moral comparison of Confucius and Kant that, "Kant's morality is based on pure reason. It is the first time in human history that a strict moral system was established according to a logical method. It makes up for the lack of moral reasoning in theological beliefs that held sway in the west for thousands of years. . . . This is also an important reason for the enduring influence of Kant's philosophy."[31]

But how do Kant's rationalizing ways supposedly lead to the Holocaust? One claim is that he made possible the positioning of duty above compassion—the result of his argument that a moral agent does a particular action because he or she recognizes by *reasoning* that it is the morally the right thing to do and therefore has a duty to do it. But this reasoning toward moral duty can be misused in alarming fashion. If you believe all Jews are vermin and that it is therefore your *moral duty* to exterminate them, what next? Rudolph Höss, the commandant at Auschwitz, wrote a terrifying description of how he had to ignore his "emotions" and murder a young Jewish mother and her two children; one could imagine a Christian crusader saying the same words as he thrust a lance through the infidels and their offspring.[32] Moral systems could be tweaked to support this particular kind of duty, for example, by labeling Jews, Gypsies, and gay men as "vermin." At Nuremburg, Eichmann famously invoked Kant to explain his own actions: Eichmann had to fulfill his duty by "setting an example within the framework of the legislation of the laws."[33] In this case, Kantian duty was created by the government, not the reasoning self, but it is noteworthy that the Italians didn't embrace Kant at the time.

Plato provides an interesting contrast. He too argues that reason is all we need for the moral life. But the process by which the two philosophers prove their claims are different. Plato "proves" that reason is the highest element of man by relying on stories, metaphors, and a priori assumptions. Kant's proof similarly rests on the a priori claim (among others) that "reason" is the highest value in humanity.[34] But in Kant, the upshot of the emphasis on reason is that we have a duty to treat others well because they, too, possess the special faculty of reason (which does not accord especially well with the Holocaust, of course). In Plato, the outcome of reason ruling in the soul is the

hierarchical society of Kallipolis.[35] Kant's either/or of rationality (you have it or you don't) seems more dangerous than Plato's view that reason is something that the individual soul has
less or more of, so that the humans coming in low on their reason content could be safely relegated to the bronze or iron
people as opposed to being dehumanized altogether.

A further, if less dramatic, criticism often leveled at Kant is
that his emphasis on rationality necessarily had an instrumental
character. As Honneth writes,

> A rational approach is inexorably linked to a perspective that
> involves the domination of things and persons. Rationality
> or reason has an instrumental character, because it serves as
> a means to know (*erkennen*) existing states of affairs and to
> make it possible to handle practical tasks. This form of the
> critique of reason . . . which found impressive expression in
> *Dialectic of Enlightenment* starts from the assertion that, by
> the capacity for rational behavior, we usually mean the abil-
> ity to know objects in order then to manipulate or control
> them in terms of the goals of one's own action. It is easy to
> show that, once it has come to predominate one's dealings
> with other people or with one's own wishes and needs, such
> a capacity for purposive-rational knowledge becomes a me-
> dium of instrumental domination.[36]

Rationality now leads to the control and domination of others.

Given all this western criticism just waiting to be adopted by
interpreters with an anti-western animus, it is not surprising
that Chinese scholarship has seized the opportunity to suggest
the horrors awaiting instrumentally rational western society.
One particular professor, the well-known scholar and former
dean of Boya College at Sun Yat-sen University, Gan Yang, in
"Freed from Western Superstition" (从西方迷信中解放出来

Cong xifang mixin zhong jiefang chulai) claims that the west has had three "enlightenments."[37] The first was the Greek victory of philosophical reason over myth. The second was the European Enlightenment and its abolishment of superstition (Christianity).[38] Finally, the west's third enlightenment is still in process. It consists of the post-Auschwitz revelation that the Enlightenment and its values were themselves forms of superstition: that the emphasis on rationality above all other values birthed instrumental rationality, which contributed to the exploitation of other humans.

As Gan continues, he identifies rationality as the religion (as it were) that was the Enlightenment's brutal new credo. "The largest superstition to be cracked is enlightenment itself, that is, the contemporary superstition caused by western enlightenment— the superstition of technology, of rationality, and especially 'instrumental rationality,' of the right of the human being to plunder and enslave nature, and of the theory that the west is the center."[39] Very much following Weber, Gan writes, "In market-oriented, highly commercialized societies such as those in the west, 'disenchantment,' the loss of the sacred, the single-minded secular pursuit of material wealth, and various forms of human alienation and spiritual estrangement constitute integral parts of the modernization process."[40] The first online version of Gan's article, which has since disappeared, featured a photo of a 1936 Nazi rally in Berlin in which an Olympic torchbearer runs up a long aisle to the dais on which Hitler awaits.[41] The accompanying Chinese text makes the picture's meaning explicit: "Measured in this huge scene, the modern Olympic Games and Nazism represent both sides of the Enlightenment."

At least there are two sides, the maligned west will be relieved to know. But we've seen this charge before: that it was rational, goal-driven thought, the machines of bureaucracy, and the valuing of efficiency over human lives that enabled the Nazis to murder millions of people in the camps. Thanks to the glorification of scientific development for its own sake, lamented Gan, we lose "the moral ground that should be our telos as human beings."[42] It is certainly convenient to beat the west with some of its own views. *Incredibile dictu,* in "Science as Vocation" Weber himself traced instrumental rationality back to Plato's Forms(!). Seeing rational argument as "a handy means by which one could put the logical screws upon somebody," and arguing that "redemption from the rationalism and intellectualism of science is the fundamental presupposition of living in union with the divine," Weber damned Platonic knowledge (in its abstraction) as the ultimate form of scientific expertise.[43] In this argument, not only did Plato lie at the basis of rational thought, his thinking also provided the necessary, if insufficient, conditions for western capitalism.[44]

In all this Weberizing, the Chinese are doing themselves a disservice. To borrow these ideas from the west to discuss China's own status vis-à-vis western culture is to borrow foreign terminology related to a historical and political tradition that has little to do with China's own rich history of thought. Using Weber cannot provide a mirror to China; at the very least, a multiplicity of social, historical, and economic phenomena (such as the industrial revolution, the rise of science and technology, capitalism, democracy, and so forth) underlie the discussion but are not placed in proper context.[45] The Chinese scholars who adopt the Weberian way seem to assume that temporally and culturally localized figures like Weber can think for all the world—thus falling into the very trap of cultural imperialism that they condemn.[46] As Liu Dong of Peking University protested, "If we should choose this 'instrumental rationality'— based on the lived historical reality of the west—as the grid upon which to examine Chinese historical sources and, even worse, if we make it the standard by which we judge 'progress' in Confucian society, then those criteria for evaluating historical progress that have emerged out of and are innate to Chinese civilization will be voted obsolete and thus be rendered invisible."[47] Indeed.

II. *Ren* Stakes a Place

The Chinese have their own—also ancient, but quite un-Socratic—answer to the central place of rationality in the western tradition. It is such an obvious value that one might even wonder just why it hasn't been a dominant feature of western philosophy as well.[48] It is benevolence, or *ren* 仁. An alternative to the abstract life of rational contemplation praised by Plato and Aristotle, *ren* reflects the necessity of treating others humanely and with good will. In the words of one scholar, *Ren* entails "a lifelong striving for any human being to become the most genuine, sincere, and humane person he or she can become."[49] Both aural analogy and visual form play a role in this meaning, since *ren* 仁 is homophonic with the word *ren* 人, which means "human" or "person," and "the distinction between the two terms [仁 and 人] is arguably qualitative: two distinguishable degrees of what it means to be a person."[50] The ideographic relationship between the two strengthens this association: *ren* as "benevolence" (仁) consists of two elements, *ren* as "person" (人) and the number two (二). In other words, man is not a political, but a social animal.[51] Another important homophone relates government to righteousness. Confucius believed that to conduct *zheng* 政 (to govern) requires one to be *zheng* 正, which means "being proper," "straight," "orderly," or "to correct" or "to make straight." The two words are not merely homophonous; they have an intrinsic affinity. Confucius writes, "If you can correct yourself [that is, be (*zheng* 正], what problem will you have in governing? If you can't correct yourself, how can you correct others?"[52]

Even explaining *ren* is embedded in consideration of context rather than abstract principles.[53] For this reason, Ni Peimin explains, "when asked about *ren*, Confucius gave different answers to different disciples according to their particular needs for personal development. This fact suggests that *ren* is more like an art that needs to be mastered, embodied, and displayed in one's gestures and manners, rather than a formula to be understood or accepted by the intellect."[54] Strikingly, in Confucian thought, identifying or theorizing benevolence does not precede practicing it.[55] The Socratic paradox of "virtue is knowledge" is totally absent—even if a charismatic teacher is doing the education in both traditions. There is no obvious relationship of morality to rational deliberation (as in, for example, Kant's universal laws validated by pure reason, or Descartes's deductive reasoning from "cogito, ergo sum"). With *ren*, how could one even begin to think of life in instrumental terms? As Confucius said, "The noble man is not a utensil," either to himself or to others."[56]

III. A Farewell to Binaries

Depending on whom we are listening to in China, the Platonic and Confucian canons do or do not look very much alike. Certainly from the perspective of the instrumental rationality argument, their output and their methods are strikingly distinct. From Plato, we have some thirty-five dialogues that lean on dialectic and the principle of non-contradiction, relieved by occasional doses of myth (the *Laws*, of course, is not a dialogue).[57] These works attempt to assert universal truths, but in practice they tend to provoke thought rather than dictate final answers. The Confucian canon consists of a book of ancient poems and eulogies, a book about divination, a book that describes court rituals, a collection of documents written by ancient rulers and officials of the Zhou period, a book on the golden mean, and collections of conversations Confucius had with students and Mencius had with kings. The *Analects*, the *Doctrine of the Mean*, and the *Great Learning* are perhaps closest in style to ancient Greek philosophy, but even so, their method is to use conversation, analogy, and elusive observations about the appropriate behavior of wise men and kings rather than dialectic, deduction, or formal syllogism.[58] Confucius himself did not privilege the acquisition of the techniques of Socratic argument, writing instead that "clever words disrupt virtue."[59] The Daoist Zhuangzi rejected the use of reason and argument as a means to "the path:" "Reasoning will not make men know about it [the Dao] . . . it is better to be silent than to reason about it."[60]

These ethical traditions did not find it valuable to front "rationality" as both method and goal for the achievement of the good.[61] Their western counterparts look and sound different. They are "infused with ideals of discursive rationality and argumentation."[62] Many comparative philosophers feel this is an important stake in the conversation, and thus grant to western philosophy what they would deny, perhaps, to the west in general. The results are still strikingly binary in form. David L. Hall and Roger T. Ames have claimed that the dominant modes of thought in classical Chinese and western cultures can be described as analogical and rational respectively. Western philosophy was unmarred by the anthropocentric mode of thinking, so it led to "the suppression of the origins of concepts formed by analogy from the human realm."[63] Arthur Waley, a translator of the *Analects*, in his introduction claims that they contain almost no sustained logical reasoning or rational argumentation, while R.E. Nisbett offers an explanation for this: in the Confucian tradition, all things are interconnected, interdependent, and ever-changing, and thus should always be seen in their context, while westerners have accepted the logical approach of Plato and Aristotle, which tends to decontextualize statements so they can remain true under all conditions (and hence be "true").[64] Angus Graham claims much the same: "It is well known that almost all Chinese philosophical 'systems' are practical, moral, or mystical philosophies of life, indifferent to abstract speculation. It is therefore not surprising that Chinese Confucianists have cared little for the forms of reasoning."[65] As Master Zeng said, "Each day I examine myself in three ways"— about his loyalty and trustworthiness towards friends, and the degree to which he has practiced what has been passed on to him.[66]

Some philosophers suggest that the disparity between the two ethical traditions can be traced to the absence or presence of the notion of the opposite as, well, opposite. We in the west might say "black is the opposite of white." But in a different perspective, black and white both belong to a single conceptual field—color—in which they share space with other non-opposites. Chinese thought in general, as Tony Fang puts it:

denies the reality of true contradiction, accepts the unity of opposites, and regards the coexistence of opposites as permanent. Belief in genuine contradiction is regarded as a kind of error. The Western Marxist dialect treats contradiction as real but defines it different[ly] from the Western Aristotelian tradition, in terms not of the laws of formal logic but rather by the three laws of dialectical logic.[67]

All too much like Socrates himself as he quizzes his interlocutors and points out their self-contradictions, sometimes causing them to melt down in the process, the west is too taken up with either/or reasoning instead of accepting the both/and approach identified with the Yin-Yang way of understanding the world.[68] The westerners want to solve the paradox they see—not let it be. The result is that they apply a standard for value that may be misplaced.

If we wish to keep arguing about rationality in the Confucian tradition, self-described defenders of that tradition point out that there is much that is based on rationalist (if not instrumentalist) thought (presumably they are still thinking in terms of these binaries, which they should not in a Yin-Yang universe). Most obviously, Confucian maxims and metaphors are often based on a hidden core of rational deduction over which lie stories and metaphors.[69] The neo-Confucianism of Zhu Xi (1126–1271 CE) and others represent a more rationalist and secular form of Confucian thought and rejected superstitious and mystical elements that had crept into Confucian thought from Taoism and Buddhism.[70] There was even a (non-Confucian) Mohist tradition in which deduction based on elements of syntax represented a sophist-like approach to reasoning.

It is very noticeable—perhaps illuminating?—that despite Xi Jinping's increasingly tight control, the whole discussion of "rationality" takes place without any mention of China's own Legalist tradition of a form of instrumental rationality in politics. "It is obvious that benevolence, righteousness, eloquence, and wisdom are not the means by which to maintain the state," wrote the prominent Legalist Han Feizi in the text that bears his name from the mid-third century BCE. As Peter R. Moody points out, however:

> The Han Feizi also makes clear . . . that acting in instrumentally (but not morally) rational ways cannot be understood in the abstract, but only in the context of what the text calls the *shi* (roughly, "circumstances"). The more useful forms of political analysis are not restricted to a reconstruction of what is rational but trace out the characteristics of the *shi*— the political, historical, cultural, and psychological context conditioning action and defining, at least in part, what constitutes rationality . . . It shares the same individualistic and instrumentalist assumptions about human behavior and political action as contemporary rational choice theory: political action can be understood as the behavior of self-interested individuals seeking to achieve their individual goals.[71]

Confucius would have been horrified: a gentleman does what is right; only a little man does what is expedient. And yet, we might be reminded of Deng Xiaoping's famous remark "Who cares if the cat is black or white?" a highly instrumentalist—and not so Confucian—approach to the Chinese economy.

Meanwhile, Plato and Aristotle (and even Descartes) had a good bit of the irrational in their texts, if by that we wish to include all the parables based on no a priori rationality at all. As Chad Hansen writes:

> If the use of analogy, metaphor, or parables to illustrate ideas makes searching for consistent, coherent interpretations a mistake, then very few of the luminaries of the western tradition could be interpreted rationally. Plato's allegory of the cave and Descartes's metaphor of the evil demon are in fact

powerful images motivating their creators' philosophical systems.[72]

But in the end, what's really at stake? If the Confucian tradition didn't privilege "rationality" as a great tool for ordering society, or for describing the nature of the soul, or for positing the existence of God himself, or even for persuading readers and would-be philosophers, why should that be a criterion for any sort of judgment?[73] There is no reason to consider abstract theories of truth better than empirical ones, and there's no winner in this description, because the binary values of the argument are all wrong to start with.[74]

There's also little reason to accept the other characteristic of the current "rationality discussion," namely, the view that the Enlightenment tradition and its harmful outcomes can be traced directly to Kant and occasionally back to Plato's emphasis on rationality as the highest principle of the human soul. Never mind if (as mentioned previously) Kant argued that no human should be used as an end by another—an inconvenient view if one wishes to make him out to be the snake-oil salesman of rationality—or if the purpose of Platonic rationality was the well-being and stability of the state.[75] Kallipolis may have relied on a form of eugenics, but despite that distasteful fact we cannot implicate Plato in the Holocaust without real effort.[76] And of course, Plato's elevation of rationality was based on a priori assumptions that were entirely irrational (to my mind, not at all like the common sense view about *ren*), and even Socrates abandoned his use of deductive dialectic now and then to have recourse to stories and myths— which often prove more persuasive.[77]

Unsurprisingly, the "benevolence versus rationality" framework that shapes this discourse has other problems as well, above all the elision of the gigantic effect of Christianity in the west. Nevertheless, and especially in the context of Xi Jinping's new nationalism, Confucian texts are now seen as the bearers of a better alternative than western philosophy, regardless if it is all a footnote to Plato. Here are ancient values that have, can, and should shape modern Chinese society. Gone is the May 4th Movement's condemnation of Confucian thought and desire for western logic. Now the story is that "the western Enlightenment brought about rationality as a tool for ruling and enslaving people," while in China, "value rationality does not rule out the need to meet the needs of contemporary people, but pays more attention to the development of our future generations, taking into account the development of immediate interests and long-term interests."[78]

I would suggest that *pace* the views penned by scholars on both sides of the Pacific, and while leaving plenty of space for yin and yang as an influential concept, there's little reason to suppose that the west is more of a hotbed of instrumental rationality these days than China. China's rapid economic rise, after all, was not based on the casting of oracle bones. And I'd also suggest that we think hard about the question, What *is* "rationality"? Is it really a tool for enslaving people? Its connection to the process of "rationalization" and to economic development notwithstanding, it is hardly so simple a thing as to lead to mass moral zombiehood in the west. Western neoclassical economics claims are based on the "rational" principle of self-interest, but what if self-interest is not viewed as rational by some? The sort of political and semantic flexibility inherent in the term "rationality," as I hope is clear by this point, lends itself to political appropriation in just about any direction. And I am hardly the first to point this out. The great comparative scholar of ancient Greece and China, G. E. R. Lloyd has argued that the tendency of scholars to lean on the binary opposition of rationality and irrationality is a reductionist, generalizing, and itself an unmitigatedly western approach.[79] The very dichotomy of rational and irrational stems from ancient Greek philosophy and mathematics, and dichotomies such as this one are poor tools to describe what is "out there," let alone in a very different culture (we have already seen the integrative thought between yin and yang). As Lloyd urges, we must avoid "slip[ping] too easily into some assumption of their [these dichotomies'] universal validity and not be sufficiently on our guard against their covert use to put down the ideas of rivals."[80] So far, we've seen it as a tool in just about everyone's hands; but it must also complicate—not simplify—our comparisons.[81]

In the end, the west does not need to receive "Chinese spirituality" any more than China needs to receive "western rationality." These empty terms act as political jabs and feints rather than as starting points for discussion and understanding. It is time for scholars to devise and communicate unique and complex—not borrowed and simplistic—responses to the many facets that characterize China and the west in the twenty-first century.[82]

5

A Straussian Interlude

Strauss turns to the root of western civilization to make us
understand that we too should turn to the root of Chinese
civilization . . . In this sense, the greatest benefit that we
acquire from Strauss is that he makes us realize that our
continuous emulation of the west over the last one hundred
years may finally come to an end.

—ZHENG WENTAO

WE NOW TURN to the peculiar phenomenon of the western
political theorist Leo Strauss's popularity among a loosely knit
group of contemporary Chinese academics. Much has already
been written about the Chinese "Straussians," whose embrace
of Strauss's writings was greeted with surprise by political philosophers in the United States when it started before the turn
of the millennium; for most western political thinkers, Leo
Strauss is a relatively marginal figure.[1] But Strauss's theories
have proven useful (whether in an instrumental or value-
rational way, it's unclear) to a cluster of Chinese intellectuals
who use his thought as a lens through which to reinterpret the
canonical texts of the west, just as Strauss himself did. Like

Strauss, the Chinese Straussians maintain that classical antiquity presents us a with a salubrious set of values that have since
been lost to modernity. In short, it's time for us western hea-
thens to let go of our modern ways and "go back to the Ancients." Never mind if this is a very particular view of the ancients, one that would hardly gain any adherents today; going
back to the ancients would come as a nasty shock to most of us.

But valuing antiquity per se is not so radical a perspective in
a country like China, in which, as we've seen, Confucius and
others are still held to be deeply relevant to present day values;
one does not need to turn to Strauss to find to feel this perspective. Moreover, Strauss was condemning the present, while
most Chinese prefer to see themselves as continuing to hold up
centuries-long traditional values. Why, then, would nationalist-
leaning intellectuals want to borrow his arguments and meth-
odologies? Adopting a foreign thinker's social and political
values as your own is a bold step. Using Strauss's claims and
methodology has enabled these scholars to provide overarching answers to the question of China's place in the world
today.[2] But the Chinese aren't just using Strauss to talk about
themselves. They like his perspective on the west as well.

I. The Prophets of Strauss

The sudden expansion of interest in Strauss took place in the
early 2000s.[3] Although several of Strauss's works had been
translated into Mandarin in the 1980s, it was not until the body
of his thought was popularized by two well-known professors
that enthusiasm for Straussian thought took off. We have already
encountered both of them. The first is Liu Xiaofeng 刘小枫,
professor at Sun Yat-sen University and Renmin University,
where he is director of the Classical Studies Center. Liu inspired

a generation of loyal students to adopt Strauss's philosophical and political arguments as the best—even the most ethical— interpretive approach to western classical texts, and provided a model for others who wished to follow his lead. The second is Gan Yang 甘阳, formerly Dean of the Boya Liberal Arts College at Sun Yat-sen University, now Dean of Xinya College, Tsinghua University.[4] Over the past decades, both scholars have carved a path for themselves from reformists to neo-conservatives, a path that mirrors that of many Chinese intellectuals from the 1980s who now support a nationalist sentiment embedded in "traditional values"—even if their claim to fame was once that they critiqued China's culture and national character.[5] Both scholars have been well-known and influential public thinkers, if also controversial ones. And both have spoken to the issue of how China should position itself today—in both cases, using Strauss.

Gan Yang and Liu Xiaofeng published extensively on Strauss's work (in Mandarin). Liu's work includes *The Docility of the Hedgehog: Five Essays in Political Philosophy*; "The Path of Leo Strauss;" "Nietzsche's Exotic and Esoteric Teachings;" and many other books and articles. Gan's writing includes a lengthy introduction to a 2002 Chinese translation of Strauss's *Natural Right and History*, which later appeared independently as *Leo Strauss as Political Philosopher*. He also published an edited volume on *Strauss and Classical Studies* in 2014.[6] More importantly, the two supervised the translation into Mandarin of practically all of Strauss's work and many books by western Straussians such as Allen Bloom and Seth Bernardete in the series "Hermes: Classics & Interpretation."[7]

Liu Xiaofeng and Gan Yang were not always Straussians. In the 1980s they were more like westernizing liberals. Both were involved in editing the New Enlightenment series "Culture:

China and the World," (文化：中国与世界 *Wenhua: Zhongguo yu shijie*) which brought works such as *The Birth of Tragedy, Being and Time* and *Protestant Ethics and the Spirit of Capitalism* to an appreciative audience hungry for western ideas.[8] This interest in important western works was typical of the late 1980s, a time of "cultural fever" that echoed many of the themes of the May 4th Movement and during which Gan Yang's and Liu Xiaofeng's political views were close to those of the student reformers.[9] Gan called the May 4th Movement "the starting point of the radical shift of Chinese culture from its premodern to its modern form" and argued that "the fundamental task of the 1980s cultural discussions in China is to decisively complete this historical shift . . . and to wholly realize 'the modernization of Chinese culture.'"[10] One of Gan's articles even touted the importance of individual freedom over democracy and science, the two catchwords of the May 4th Movement—out-westering the prior reformers, as it were. "If today's Chinese intellectuals are still unwilling to hold high the banner of 'liberty comes first,'" Gan wrote in 1986, "then China will have no luck in welcoming the twenty-first century."[11] Gan exhorted those same intellectuals to take pains "to reintroduce the basic values in modern western culture, and in particular freedom, democracy, and rule of law, that have been crudely rejected and excluded."[12] All this stands in contrast to his stance from the late 1990s onwards; in 1997, for example, Gan described the biggest obstacle to China's emergence as its feeble central authority, and a year later he remarked that, "In general, Chinese intellectuals' reflections (and self-reflections) on revolution and radicalism have come to an end. Those reflections and self-reflections did not deepen the understanding of liberalism in the Chinese intellectual world."[13]

Liu likewise left China at the time of the suppression of the student and worker movement. In the 1990s he returned to

China in a different guise, self-avowedly in search of universal ethical values not dependent on western democratic ideals. Liu decided they were to be found in Christianity, announcing his status as a "cultural Christian" with the publication of a number of books proclaiming his new views: *Dao and Logos: The Meeting of Chinese and Christian Cultures; Approaching the Truth on the Cross; Individual Faith and a Theory of Culture;* and *Delivering and Dallying.*[14] In the final work in particular, Liu contrasted the Chinese, who were "dallying" in complacency, to the ideals of the Christian west.[15] Liu argued that his fellow countrymen should not turn to China's bloody dynastic history in their search for a model for society—a history in which "the mandate of heaven" was invoked to cover up blatant injustice among humans. A meaningful life could only come from Christianity's transcendental God, not Confucian traditions, even when they were blended with Christianity (as he accused Chinese theologians in Hong Kong and Taiwan of doing).[16] Liu even repeated the old criticism of the Chinese sages as not emphasizing logical structures and not being interested in analysis.[17]

This desire to find a source of ethical values—or at least to banish nihilism—also informed Liu's subsequent engagement with Strauss, whom he came to after reading Weber, Schmitt, and others, and with whom he recognized a deep intellectual affinity. Upon reading the Preface and Epilogue of Strauss's *History of Political Philosophy* in 1994, Liu was shocked (he said) because he felt that "Strauss's unremitting struggle with value relativism and nihilism [were] the same as my stance in *Delivering and Dallying.* How am I so close to this man!"[18] As it happens, Liu had a good medium for spreading his own/Strauss's views—his series "Hermes: Classics & Interpretation," mentioned previously, which to date consists of some 500 works, including many classics of western political theory, translated into Chinese under his editorship.[19] The series includes studies of Plato, Homer, Pindar, Aristotle, Hobbes, Nietzsche, and others. In the bulk of these translations, Strauss's theories are often cited in the introductions, and the series contains all of Strauss's major works, including *The Political Philosophy of Hobbes, On Tyranny,* and *Natural Right and History.*[20] The series also contains essays and books by western Straussians such as Allan Bloom, Karl Heinrich Meier, and Harvey Mansfield. Liu also created the (now discontinued) *Chinese Journal of Classical Studies.* (We encountered its mission statement already in Chapter 3). Liu's fellow Straussians, some of them at one point his students, wrote many of the journal's essays. Liu himself edited a 775-page volume on the man, *Strauss and Ancient Political Philosophy.*[21]

As with his friend and colleague, until quite recently Gan was a neo-conservative very much in the Straussian school. His ten years in the PhD program at the University of Chicago's Committee on Social Thought, a hotbed of academic Straussianism, must have been deeply influential. In his 2002 introduction to the Chinese translation of Strauss's *Natural Right and History,* for example, Gan spoke of the importance of Strauss's political philosophy to the American conservative scene of the 1980s. Gan emphasized Strauss's insistence on "critically examining western modernity and liberalism from the perspective of western classics." Quoting Machiavelli, Nietzsche, Kant, Heidegger, Rawls, and others, Gan paraphrased Strauss's message for any unfamiliar Chinese readers:

> western modernity has reversed this moral foundation [from antiquity] and increasingly disrespects ancestors and old age, because "modern ideas" instinctively believe only in so-called "progress" and "future" . . . The biggest irony of modernity is therefore: "The higher the development of rationality, the

more nihilism develops, the less we can become loyal members of society." Since the 1930s, Strauss believed that the most profound problem of modernity was this so-called "intellectual probity" or "philosophical freedom."[22]

Somewhat puzzlingly, Gan added that, "American conservative scholars often compare the United States in the 1960s with the 'Cultural Revolution' in China in the 1960s, saying that the social changes in the United States since the 1960s are the 'American Cultural Revolution' that also caused catastrophe to the United States." He cited "the famous intellectual historian Paul Kristeller" in support of this view (the Paul Kristeller I know is a Renaissance scholar). In any case, the message is that, like Weber, Strauss conveyed a negative message about modernity that these scholars were keen to adopt.

Strauss's emphasis on the moral gulf between the ancients and the moderns was seen by his Chinese readers, rightly or wrongly, as enabling both a condemnation of liberal democracy and an upholding of the value of Chinese nationalism.[23] As Leihua Weng points out:

> [The Chinese Straussians] are immensely interested in finding an alternative to democracy, which is not always present in Leo Strauss. Even according to Drury, the most vigorous critic of Strauss's political philosophy, Strauss is elitist but not anti-democratic [Drury PILS 194]. However, in the readings of Chinese Platonists, the intention of cultivating an elitist ruling class coexists with a criticism of democracy and a strong urge to find a political alternative in Confucian political tradition and Maoist heritage.[24]

Strauss's views on the liberal democratic present of the west thus could be used against contemporary Chinese who were attracted to the west in its current democratic and capitalist form.

Finally, turning to Strauss enabled Liu to engineer a meeting of two ancient bodies of thought—the Platonic and Confucian traditions—which could now be made to agree with each other in their most important aspects.[25] In "Strauss and China," for example, Liu argued that the mutual encounter of Strauss and China (which also meant the mutual encounter of classical western and Confucian philosophy) is a "meeting between classical mentalities."[26] Together, these two traditions could provide an ethical alternative to the west's annoying "universal" values like democracy and equality.[27] Another scholar, Tang Shiqi, suggested that we can compare Confucian and Straussian philosophy in three ways: the hierarchy of the soul, esoteric writing, and the relationship between politics and philosophy.[28] However, according to Tang, since Strauss did not understand that the Chinese "to be" is not existential, he wasn't perfect.

This equation of Confucius and the western classics (in their Straussian interpretation anyway) provides a powerful argument, Strauss's fans believe, for the values of ancient civilizations over modern ones. We must take Strauss as our moral leader lest we wander from the path of what is ethical. In Liu's own words, "the reason we appropriate Leo Strauss is that modern education doesn't teach you to distinguish between right and wrong, justice and injustice. He shows us to look at the great works of antiquity, and we should build on it a moral system, whether Chinese antiquity or western antiquity."[29] That system should be based, not on freedom, but on virtue, and ignoring this imperative (Liu claimed) heads indubitably to nihilism.[30] "A few Chinese intellectuals need to make a crucial choice: either continue to be corrupted by western modern thoughts, or accept reeducation through Plato," argued Liu.[31]

Thus Liu, Gan, and other Chinese Straussians switch the former opposition of China and the west into a new opposition of Antiquity and post-Enlightenment thought. Now Confucius can be brought into the picture as contributing to the collective wisdom of the ancients.[32] The modern post-Enlightenment quest for further developments in science, considered as the source of certain knowledge, has led us to discard not only ethical values but ultimately even the notion of truth itself. How to backtrack from the precipice? The Chinese Straussians argue that we must eliminate our modern prejudice that pre-Enlightenment philosophy has little to offer; we must, in effect, read the ancients (but only esoterically) and learn from their values.[33]

The esoteric/exoteric approach that leads to this message runs rampant in the pages of *The Chinese Journal of Classical Studies* (*Gudian Yanjiu*), whose editor (before the journal went out of publication) was none other than Liu Xiaofeng. In its pages, we read more than once that Plato's *Republic* is not about the possibility of the just city, nor a text about transcendent values represented by the Forms of the Good and of Virtue. It is instead a text about the *impossibility* of the just city, the philosopher's refusal to rule or participate in politics, and the necessity for a strong ruler with a strong myth behind him to control his fallible and wayward human subjects.[34] For example, Cheng Zhimin argues that, in Plato's view, the Noble Lie is justified because there is an eternal conflict between the city-state and the philosopher: the philosopher and the city-state have different orientations, and the philosopher's thoroughness or "sacred madness" also affects the city-state. Philosophy's potential for harm, and the safe use of its enlightening function, is the main subject of Platonic political philosophy.[35] Wang Jin summarized this thought, "The nature of philosophy is pursuit of the truth, but when faced with political reality, philosophers must refrain themselves from the drive to pursue universal philosophy in order not to undermine the realistic foundation of political community."[36] Just so, in an example of esoteric reading at work, Zhang Bobo suggested that Cephalus leaves the scene so early in Plato's *Republic* because he cannot be exposed to logical argumentation—from which, as Strauss argued, the political leadership (here represented by Cephalus's status as an aristocratic) must be defended at all costs.[37] Even Vergil, though no philosopher himself, is converted to the message: his ultimate goal in the *Aeneid* was to advance religious obedience and piety, to imbue people with a national myth, and to promote a strong and military government.[38] The inevitable tension between philosophy and the citizen is likewise the main point of Wu Fei's interpretation of the *Apology* in the Hermes Series. And so on.[39]

One of the best-known works in the series is Liu's own "interpretive translation" (his description) of Plato's *Symposium* (*Huiyin*). In his preface, Zhang Hui emphasizes the dramatic qualities of the *Symposium*: "we should pay attention not only to speeches . . . but also, in Leo Strauss's words, to their deeds, which are of great importance."[40] Zhang Hui tells us that Plato composed the work as a play to obscure his own views and to escape persecution. As Weng points out, Liu avoids describing the text as a *pian* (treatise) in order to suggest that we are watching a drama, then uses the traditional form of Chinese Confucian commentary to insert his own Straussian explanations of the drama, thereby suggesting a certain historical authenticity for these interpretations.[41] And when Liu discusses Socrates's death in *The Docility of the Hedgehog*, Strauss's influence colors his extrapolation of that philosophical self-sacrifice to China. In Liu's view, Socrates would stay in Communist

China even if condemned to death, and not flee to bourgeois nations.[42] This is because Socrates would prefer to die in order to preserve the integrity of the philosopher, just as he did in Athens.[43] The moral of the story? That a philosopher who shares his truths in the public realm will always face the repercussion of the state—and only a few are willing to accept this cost.

Interestingly, even the translation of the title of Plato's *Republic* carries particular meaning in this Straussian context. As Wentao Zhai points out, although it is usually translated as "the ideal state" [理想国 *lixiangguo*], "Liu Xiaofeng favors 'the rule of king,' [王制 *wangzhi*], since he believes the proto-Confucian 'way of the (sage) king' is what Plato is getting at with 'politeia' . . . Less disruptively, he [Liu also] translates *nomos* (custom, law) as *lifa* 礼法, setting up an explicit comparison with Confucian rituals (*li*) and Legalist law (*fa*)."[44] In this way, critical terminology that has a specific meaning in the Greek context can be made to "merge" with the Confucian belief-system, a transformation that we might think of as an esoteric translation.

Of course, this is a Plato the west may not recognize.[45] One major feature of the reeducation offered by Plato is the necessary endorsement of Strauss's view that the philosopher should not speak truth to society: his rationally formulated ideals are dangerous in their unadulterated form, and will break down the bonds of custom or religion. The Straussian reeducation also calls for much hand-wringing about the problems of modernity and the abyss of meaninglessness that characterizes it. Finally, reeducation entails believing that Strauss's thought is not a theory. In Liu's view, using Strauss provides Chinese intellectuals with an escape from western "isms."[46] Asked whether Strauss's thought does not itself constitute an "ism," Liu answers emphatically in the negative. Strauss's "classical" imperative is literally directed against the collections of "ism"-discourses of modernity and represents an orientation towards antiquity rather than any interpretive straitjacket.[47] This answer allows Liu, somewhat disingenuously, to lay claim to something like a view from nowhere, an Archimedean point from which he and Strauss will view the classical world anew—and this time correctly.[48]

Given that Strauss's interpretations are united by the essential themes of the tension between truth and social values, between philosopher and politicians, and between antiquity (narrowly defined) and modernity (broadly defined), it's an interesting move for these thinkers to claim that Strauss's thought is somehow both natural and universal. But there may be a method to their madness. Strauss rooted his own view in the classical past by reading its ancients texts as if they had both esoteric and exoteric meanings. In his article "Persecution and the Art of Writing," Strauss argued that a close reading of the great texts of Al-Farabi, Maimonides, Spinoza, and others would unveil the hidden, esoteric layer of their teachings: views too dangerous to the current political regime for the authors to state openly. Most readers, however, would only see the surface/exoteric meaning, which was perfectly harmless to both its authors and its audience. Strauss went on to theorize about the esoteric meaning he uncovered in these texts, which contained variants on the basic idea that voicing philosophical truths would do no public service and was in fact dangerous.

Liu was able to "naturalize" this methodology (that is, the contrast of esoteric/exoteric writing and reading) by finding it in his own Chinese context. In Confucius's *Analects*, Liu pointed out, a distinction is made between *weiyan* (微言) and *dayi* (大义), literally "subtle words and big meanings"—so that Strauss's view is already Chinese.[49] Then there are the writings of the Legalist Li Si, who in 213 BCE assaulted "private learning" as

MAIMONIDES

dangerous to the state, a very Straussian view. Liu also argued (and he is not the only one) that in the course of the history of the globe, many political or philosophical thinkers have written tracts to simultaneously reveal and conceal their views.[50] What could be more obvious? To the uninitiated, however, Straussian readings can seem highly subjective, privileging the middle of a statement or paragraph over other parts, focusing on a single word and blowing it out of proportion, or looking at contradictions as keys, and generally avoiding citation of extant scholarship.[51]

Once they knew to look for esoteric meanings in ancient texts, Gan, Liu, and the other Chinese Straussians read classical western texts in support of particular philosophical and political viewpoints. For example, when discussing *Maimonides' Guide for the Perplexed* Strauss argued that Maimonides wrote for two audiences at the same time in order to avoid persecution. A non-Straussian audience would read Maimonides as trying reconcile Aristotelianism with Rabbinical Jewish theology by offering rational explanations for religious phenomena—thereby assuming that philosophy and revelation are reconcilable. In Strauss's interpretation, however, this is merely the surface, exoteric meaning of the text. Esoteric writing serves multiple purposes, including the self-protection of philosophers against the retribution of society; the protection of generally held social values from the corrosion of philosophy; and providing philosophical training for potential readers.[52] They argue that because philosophical truths destabilize the political world, which must offer its citizens security based on shared laws and customs (what Strauss called *nomos*), the philosopher must hide his message—a theme of Strauss's discussions of Plato, Aristotle, and Xenophon as well as of later philosophers.[53] According to these ancient philosophers, the irreconcilability of law and philosophy, or practical values and abstract reflection, or society and the isolated philosopher, is always lurking in the text—if read esoterically.[54] The fact that Confucian mandarins were traditionally close to those in power throws a bit of a wrench into this view, or maybe it supports it. Did they write exoterically for the emperors while hoarding esoteric knowledge for themselves? At first glance it seems unlikely, but one could always argue that the court chronicles they habitually wrote revealed something to their fellow Confucians. That is a whole different question.

II. An Esoteric Paradox

In reality, the Chinese Straussians don't say much about the esoteric reading approach in their agenda. It does, after all, suggest subjective interference in a text—the risk is of producing what will be taken as an individual view in contrast to eternal truths. Perhaps tellingly, Tao Wang (at the time of his essay, a fellow at the Center for American Political Studies of Harvard University *and* a lecturer in Fudan University in Shanghai, now a professor in Iowa State's Department of History) steered away from discussing esoteric/exoteric readings as the tool of the Chinese Straussians. Instead, Tao Wang argued that Strauss's popularity came from other fundamental aspects of his thought, including an animus against "western rationalism" (once more unto the breach!), the contrast of the values of the ancients and the moderns, and a new *Chinese* understanding of the gulf between philosophy and politics, because philosophical ideals cannot be interpreted into political life without disasters such as that of the late 1980s. (Gan Yang and Liu Xiaofeng might say so too!) According to Tao:

> Leo Strauss has influenced Chinese scholars in three ways. First, his interpretation of the conflict between revelation

and reason in the western tradition made Chinese scholars aware of the problem of modern rationalism. Second, Strauss's emphasis on the quarrel between the ancients and the moderns showed Chinese scholars the connection between the origins of modern rationalism and the drastic turn from contemplation to action, providing them with a new lens through which to reconceive modernity. . . . Finally, Strauss's explanation of the relationship between philosophy and politics lets Chinese scholars understand the inevitable conflict between these ways of life, as well as the importance of the philosophic life that transcends politics. Through his influence, some Chinese scholars have been able to overcome the narrowness and trendiness of the modern academy, and discover a very broad and deep way of understanding the future of Chinese civilization, and even of human civilization.[55]

If I read Tao correctly, it becomes clear that Strauss *has* been a nationalistic political tool, because using his theory shows the government that, as an intellectual, you are going to keep your mouth shut about certain issues in the interest of political stability.[56] This is perhaps all the more reason that liberal intellectuals linked to Tiananmen Square turned to Strauss upon their return to China. Their move is an intellectual offering— not to their leadership, who may or may not care about Strauss, but to their politically correct colleagues. The problem with their loyalty is the interpretive old rabbit hole it sets up (like the Noble Lie!). If you endorse esoteric reading, aren't you also endorsing the esoteric reading of your own words? So, are you conveying a secret message unpalatable to the government? If so, what is it? The very idea that the intellectual must write obliquely certainly makes more sense in the Chinese context than in the contemporary western one, given that the severe restrictions on free speech ("word-crime," *wenziyu*) in the Ming and Qing dynasties and the Maoist era are firmly in the culture's memory.

What is at stake for the west in this argument? For one, Liu and Gan have long had a high profile in China, and the choice of Strauss[57] has something to tell us about contemporary Chinese culture—because, as we have seen, and as Kai Marchal puts it, "the interplay of China and Straussianism is . . . never purely scholarly or academic; in the destabilizing context of social and cultural globalization, it is driven by increasingly political dynamics, especially the wish for a new 'rootedness' (*Bodenständigkeit*) in Chinse culture."[58] The authors in *Gudian Yanjiu* may not attract much attention, but Liu and Gan and other prominent Chinese Straussians do, and they have used their exoteric readings (inter alia) to speak in praise of the Chinese government, in the process leaving Leo Strauss in the rearview window—but still leading one to wonder just what they intend to be saying.[59]

Liu in particular has taken a drastic step in this regard. In May 2013 he publicly dubbed Mao Zedong as "Father of the Nation" (国父 *guofu*) and he has gone on to portray him as the Confucian *Shengren* 圣人, or sage, as well as the Platonic philosopher-king.[60] This has upset more liberal Chinese scholars who feel it is important to remember the bloodshed and famine of Mao's regime. Adding to the turmoil caused by this pro-Mao position, the epithet "Father of the Nation" had until then been reserved for the first president of the Republic of China, Sun Yat-sen.[61] In the opinion of one western-trained scholar of the classics in contemporary China, "Liu seems to support the legitimacy of the current rule of the Chinese government as well as its role in preventing democratization in other countries."[62]

This is slippery too. What if Liu is just trying to be a good Straussian philosopher, mouthing the necessary words in public to praise a problematic authority figure?[63] In theory, one could have philosopher-king-like-academic thought that would disrupt the government's legitimacy and as such would have to stay quiet, or prop up the system—the latter being what Strauss thought would be the only safe path for intellectuals. Can we say, then, that these Chinese Straussians are actually pointing to the fact that they cannot speak freely? Perhaps not. Like a quantum particle, this possibility both is and is not in Liu's writings at the same time.

Gan too seems to be implicated in nationalist rather than philosophical thought, as some of his contemporaries have noted. A much-circulated but anonymous 2017 article by a self-described "academic terrorist" attacked Gan as corrupt for joining the New Left and turning his back on his former liberals. A special source of the writer's ire was Gan's description of the Maoist period as representing "equality and justice." Equality is built into the CCP's constitution, but Mao's leadership and his cult of personality (not to mention the horror of the Cultural Revolution) are difficult phenomena to whitewash in the name of "equality and justice."[64] The anonymous author also accused Gan of cherry-picking his western authors and thereby not representing the west to China in an authentic way.

These days Gan Yang has mostly (or purportedly?) abandoned his earlier enthusiasm for Strauss. His new contribution to public political discourse is a plan to recover the values of Chinese tradition via a blend of three bodies of thought that would be authentically Chinese. This is his plan in *Tongsantong*, a 2007 book in which he proposed to unite the Confucian tradition (described as valuing elitism, affective personal, and local relationships), the Maoist tradition (to which he too ascribes equality and justice!), and the Dengist tradition (with markets and competition).[65] Gan argues that "we will perpetually remain in a culturally rootless situation, unless the general attitude and actions that oppose Chinese tradition in the twentieth century are completely changed in the twenty-first century."[66] Even if we are skeptical that there has been "one continuous tradition of Chinese history," Gan Yang's idea has galvanized many Chinese intellectuals into thinking about ways in which a new Chinese periodization might replace the historical categories of the west. Since the western classics are no longer directly involved, I will not linger here, except to point out that Gan publicly and actively advocates for a particular form of Chinese nationalism while Liu's work continues to stress that the philosopher and society should be separate.[67]

Strauss himself, meanwhile, has tumbled from his pedestal, if recent graduate students provide any evidence: it is easy, now, to find articles that concentrate on his flaws as a thinker rather than a substantiation of The Way. A 2019 master's thesis criticizes Strauss's "classical rationalism" and his reliance on a Platonic concept of the soul. Strauss cannot help with the crisis of modernity because he has left no room for compassion.[68]

In closing, let's turn to the actual professorate of classics in China, many of whom were strictly trained in western classics departments and who do not look upon Gan Yang and Liu Xiaofeng with great enthusiasm. The Straussian turn of these two scholars—and especially of their students—is critiqued as a way of approaching the ancient texts without becoming familiar with any of the extant scholarship on them, and the result is criticized as a shallow and insufficiently trained appreciation of the ancient corpus. In the same interview I cited in Chapter 2, Nie Minli commented that those who entered the study of western classical studies through Leo Strauss devoted

IDEOLOG.

too little of their time to the classics per se and always approached the field from a political angle. Before these scholars even have time to mature, suggests Nie, they turn from their Strauss-influenced explication of ancient philosophy to the traditional Chinese classics, seeing affinities in both and arguing for the creation of a uniquely Chinese form of government. Such research, Nie says, is "essentially ideological."[69] In the same interview, Nie's colleague Gao Fengfeng spoke up when discussing the same Straussian scholars to emphasize that academics require truth, not "fun and influence."

Nie's words imply that the mainstream classicists (whether in China, Europe, or the US) are free of ideology (we may or may not choose to agree with this). The cost of staying true to the texts, however, is that they (and we in the west) remain comparatively invisible to the general public while the dervishes of ideology sprinkle their Straussian magic and gain influence across a broad sphere that even extends into the political—having much fun in the process.[70] And yet, as I sit typing these words, it strikes me that those who study classics in the west should be so lucky as to be derided for our fun and influence across the US. One message to emerge from the Straussians, however, is a troubling one: if "elite" western classicists cannot make these texts speak to everyone, we will become increasingly marginalized. (Of course, the original Strauss did not wish to speak to everyone.) But yet we cannot distort our interpretations by consciously reading what we want into our classics. What will the compromise be?

6

Harmony for the World

Only Chinese civilization can save China and eventually help save the world, because it was not developed from a religious form. Confucian respect for universal harmony and collectivism in Chinese culture should be especially instrumental for world peace and development.

—SHEN HONG

ON OCTOBER 29, 1989, roughly five months after the unharmonious crackdown at Tiananmen Square and across Beijing, the Vice-Chairman of the Chinese People's Political Consultative Conference, Gu Mu (谷牧), gave a formal speech in a government-sponsored celebration of the 2,540th year of the birth of Confucius. Gu reminded the Chinese people that recent progress in technology necessitated even more attention to the social value of harmony (和谐 *hexie*):

Due to the rapid progress of modern science and technology, humanity is entering a new age. In this new era, all people seek peace and development. The development of science and technology offers a future with limitless promise to mankind, but at the same time confronts humanity with new problems. This reminds everyone of the necessity to diligently strengthen the building of culture and broadly increase the cultural sophistication and degree of civilization of humanity, in order to achieve "harmony" among men, as well as between human society and nature. This alone accords with the fundamental interest of all humankind.[1]

Gu Mu concludes by arguing for the urgency of a return to "Confucian values" and by pointing out that harmony among men can be only be achieved as long as students, protestors, and other "bad elements" refrain from damaging the fabric of society—by demanding such western evils as freedom of speech, liberty of the press, and so forth. As John Delury wryly comments, "These grand words sound like something Chinese Communist Party General Secretary Hu Jintao or Premier Wen Jiabao might say in explaining their agenda of 'constructing a harmonious society' as they manage China's 'peaceful rise' to great power status."[2]

The return to Confucius has been striking. As Jiang Yi-huah relates, Xi Jinping visited the birthplace of Confucius in Shandong in 2013 and praised his teachings.[3] In 2014, further pro-Confucian activity was timed to coincide with the anniversary of the May 4th Movement of ninety-five years earlier, and Xi delivered a keynote speech at the international conference in memory of Confucius's 2,565th birthday. In Jiang's estimation, "These three consecutive events are generally perceived as the CPC's intentional moves to show to the world that it is promoting Confucianism." At the conference, Xi spoke of this philosophical tradition as "an essential part of Chinese culture that 'recorded the Chinese nation's spiritual activities, rational [ahem!] thinking and cultural achievements in building their homeland, reflected spiritual pursuits of the Chinese nation, and provided a key source of nutrition for the survival and continuous growth of our nation.'"

I. Harmony Contains Multitudes

Mao's Communist regime relegated a foundational concept in Confucianism—harmony—to the sidelines, not surprising, given that Mao himself was more interested in manipulating conflict and dissolving rather than creating harmony. (His political philosophy has often been compared to Legalism).[4] During the Cultural Revolution, when Mao launched a full-on attack on the remnants of the "feudal" Confucian belief system, "Red Guards overran Confucian temples, defacing statues of the sage, and chanting 'Down with Confucius, down with his wife!' ... The graves of the Kong family were trashed and looted. Corpses were once dug up from their graves at the Kong family's cemetery and hung from trees. More than 6,000 artifacts were smashed or burned."[5] An unverifiable tradition has it that Mao's nephew, Mao Yuanxin, reported Mao saying, "If the Communist Party has a day when it cannot rule or has met difficulty and needs to invite Confucius back, it means [the Party] is coming to an end."[6]

But the Party was still in full swing (as it were) when Secretary General Hu Jintao invited the old sage back. Pulled out of exile, Confucius was dusted off and put to work. The policy turn came in response to an increase in social and political unrest under the new economic order. Harmony needed to take a stand: it was time to appeal to a principle already deeply embedded in an ancient tradition. Starting in the late 1980s, then, the Confucian concepts of harmony and a "harmonious society" (*hexie shehui*) steadily gained ground in Party propaganda.

On October 11, 2006, President Hu Jintao formally endorsed the creation of a "harmonious society" as a Party goal. In the words of Maureen Fan in the *Washington Post* the next day, this represented "a shift in the party's focus from promoting all-out economic growth to solving worsening social tensions."[7] A statement released after the plenary said, "China is a harmonious society in general, but there are many conflicts and problems affecting social harmony. We must always remain clear-headed and be vigilant even in tranquil times."[8] By invoking harmony as a priority for his time in office, Hu was giving it the same importance as the Party's other important goal of fostering economic advance.[9] As one op-ed author wrote somewhat floridly:

> In the new century, China defines a harmonious society as a "democratic rule of law, fairness and justice, unity and friendship, stability and order, full of vitality, and harmony between man and nature." We cannot deny that this definition indeed reflects the new problems and challenges faced by mankind in the new historical stage. And it does depict a beautiful vision of happiness, which I believe will become a reality, just as I always believe that communism will eventually come true.[10]

Hu eventually extended the ideology of a harmonious society to his foreign policy, where he stressed peace and cooperation between other countries. (*This* harmony may have been more of an example of soft power than Confucius would have wanted.)

Hexie is a concept that reaches back to all the major Chinese traditions (Confucian, Taoist, and Buddhist), but it plays a particularly central role in the Confucian classics.[11] *He* 和 (the first half of *hexie*) appears in all of the "Five Classics" and three of the canonical "Four Books."[12] It originally designated musical harmony, a key element in the proper conduct of *li* (ritual). This harmony resulted from the coming together of different sounds, tempos, and pressures into a melodious whole, and, therefore, was seen as a quality that relied on differences combining into a beneficial synthesis. Among musical notes, "there are clear and broad, small and large, slow and fast . . . —all of which balance one another."[13] We can already see that this musical meaning, when applied to social interactions and the governance of the state, implies that harmony must rely on diversity and may even include opposing elements; a single humming noise is not "harmonious." The text continues, "A gentleman listens to such music in order to calm and settle his heart and mind. His heart and mind are calm and settled and his virtue is harmonious." In the fragments of the lost *Book of Music* included in the Li Ji, it is said that "the early rulers formed the *li* [rituals] and *yue* [music] not to satisfy the mouth, stomach, ear and eye, but rather to teach the people to moderate their likes and hates, and bring them correct direction."[14] As Confucius said, "Be aroused by poetry; structure yourself with propriety, refine yourself with music."[15]

Harmonious music also educates the people—but always by containing differences, not ironing them out. In the *Book of Rites, yayue* supports the hierarchical nature of the harmonious society: "When there is music in the ancestral temple, both ruler and minister, superior and inferior listen to it together, and none fails to be harmonious and respectful. When there is music among the clan elders and townspeople, elder and younger listen to it together, and none fails to be harmonious."[16] Even a ruler, or a *junzi* (gentlemen) should not strive for the sort of harmony that consists of only one opinion, shared by all.[17] As Confucius put it, "The noble man is in harmony

[*he*], but does not follow the crowd [*tong*, be the same as]. The inferior man follows the crowd, but is not in harmony."[18] In other words, only the inferior man looks for acquiescence rather than harmony. This is why in the *Zuozhuan*, a commentary on the Spring and Autumn Annals, the statesman Yanzi criticizes the "wrong" harmony of the courtier who agrees with his king:

> When the duke says "yes," Ju also says "yes;" when the duke says "no," Ju also says "no." This is like mixing water with water. Who can eat such a soup? This is like making an entire orchestra out of one kind of instrument. Who can enjoy such music? This is why sameness is harmful.[19]

In the *Analects*, Confucius quoted a saying, "'I do not enjoy ruling; I only enjoy people not disagreeing with me,'" and then corrected this erroneous view by adding, "Now if you are a good man and no one disagrees with you, it is fine. But if you are evil, and no one disagrees with you, perhaps you could destroy the country with a single utterance."[20]

Plato too drew a connection between music and the well (or badly) ordered soul, though his emphasis was on the ways in which bad music (like bad poetry) can corrupt the soul and encourage the desires. Just so for Confucius, who contrasted a "pure" or "elegant" music (雅乐 *yayue*) with vulgar music (俗乐 *suyue*), the latter of which would lead to confusion and disruption.[21] Again, as in the Confucian texts, this tie between music and the nature of the soul has implications for social harmony. Socrates frets in the *Republic* that:

> The overseers of our state . . . must throughout be watchful against innovations in music and gymnastics counter to the established order, and to the best of their power guard against

them, fearing when anyone says that "That song is most regarded among men/Which hovers newest on the singer's
lips," lest haply [sic] it be supposed that the poet means not
new songs but a new way of song and is commending this.
But we must not praise that sort of thing nor conceive it to be
the poet's meaning. For a change to a new type of music is
something to beware of as a hazard of all our fortunes. For the
modes of music are never disturbed without unsettling of the
most fundamental political and social conventions.[22]

In Plato's *Laws* especially, the connection of music, text, and
chorus to social order seems strikingly Confucian. We are told
that in Egypt political and moral stability issued from the fact
that the Egyptians set up musical and political laws (*nomoi*) in
their temples for the citizens to follow. As the Athenian says:

> So, let's assume we've agreed on the paradox: our songs have
> turned into "*nomoi*" . . . let's adopt this as our agreed policy,
> no one shall sing a note, or perform dance-movements, other
> than those in the canon of public songs, sacred music, and
> the general body of chorus performances of the young—any
> more than he would violate any other "*nomos*" or law.[23]

But the similarities must be contextualized. Plato discussed
the order of the soul, city, and university using the term order
(*kosmos*) rather than harmony (*harmonia*), the latter of which
comes up only once in the *Republic* in reference to the soul.[24]
Socrates discusses how the just person "harmonizes" the three
parts of the soul, and even makes an explicit comparison to the
tuning of a lyre.[25] But in the earlier dialogue *Phaedo*, Socrates
rebuts the idea of the soul as a harmony, and in the *Gorgias* he
only uses the language of order.[26] Second, in the *Laws*, as we
just saw, the text references the connection of music to the

state's unchanging laws and not to its poetry; the written law, set to a chorus and lyre, reflects the cosmic principle guiding the heavenly bodies.[27] This would not do as an analogy for modern China: a leadership that wants the people to be guided by the principles of harmony would not have been keen to invoke the rule of law, one assumes. Nor would Confucius:

> If you govern the people legalistically and control them by punishment, they will avoid crime, but have no personal sense of shame. If you govern them by means of virtue and control them with propriety, they will gain their own sense of shame, and thus correct themselves.[28]

Finally, and on a more theoretical level, the distinction between harmony and order must remind us that these two concepts simply do not connote the same thing; we are using English translations of Greek and Chinese concepts, none of which properly overlap with the others.

Ironically enough, *modern* western harmony knows that it must rely on each individual instrument playing slightly out of tune because of the compromise represented by the eighteenth-century ideal of the "well-tempered clavier." As Sam Whimster and Scott Lash put it, "the pure, mathematical rationalism of harmony cannot be fully realized in practice . . . harmonically it doesn't sound 'right.' The Western practice of keyboard tuning, temperament, is an example of the empirical fudging that takes place."[29] One wonders what Plato would have made of this impossibility of harmony through rational mathematic proportions, poor man.[30] Temperance, as it turns out in western music, is actually the product of "the imperfection of the rationally closed unity of western music."[31]

Perhaps by now we will not be surprised to see that Chinese scholars describe Confucian *hexie* as the fundamental goal of

Plato's *Republic*! Although this involves some fudging with *hexie* and *kosmos* (order), it is a common topic in Chinese treatments of the *Republic* and the *Analects*, on the basis of which Plato and Confucius are considered similar both in their impetus to improve their corrupt societies and in their emphasis on harmony.[32] Wang Yong, for example, assimilates Plato to Confucius by describing them both as looking back on a troubled period: "the original stable social and political order and fine moral traditions no longer exists, the spiritual life of city-state society has disintegrated, and all kinds of evil behaviors fill the whole society."[33] Both Plato and Confucius were trying to restore their respective societies for the better "by reflection on the political, economic, and cultural issues of their day." And both saw that "The ultimate secret of justice is the overall harmony achieved through mutual limitation and temperance."[34] Moreover, Wang argues, rule of virtue and rule of law are not absolute opposites. The two permeate and merge with one another. There is morality in law, and there is law in morality. "The rule of law needs to be based on the rule of virtue, and the rule of morality needs to be supplemented and guaranteed by the rule of law." In this sort of quest for, er, *harmony* between Plato and Confucius, poetry, virtue, harmony, morality, and justice simply become synonyms for each other.[35]

This is a broad perspective on the *Republic* that is repeatedly echoed in articles that identify *hexie* as what's *really* at the bottom of the *Republic*, despite the text's framing concern being justice. "It can be seen that the establishment of a well-ordered harmonious society is the ultimate goal of Plato's 'Utopia' [Kallipolis]," writes Hou Dianqin.[36] "Justice is essentially a kind of order and harmony," emphasizes Wen Tao, adding that "The essence of justice lies in harmony."[37] "Justice is harmony and order," says Rong Guangyi.[38] Zhang Xiaomei argues that "justice was the benefit of harmony. . . . Justice was overall harmony."[39] Wang Bei details that Kallipolis conveys a sense of harmony and throws light on "law" as being based on autonomy, order, rules, unity, and righteousness. Politicians need special training to strengthen the country and must emphasize the shaping of citizens according to the needs of the country.[40] And so on.

These scholars are not necessarily classicists, but that's the point. The primacy of ancient harmony (without the need for law) is a general theme, and not only in academic articles. Shortly after Hu Jintao came to office, *The Asia Times* published an article on "The Abduction of Morality" worth quoting at some length:

> Western perception on the alleged underdevelopment of law in Chinese civilization is based on both factual ignorance and cultural bias. Chinese dismissal of the rule of law is not a rejection of modernity, but a rejection of primitiveness. Confucian attitude places low reliance on law and punishment for maintaining social order. . . . The Confucian Code of Rites (*Liji*) is expected to be the controlling document on civilized behavior, not law. In the Confucian world view, rule of law is applied only to those who have fallen beyond the bounds of civilized behavior. Civilized people are expected to observe proper rites. Only social outcasts are expected to have their actions controlled by law. Thus, the rule of law is considered a state of barbaric primitiveness, prior to achieving the civilized state of voluntary observation of proper rites. What is legal is not necessarily moral or just.[41]

This of course turns much western legal thought on its head.

Harmony and the harmonious society met each other in the new slogan, "building a community of human destiny" (人类命运共同体 *Renlei mingyun gongtongti*), which, like *hexie*, is basically unlimited in scope.[42] A major conference on "the community of human destiny" in Beijing on the 2,570th anniversary of Confucius's birth (2019, thirty years after the conference with which this chapter opened) featured dignitaries and scholars from some eighty nations. As the conference description notes, Confucian values played a role in developing the slogan:

> Through heated discussions, experts and scholars have gained important insights on how Confucian culture can provide ideological nourishment and cultural support for the promotion of "building a community of human destiny" in the fields of politics, security, economy, culture, and ecology. . . . The Confucian culture's unremitting pursuit of "Harmony" and "Universal Unity" can provide a historical mirror for "building a community of shared future for mankind."[43]

This slogan represents the CCP's desire to create a new framework of international countries, a series of ties which would improve governance around the world. Some analysts hailed it as an important new amendment to China's foreign policy, while others have simply seen the slogan as a bid for global influence. As one might guess, "building a community of human destiny" is also the rhetorical face of China's Belt and Road Initiative, which could be seen as alternatively colonizing or boosting (or both) the poorer countries whose infrastructure China is supporting (or acquiring).[44]

The Community of Human Destiny plays a significant part on the world stage. In a foreign policy statement of 2014, Xi Jinping noted that:

> The major powers must respect each other's core interests and major concerns, manage contradictions and differences, and strive to build a new type of relationship that is free from conflict, non-confrontation, mutual respect, and win-win

cooperation. As long as you insist on communication and sincere coexistence, the "Thucydides trap" can be avoided. The big powers should treat each other as equals, and not engage in the hegemony of being alone and strong.... We must uphold the principles of peace, sovereignty, inclusiveness, and common governance, and make the fields of deep sea, polar regions, outer space, and the Internet a new territory for cooperation among all parties, rather than an arena for mutual gaming.[45]

In the west, of course, "Building a community of human destiny" is regarded as a rhetorical slogan invented to shine a moralizing light on the CCP's desire for soft power abroad—influence-peddling packaged as helping communities and nations prosper. What if a "community of common destiny" actually represents a direct threat to the current world order of alliances and organizations which hope very much to maintain that position, as they have since 1945? Jacob Mardell pushed back on this view: to dismiss "the community" so easily does not do justice to the complexity and pull of an idea that has been so long-lived. "To the cynical western mind," he wrote, "oft-wheeled out phrases like 'win-win cooperation' and 'peaceful development' form part of a meaningless lexicon of diplomatic jargon. But such slogans, are not used without purpose. Theory and ideology are more important to the CCP than an international audience might be led to believe."[46] In emphasizing that China will commit to international aid while letting each member of the community "choose their own development path," the phrase sets China up as a moral agent who will replace the US (and US democracy) in its old post-WWII role. China will do so, to be sure, without the western norms of rule of law, of one-vote-one-citizen, of respect for human rights, and more. Will the Chinese find other norms that they prefer? One China-watcher observed, "The path that the Chinese regime has chosen for itself—a disinhibited authoritarian one-party system fully integrated into the global economy, showing no intention of evolving into a liberal democracy—is now being offered as 'a new option for other countries and nations who want to speed up their development while preserving their independence.'"[47]

Given the attention we have already paid to Plato's Noble Lie and the Chinese arguments that a government will inevitably have to lie to the people, it may be tempting to see the Community of Human Destiny as a parallel to Plato's Kallipolis, in other words, a society whose stability relies on Xi Jinping's Noble Lie ("if you behave, we'll all get along"). The goal of this slogan is to unite the state, stop conflict between different socio-economic ranks, and unite the "polis." Only the person behind the lie and his courtiers know the truth—that they are creating a fiction—but to do what? To increase patriotism while diverting eyes from abuses by the CCP? (I do not suggest this tactic is unique to China.) In praising the Chinese people in particular as peaceful and wise, the phrase also unites them; and in emphasizing that China will not interfere with countries' internal politics the way the US has, the phrase also sets China up as the new global moral agent, the one that will replace the United States. Maybe all governments have leant on a Noble Lie. The question is now: will China be bound by its own new adherence to new Confucian values to become a moral leader for the world, or will it revert to the abusive authoritarian tendencies shown by Mao Zedong?

II. The Uses of Confucius

These days, Confucius has many different manifestations—he has become a jack of all trades.[48] Given his leading role as part of Xi Jinping's initiative to promote Chinese nationalism by rooting it in China's cultural tradition, the philosopher has had to straddle a gap over two millennia wide, occasionally sounding very modern and occasionally very ancient.[49] As Roland Boer wrote of the above-mentioned Party conference on Confucius of 2019, "As I listened to papers and spoke with many there, it became clear that the Confucius of today is a rather truncated sage. We heard of harmony with diversity, of welcoming friends of like minds from all over the world, of peace over the four seas (there seemed to have been fewer of those 2,500 years ago)."[50] Anything objectionable or antiquarian in Confucius's views tends to disappear (it has been harmonized!). The sage's insistence on the centrality of ritual and the ancestor cult, his low regard for women, his distaste for profit—these are not useful for a modern Chinese nation.[51] On the other hand, the CCP has made sustained efforts to depict its own leadership as a group of Confucians on steroids, as "aggressive corruption fighters who adhere to the Confucian values of propriety, ethical behavior, self-discipline and cultivation, and dedicated public service."[52] Here the modern state imposes its own anachronistic views on those of the past, since the contemporary nationalist idea of the citizen serving the state is not, of course, Confucian in nature.

The harmonized Confucius appears differently according to the political and philosophical needs of his readers. Some modern neo-Confucianists have found in the philosopher a version of Max Weber's "Protestant ethic" driving economic success.[53] The harmonized ancient also can be easily enlisted in support of the ethical values of the Chinese political system. He can stand in the role of an advisor to the attentive Chinese government itself, reminding all of the need to fight corruption.[54] For still others, Confucius is a standard bearer for environmental ethics, an idea traced back to the Confucian idea that man should not try to overcome nature, but rather to live with it in harmony.[55] Bringing together several of these ideas, the New Confucianist Tu Wei-ming, leader of the International Confucian Ecological Alliance (ICEA) and a professor at both Harvard University and Peking University, has called for "the creative transformation of Confucian humanism with a view toward the future."[56] According to Tu, Confucianism transcends the concept of rationality that derives from the Enlightenment mentality and provides a philosophy of life rooted in the sensitivity, sympathy, and compassion inherent in human nature. The Earth is alive. The "Golden Rule" and the *ren* that Confucianism champions apply not only to other people but also to nature.[57] But Feng Yongfeng, an environmentalist and founder of the Beijing-based NGO Green Beagle, doesn't hide his doubts about using Confucianism or Daoism to fix the environment, calling it "pure nonsense."[58]

The New Confucians (including Tu Wei-ming)—very few of them currently writing in mainland China—argue that Confucianism supports human rights and offers liberty without encouraging the individualistic excesses that, as they see it, plague America and Europe.[59] The twentieth-century *neo*-Confucians, on the other hand, are very much in China.[60] Like Zhu Xi and the original Neo-Confucians, these more recent neo-Confucians describe themselves as committed to the foundation of a moral society, which (they say) is the only conceivable foundation for good government. Staunchly anti-democratic, they bring Confucius into play to criticize the automatic assumptions of the west. Both groups have been criticized as propagating a disembodied Confucianism, without historical or social context, that simply reproduces the essentializing procedures of Orientalism itself: now the modern Confucians spout the same clichés about what it means to be

Chinese as the Orientalizing west.[61] Radical conservatives would like Confucianism to be a religion, presumably because it offers the government a means of control. And yet it's not clear that just stating it is a religion makes it so. The west may have largely lost its God, but the Chinese never had one. They have not encountered the Christian need for a leap of faith.[62]

Other critics are not so concerned with the deviation from Confucian orthodoxy as they are with the danger of China's government returning to any form of Confucianism, which they regard as a justificatory mechanism for feudalism—or perhaps for an absolutist state. Jerome Cohen, faculty director of the US-Asia Law Institute at New York University, argued that:

> intermittent attempts by Xi to invoke China's traditions to fill the void with nationalist pride have won little acceptance. The hoary maxims of Confucianist humanism, long denounced by the party as pernicious feudalism but now revived by Beijing, do little to meet contemporary demands. And Xi's occasional invocation of . . . the legalist version of Confucianism, a philosophy of government that involved dictatorial rule over China's first imperial dynasty more than 2,000 years ago—is too close to today's reality to do more than enhance the fear that already exists among the increasingly sophisticated Chinese people and even many party members.[63]

We have wandered from our path—where are the western classics here? To answer that question, we turn to another area where the value of harmony and a community of human destiny has cut a noticeable figure, and seems to reflect, *in nuce*, some of the government's higher aspirations. In 1998, 2000, and 2002, three diplomatically arranged conferences about Socrates and Confucius were co-hosted by Greece and China.[64] The conferences provided a forum for scholars from the two countries to compare and contrast the ethical teachings of their respective ancient sages and to express their ideals of mutual friendship and a harmonious future. The expertise on display was sometimes a bit perfunctory, but perhaps precisely for this reason, the speakers' gathered papers provide an interesting, if not excessively academic, window into how Confucius and Socrates fared in their match-up, and also into the stakes involved in having such encounters in the first place. When the representatives of two ethical ancient traditions meet in this context, do they box it out or harmonize?[65]

The conference volume starts with some comments by Chen Haosu, a Party official and honorary professor at several Chinese universities who presides over CPAFFC, the Chinese People's Association for Friendship with Foreign Countries. In his written preface to the volume, Chen reminded his readers that "In the Athens conference of 1998, I gave a speech, 'Keeping on Learning, Becoming Mature in Harmony,' which represented my understanding of the initiative [sic] positions of Confucius and Socrates in the East and the west ancient philosophy histories."[66] The reference to the "positions" of the two is a hint at what is to come in the volume, because it appears that the two itinerant ethicists (a) share their views, and (b) are oriented towards goals that are more Confucian than Socratic. We are told, in effect, that Socrates has borrowed much from Confucius—especially in the area of moral values—even if these values would not normally be associated with the Athenian philosopher. (This borrowing never occurs in the opposite direction during the three conferences). As Chen said when he quoted himself once again from the first conference:

Now it is the time to let them have both (time and space); the treasure of their thoughts should be comprehended by their later generations, so that we can come much closer to the realization of the great harmony of human beings they expected![67]

Chen is full of diplomatic goodwill. But the language of harmony that he uses here is very close to the official rhetoric about the community of human destiny and, ironically enough, contributes to the disappearance of the real Socrates, producing instead one that seems to support Xi Jinping's policies. Who needs the querulous Socrates in the context of diplomacy anyhow? If we want harmony between nations, the implication is that China's native traditions (not those of the west) are the best path to this goal. In a telling parallel, Chen's statement also seems to quote Jupiter's famous lines about Rome in Vergil's *Aeneid*: she shall have no boundaries of time or space.[68] Whether the reference is deliberate, the scope is definitely imperial. Confucian harmony shall prevail—everywhere.

Following similar diplomatic comments from the Greek side that stress the importance of philosophical dialogue and political good will, many of the papers fall into one of two categories: either they harmonize Socrates and Confucius by emphasizing everything they had in common, or they distinguish between the two by emphasizing how little they had in common. The "harmonizers" draw attention to the real and manufactured convergences of Confucian and Platonic/Socratic thought to make their point. While both Greeks and Chinese take interpretive liberties here in the name of international friendship, the harmonizers, interestingly, are all Chinese. Another interesting observation is the fact that it is the Platonic Socrates, not Xenophon's homelier version, that received all the attention— presumably because Plato is seen as a more authoritative representation of western values. Ironically, Xenophon's busybody

Socrates would be far more likely to have opinions in family matters, and he is conventionally pious as well—but he was of less interest to the conference speakers.

As an example of the harmonizing approach, let us turn to Professor Yao Jiehou.[69] In his presentation he stresses that Socrates and Confucius share details of biography as well as philosophy. Both men are characterized as living in a time of chaos, neither left behind any writing of their own, and they share the common ethos of improving society. Yao also asserts that the Confucian *ren* (benevolence) is commensurate with Socrates's notion of "the good" (*to agathon*). There are some difficulties here, especially since Socrates's good is ultimately the *form* of the good, an intellectual concept rather than a societal practice. It is via the contemplation of this form, or idea, that one can realize the other forms and become a philosopher-king.[70] Yao's Socratic "good" turns out to be predicated on order and rule, and his Socratic wisdom (*sophrosyne*) entails loyalty to kings, reverence for hierarchy, and ethical relations within the hierarchical family.[71] Indeed, Socrates saw the state as an expanded family and viewed the function of ethics as "normalizing social order, maintaining sustainable development, educating humanity, and cultivating moral personality."[72] It becomes more and more difficult to see Plato's Socrates behind these words, and as Yao himself pointed out, all of these goals belong to the twenty-first-century Chinese-Confucian state: "Along with perfecting the legal system of market economy, China is unfolding the construction of ethics and morality so as to make the same system of market economy and social life beneficial to the development of society and perfection of personality."[73] And despite his approval of Socrates, Yao nevertheless ended his presentation with a rousing critique of western logic, technology, and the rupture of its knowledge-value system.

In the same way, other Chinese scholars at these three conferences seemed to downplay serious philosophical differences between Socrates and Confucius by various means—for example, by forcing Chinese and Greek terms to mean the same thing, or by relying on vague generalities, or even by just baldly making claims. Ye Xiushan notes "the common ideal of harmony between Confucius and Socrates," both of whom wanted to "reconstruct society in a harmonious stability."[74] He adds the impenetrable claim that, "The ancient Chinese worshipped the Heaven just as the ancient Greeks did." Zhao Dunhua compares *ren* and the Socratic idea of "excellence" (*arete*) and concludes that, if Confucius was harmony, Socrates represented the soul, rendering the two inseparable.[75] Li Qiuling comments that "Both Confucius and Socrates recalled affectionately each golden age though passed away."[76] In Confucius's case, this golden age was under the duke of Zhou; there's no such nostalgia from Socrates's viewpoint.[77] And Chen Haosu reappears to carry out more harmonizing: both Socrates and Confucius recommend that we live in harmony according to the Doctrine of the Mean (of course the Doctrine of the Mean in the western tradition is more Aristotelian than Socratic).[78] To this end, Chen exhorts us to master the thought of the two sages: "then harmony won't be far from us."[79] Full steam ahead![80]

The Greek speakers (apart from the diplomatic conference openers) are more interested in differences than in harmony.[81] If the Chinese are enacting Confucian harmony, and thus hope to blend the two schools, the western scholars represented here interpret the two traditions quite differently. As Marianna Benetatou points out in her paper, unlike Socrates who desired to question tradition, Confucius embraced it, and even claimed to transmit it rather than to innovate it.[82] Confucius's goal was to invigorate past traditions, rites, poems, songs, and institutions, but unlike Socrates, he showed little interest in any abstract "truth." In the repeat conference two years later, Kyveli Vernier-Tsigara noted essentially the same differences, pointing out that where one thinker focused on content, the other focused on method. (Nevertheless, she too saw "parallel tracks" and hoped the two philosophies will bear each other's fruit).[83] Moreover, Socratic dialectic and its sharp probing lie in direct contrast to Confucius's generally declarative sentences.[84] As the Neo-Confucian Tu Wei-ming has remarked (he for one does not want to harmonize Socrates):

> There is nothing in the *Analects* that resembles the elaborate reasoning in the Socratic dialogue. Indeed, Confucius distrusted mere verbal persuasiveness, he despised glibness, and he resented clever expressions. Although he highly valued eloquence in diplomacy, lucidity in thought, and articulateness in literature, he preferred tacit understanding to effective argumentation. The former reminded him of the trickery in legal disputes, even litigiousness.[85]

Jiyuan Yu, a US-trained professor of classical philosophy *not* writing in the context of a diplomatic event, is not interested in easy harmonizing either.[86] As he points out, Socrates—that annoying gadfly—was critical of traditional values and the lives led by others. He was willing to embarrass people in order to show that their moral beliefs were contradictory: ethics comes through critical examination. For Confucius, on the other hand, tradition supplied the path, and it is the very historical rituals and practices he wished to restore that Socrates would want to refute. Nor does Confucius regard virtue as a matter of the intellect alone. Yu writes of him that:

> the pursuit of *ren* (human excellence) involves a full-fledged development of moral character. It requires one to cultivate

traditional ritual practices [c.f. *Analects*, 12 :1], to love his fellow men [12:22] in a way rooted to filial piety and brotherly love [1.2], and also to develop an intellectual aspect of knowing what is appropriate in applying the general requirement of traditional values in particular circumstances [4:10].[87]

Here we have ethical guidance and rules for life rather than the destruction of values via cross-examination.

At the conferences, of course, even if the Greek delegates may have spoken of the important distinctions between Socrates and Confucius, they could hardly elevate that difference in values into a statement about the radical differences between Greece and China. Presumably the Greek speakers also hoped for a peaceful future (how could they not?). And so, they too made statements hoping for harmony and peace between the two nations in the future. As Pavlos Yeroulanos, Minister of Culture and Tourism of Greece, eloquently remarked of our two sages, "Reaching back in the elements that these thinkers have in common we shall find what we need to build our world forward."[88] There is a sense, then, in which Confucius won the unspoken contest between the two in preaching peace and harmony. If that's what we want, Socrates's aggressive questioning must be subsumed into Confucius's all-inclusive vision of the harmonious and well-ordered society.[89] Perhaps none of this is surprising given that the emphases of the two traditions tilt to community/harmony and individuality/self-interest, respectively (of course communities, friendships, and individuals appear in both).[90]

The harmonizing tendency of the speakers is repeated even in newspapers; what Socrates and Confucius can both contribute to the good society seems to be of real public interest in China. For example, the *Guangming Daily* featured "A

Comparison of Confucius and Plato's Conceptions of a Harmonious Society" by Zheng Xiaowu and Zheng Jianping, its stated goal being to educate the good citizens of Beijing about the harmonious society.[91] Plato and Confucius both brought something to the table: "In Plato's view, the so-called good society is a just society, and social justice is the formation of all sections of society," while Confucius's ideal "is based on the principle of benevolence." So, the authors concluded that the approaches of the heart and mind are both needed—but specifically to deliver Xi Jinping's goal of the harmonious society, or more specifically, to "construct a broad, open, and benign harmonious society with both internal and just order and external tolerance and harmony. And that is what is really needed today as a broad exchange between people and nations."[92] Who could disagree?

III. Whose Republic Will It Be?

The modern Confucianists most relevant to this book are yet another group (although these borders are permeable): the "political" Confucians. Their aim is to reconcile Confucianism with the contemporary Chinese state and its leadership and to suggest that China is already on the way to the best Confucian-communist form of government.[93] The political Confucians are often scholars familiar with western political philosophy who compare western values (and practices) to Confucianism and argue that the latter is a better method for electing knowledgeable and qualified leaders (very much in contrast to, say, the popular franchise).[94] They also emphasize the Confucian view that hierarchy is a natural state in human societies. The Canadian political theorist Daniel A. Bell, Dean of the School of Political Science and Public Administration at Shandong University and professor at Tsinghua University, has written several critically praised books making this argument (the most recent with his colleague Wang Pei).[95] And even westerners in the west have tackled the topic. In their book *Intelligent Governance for the 21st Century*, Nathan Gardels and Nicholas Berggruen have suggested "a Middle Way between West and East" that would combine aspects of Chinese meritocracy and western democracy, improving the latter by reducing its vulnerability to wealth and the former by incorporating more participation, accountability of government, and the rule of law.

But it is Bai Tongdong, professor of philosophy at Fudan University, who explicitly takes up Plato as offering an alternative to a Chinese-Confucian meritocracy. His 2020 book, *Against Political Equality—The Confucian Case*, grapples with the question of whether a Platonic or a Confucian republic would serve its citizens better.[96] Bai's core argument is that all societies have an honor-seeking segment for which a place must be made in any hypothetical state. In the US, that segment has focused primarily on the accumulation of wealth, which has had a corruptive effect on democratic politics. A Confucian-influenced system, however, would seek status rather than money, relying on a meritocratic politics that would provide a real alternative to American electoral democracy in combining a meritocracy at the highest levels and a democracy at the lowest. The meritocratic element draws authority from the well-established dynastic tradition of selecting officials through rigorous examinations based on the memorization of Confucian works.[97] Since people are not all equal, not all citizens should be equally influential.

Confucians only deny the equal voice in the political decision-making process due to the actual differences among human beings with regard to their moral, political, and intellectual

capacities. For Confucians, the right to govern is not an in-
born right but a right that must be earned (and it is "earn-
able" by all). Their position is close to the concept of "equal
opportunity," and is also close to what is argued in Plato's
Republic, where to rule is a burden that should be left to the
wise and virtuous.[98]

As for one-person-one-vote, Bai acknowledges that Confucius
and Mencius believed that "the legitimacy of the government
resided in service to the people"—but, as he stresses, not *by* the
people.[99] Mindful of the horrifying excesses of the Cultural
Revolution, Bai argues that China needs to be wary of political
ideologies that have the character of religious belief, because
the ability of religions to create deep bonds among citizens also
makes them liable to intolerance of a kind that does not work
well in large, pluralistic societies such as China.

Bai argues that even the policies of American democracy at
its origin were "specifically for preventing the uninformed populace from having too much influence and harming people's
true interests . . . In this sense, the American regime at its early
stage, especially with regard to the aspects mentioned above,
can be considered an (imperfect) example of the Confucian
hybrid regime."[100] However, modern electoral democracy, with
its emphasis on "one person, one vote" fails to realize that
people as a whole are gullible and lack sufficient vision into the
future (we recall here Thucydides's critique).[101] Bai refers to
Plato to cinch the point: even with the reliance of the Athenians
on slave labor to free them up for political activity, the philosopher had a dim view of the democracy's competency to make
good plans.

For Bai, the Platonic Kallipolis has several flaws that are absent
from the Confucian account. For one, there is the destruction

of the nuclear family.[102] To become a member of the ideal city-state, in Kallipolis, men and women must overcome their natural love for their offspring, who are whisked away at birth to join a general pool and never know who their true parents are. From a Chinese perspective, this is untenable. In Confucian thought, the family is the training ground of ethics and compassion, and in the absence of the family, adherence to the good of the society as a whole will eventually break down.[103] Can philosopher-kings emerge from orphanages, however well educated? Without the family, can compassion thrive? The loyalty to family and country that is natural in the Confucian state has to be manufactured in the Platonic one, where love of Kallipolis, when not philosophically grounded, is born out of a Noble Lie. "The early Confucian model begins with something very accessible to ordinary human beings (the cultivation of family relations), while the model in the *Republic* is radical from the beginning."[104]

In Bai's argument for the practical benefits of the Confucian tradition, the Platonic concept of the good also comes in for criticism as excessively abstract.[105] The Confucian good is practical: serving the people, observing ritual, and practicing *ren*.[106] The Platonic Good is analogous to the sun: it is the medium through which we see or understand the world.[107] Just as "sun is not sight" but rather the cause of sight, so too the Form of the Good is "what gives the power of knowing to the knower." This probably has less curb appeal to a general public. Nor does the justice observed in Kallipolis seem to make anyone happy, notes Bai, apparently agreeing with Adeimantus's reproach to Socrates in the *Republic*.[108] And then there is the Noble Lie. "Simply put, the unity the latter model tries to achieve is rootless . . . It may work to some extent through brainwashing and through quite radical arrangements such as the community of woman and children, but without some proper root, devotion to the public and to a set of laws and codes of contact will eventually wither."[109] Unsurprisingly, *Against Political Equality* ultimately decides in favor of a modified Confucian system with socialist characteristics.[110]

But unlike the other models for a modernized Confucianism in China, Bai's regime is meant to be universally applicable to any state, *including* modern democracies. As James Hankins observes of Bai's model:

> Confucian political ideals are a cure not only for the moral failures of the Communist totalitarian state, but also for the ills of liberal democracy. . . . The Confucian alternative of social and economic equality coupled with political meritocracy, "government of the people and for the people but not *by* the people," would produce fairer and more enlightened outcomes. The tumultuous and morally debased public life of modern democratic societies would become orderly and stable.[111]

In other words, the Confucian hybrid regime is just what the United States needs. But there is an implementation problem: because of its staunch commitment to electoral democracy, argues Bai, this regime could only be established through "skillful disguises."[112] It sounds as if the United States needs a Noble Lie, and the sooner the better. Presumably, it would lead Americans to embrace Confucianism while mistakenly believing all along that they were practicing democracy? Of course the Americans would be happy under the Lie, but one can imagine the indignation if the truth got out that the US had been deluded en masse by China for its own good.[113] On the other hand, there are those who believe the American government did just that to the Americans under George W. Bush, whose cabinet was openly called Straussian in the press—that is, as practicing a "tell the people what they need to hear, but not the truth" approach.[114] Ron Suskind's famous 2004 "We're the authors of reality" interview with an unnamed member of the Bush administration in *The New York Times Magazine* revealed an arrogance appropriate to the those who believed themselves philosopher-kings. The anonymous official disparages the "reality-based community," which he defines as people who "believe that solutions emerge from [the] judicious study of discernible reality. . . . That's not the way the world really works anymore. We're an empire now, and when we act, we create our own reality. And while you're studying that reality—judiciously, as you will—we'll act again, creating other new realities, which you can study too, and that's how things will sort out. We're history's actors . . . and you, all of you, will be left to just study what we do."[115] As the social scientist Jim George notes of the second Bush administration, "the notion that elite rule is crucial if post-Enlightenment liberalism is not to further threaten the (classical) democratic model of governance, and that the neoconservative elite has the right and indeed the obligation to lie to the masses in order that the 'right' political and strategic decisions be made and implemented" is completely out of Strauss's playbook.[116]

Rather than end with the worry that the US will be tricked into becoming a new Confucian nation, let's return to *hexie* (harmony) to see its latest deployment in the Chinese media. Given the Chinese government's interest in imposing harmony on the citizens in order to suppress "notes" that don't agree with its own, *hexie* has come to lose some of its original sense of "harmony through diversity" and to resemble a single tone—a C, but not a C natural, if you will. If you don't agree with an official perspective, you may be required to harmonize. In the hands of some netizens, then, references to harmony have taken

on something of an ironic tone. Since *hexie* is the apparent justification for state actions aimed at silencing voices, it reneges
on its implicit promise of "a hundred schools of thought," in
return for which the younger generation of bloggers and internet users has turned it into a shorthand for government control
of public expression. For this new generation, *hexie* means the
erasure of opinions inconsonant with CCP ideology—the very
opposite of its original meaning. Use of the word harmonious
in an internet post can now refer to items deleted by China's
vast internet security force for objectionable content or sensitive matter. An article censored in this manner has been "harmonized" (被和谐了 *bei hexiele*).[117] So yes, to use the word
"harmony" can be a way of protesting the very acts of censorship that are necessary to create a harmonious society.

7

Thoughts for the Present

THE FRAME ON which this book hangs is a study of broad and mostly nationalistic interpretations of a number of ancient Greek philosophical and political texts in China.[1] We started with the Jesuit mission to China for a first example of the appropriation of the classics by users eager to have them serve an agenda: Catholics citing pagan Stoics to show the Chinese court and its mandarins that this new religion, Christianity, was largely Confucian, but also incorporated the figure of Jesus and an anthropomorphized God. Whether the Jesuits did so in earnest, believing Stoicism to have inklings of "the ancient theology" or to represent an ethical system that anticipated Christianity, or did this more as a sleight of hand, is not only impossible to answer but possibly also a false opposition (we return to Yin and Yang!). We all believe what we want to out of our core texts once we use them as such, and we are always using those beliefs for *something*, however simple or neutral it seems.

The Chinese succeed the Jesuits as the object of study, their own appropriation of the classics perhaps not so unlike the missionaries. For the Chinese reformers associated with the May 4th Movement, and for the idealistic students and workers of the 1980s, Aristotle was right about the importance of the citizen's political participation, and right that citizens should exist in the first place, not just be subjects of dynastic rule. Aristotle *would* have said democracy was best if he'd just been up-to-date on the twentieth century. But if we look at Chinese public intellectuals today, when Aristotle is cited it's to show that the west has taken as its political Bible a work that naturalizes slavery, encourages the deceit and manipulation of one's fellow citizens, and inherently encourages military aggression(!). It's just as Plato and Thucydides showed us: the people are not fit to rule. Either they can't control themselves, or they'll fall prey to some demagogue, or both. In a rather both/and leap from this position, government spokespeople and nationalist thinkers *also* argue that, if democracy is good, well then, China is the best example of it, and not the democracy practiced by the United States. Only a few lonely voices from the past pipe up to protest the new orthodoxy.

The Chinese have also found Plato's *Republic* very good to think with. Kallipolis's supposedly merit-based division of humans into different ranks based on their capacity for rationality appeals to the Confucian notion of keeping one's given role in society (even if not based on one's capacity for rationality), and the philosopher-kings who look to hierarchy for their subjects' best interests offer a close copy of the ideal Chinese emperor. Conveniently, the position of Plato (rather than, say, the pre-Socratics) at the head of the western tradition means that ancient Greek and modern Chinese thinkers have come up with similar "basic truths" that they rely on—truths to which the contemporary west is stupidly closing its eyes. But when Chinese writers endorse Kallipolis's Noble Lie as an obvious necessity for all stable societies, they are presumably including their own, in which case the citizens know the lie—in which case it should be impossible to believe in it. There's no figuring out what lies beneath this.

If Plato is "good" on these fronts, he is "bad" when he represents the rationality-based western philosophical tradition (or, more accurately, the so-called rationality-based western philosophical tradition). Following Weber, a large group of scholars are denouncing western society as driven by an instrumental form of rationality that is by a nature amoral and unlinked to older ethical traditions. Looking back to Kant in particular as a paradigm of the Enlightenment, these scholars contrast the rationality-based rules for duty that helped to create the technologically advanced but "disenchanted" west to their own tradition of Confucian benevolence for other people. These texts, unlike the Platonic dialogues, do not rely on argumentation and logic-based deductions. Of course, there are those who do want to stress the presence of logic in Confucius and the presence of the mythical in Plato, in which case they invert the argument but keep the terminology intact. No one suggests that the logic in Confucian texts has contributed to the Holocaust, though. In the end, "rationality" turns out to be too vague a tool with which to be bashing anyone. It's time for this pillow-fight to be over.

Good Plato and bad Plato are complemented by Straussian Plato, who seems to exist mostly to give a group of intellectuals special status. According to this group, by using Strauss they can make classical antiquity relevant to China's current path (but then much of the country's intelligentsia seems to be doing this!). Moreover, as Straussian philosophers, they are also the people "in the know." Furthermore, what they know is what Strauss "knew," namely, that throughout history philosophers who could not speak freely wrote esoteric messages in their texts intended for recipients who could read between the lines. Additionally, they know that the content of those esoteric messages was that philosophers know harmful things that they can't say, because it would be harmful for the state—if this is what the Straussians claim to know, then one wonders what exactly they are *not* saying openly. We would have to be Straussians to find out.

Plato's final manifestation (and Socrates's as well) is as an alternative Confucius. Surely taking Kallipolis more seriously than any western political theorist, one of China's most famous intellectuals compares it to his own recommendation for the ideal state and found much that is similar between the two. But there is not enough: the Confucian-influenced model proposed is better on several fronts, Bai Tongdong argues, and it's just what the United States needs. Meanwhile, others have seized on the *Republic* as an example of the ancient west advocating nothing other than harmony (they must do so by harmonizing justice and harmony). And if Plato has been put to use for this Chinese moment, we should justly point out that so has Confucius, his own teachings harmonized into what the CCP needs.

Where does this leave us? Most immediately, there's the obvious point that a study of the reception of the Greek classics in contemporary China can actually put into focus issues that dominate public and political discourse in both nations. More broadly, using the lens of classical antiquity throws light on the changing self-representation and claims to moral authority of both China and the US. There are thus implications both for the field of classics in modern US universities, and for the war in words and concepts currently in play between China and the west.

I. Classics

What should the west do with a classical culture that seems so amenable to the Chinese, but not to the west? First of all, it bears repeating that Plato and Aristotle can hardly stand for the entire classical tradition, which includes figures like Sappho and Herodotus, genres like satire and elegy, and everything from practical manuals to the scribblings of graffiti all over the Roman empire. As a field, classics has room for local cultural values, flexibility in gender norms, and challenges to authority. Indeed, the texts of this reception study have shown themselves to be almost infinitely flexible. Epictetus can serve Christians proselytizing to Confucians; Plato can emphasize rationality or harmony; Aristotle can call for democracy; and classical Athens itself can be a locus of the *absence* of freedom. Since the Chinese have taken what they needed, both in the twentieth century and in the twenty-first, it is curious to me that we (by which I mean the teachers of classical texts) cannot do the same. Am I advocating misreading? Of course not. I have already commented on how we always read to our interests anyhow, even at our most sincere.

It is also very much worth noting that many of the interpretations of Plato, Aristotle, and others in this book *are not intellectually sophisticated*. Simple interpretations can be made to support crude or simplified claims—precisely the kind of claims that we are hearing today on both sides of the globe and that currently drive major international political agendas.[2] The interpretations we have seen here are for the most part not scholarly essays striving to make a dean's *summa cum laude* list. Instead, they exist to support broad knowledge-claims about humans, hierarchies, histories, nations, and ethics. Especially in a culture like China's, with its respect for antiquity, the fact that these interpretations hark back to ancient Athens brings them a certain legitimacy. But Plato and Aristotle are not the only thinkers who have been boiled down to a few simple points in these readings, the complexity of their thought abandoned in favor of easy slogans. The resuscitated Confucius has suffered the same reductionism—or is it expansion?—at the hands of his new adherents, who can mold the ancient sage into a Chinese Greta Thunberg wringing his hands about climate change, his less popular or useful views (just like those of the Stoics!) left discreetly by the roadside.[3]

II. Cultures

This book's imaginary audience and interlocutors are readers in both China and the United States. It is not addressed to western classicists in particular, nor do I need to inform Chinese intellectuals of what they themselves have written. My hope is that in the crucible of classical antiquity we can see emerging deep cultural and political values and assumptions that claim for themselves a timeless authority, and that seeing this process in action will make us think about how regimes justify their existence, even if they are very much linked to finite time and place. My goal has not been to be a spokesperson for one government rather than another, and if I have occasionally failed at this, it is because I am myself schooled in western, but not eastern, points of view. Perhaps the lack of a platform from which to issue judgments suggests, as one reader complained, that this book has no moral compass. But I hope I can persuasively make the argument that its moral compass rests on (as it were) the absence of a moral compass, or more exactly, on the belief that studies like this one can contribute in some small measure to national introspection and greater understanding of different cultures, that they can show us (and others) a mirror to our moral assumptions, and that they can also lead to an interrogation of the assumptions that the west is inflicting on its own interpretations of China and her cultural traditions (and vice-versa). Now that we see how it's done, in other words, can we in the west see ourselves doing it too? Can we be attuned to the way the language of our questions already shapes and restrains the possibilities for answers—questions such as, "Is this rational?" or "Are we citizens?" or "What is democracy?"

III. Myths

Having a richer viewpoint on the core values of other cultures also helps us to shrug off the claims of some widescale theories—and since I have singled out Chinese nationalism in this book, maybe it's time to include a few western narratives about the place of democracy in a global world, such as Francis Fukuyama's "end of history," Samuel Huntington's "clash of civilizations," or Graham Allison's "Thucydides Trap." The last of these has given the Chinese government fodder to argue that the United States sees everything through the lens of aggression. In his 2017 book *Destined for War: Can America and China Escape Thucydides's Trap?* Allison argued that the likelihood of war will arise every time an emerging power seems on the verge of displacing an extant power as globally hegemonic. A rising China is therefore irresistibly on course to collide with an immovable America—the scenario Thucydides described at the beginning of the *Peloponnesian War*: "The growth of the power of Athens, and the alarm which this inspired in Sparta, made war inevitable."[4] This political model for current Sino-American tension around moral and economic status in a globalized world appeals because it grounds itself in learning from history and also contains implicit judgments of the actors, not to mention offering everyone a way of predicting the worrisome future of global conflict. While foreseeing and thus preventing this conflict is Allison's stated goal, the analogy itself supports the notion that war is likely.[5]

The Chinese feel that this a dangerously antagonistic way to conceptualize the US and China and urge the Americans to drop the analogy for their own good.[6] In a 2019 editorial entitled "There is no 'Thucydides trap' in the world: Comments on the danger of some Americans' strategic misunderstanding," Guo Jiping 国纪平 (a pen name attributed to the *People's Daily* editorials on China's viewpoints on major international issues) wrote that:

> The "Thucydides Trap" concept is commensurate with the zero-sum game political view of the United States and its "Keep America First" motto . . . In the eyes of the former chief strategic adviser of the White House, China poses the "most serious existential threat" to the United States, and the core issue of the trade dispute is China's intentions on the world stage and what these ambitions mean to the prosperity of the United States. . . . Regarding the future of Sino-US relations, the world not only does not want to see the "Thucydides trap," but also expects great powers to devote themselves to the great practice of improving global governance and promoting common prosperity with far-sighted decisions and actions.[7]

For Guo, this very analogy—the idea that the US can no more stand the growth of Chinese power than the Spartans could tolerate Athens—provides a dangerous framework. The US should not turn to aggression in the face of the lotus extended from the peaceful *ren*-loving Chinese. Instead, the west should *correctly* learn from its classical past. Guo cited Thucydides again to offer ancient wisdom against the folly of those who would believe we face a Thucydides Trap: "Many times people have the ability to foresee the danger ahead. But they let the idea of enticing them into irreversible disaster . . . because of their own stupidity, not misfortune."[8]

From a different point of view, it would be just as easy to argue that China is Sparta and the US, Athens.[9] Like the

Spartans, until recently China was an inward-looking land power, while the US has long supported a powerful navy. As Jack Bowers of the Strategic and Defense Studies Centre at Australian National University pointed out, Sparta's loose confederacy of alliances could be analogized to China's use of soft power across the Pacific and Africa.[10] The Chinese have even bought the ancient Athenian port of Piraeus as part of the One Belt One Road initiative. Perhaps the drive with which China conceals domestic issues while showing strength to the world may even remind us of the Laconian boy who let a fox eat through his stomach without showing any pain.[11] Probably the best perspective, however, would be one that disavows the analogy altogether. As James Palmer has suggested, maybe Western strategists need to learn some new history: it is shortsighted that, "even when strategists move beyond Athens, they're still writing about Europe. In all the takes on the US-China relationship, the history of Chinese warfare itself—and the vast span of Asian conflict, warfare, and political contention over the last 3,000 years—goes virtually unmentioned."[12]

Samuel Huntington's theory of the "clash of civilizations" argues that that people's cultural and religious identities, not their national identities, will be the main source of conflict in the post-Cold War period.[13] This idea has not fared much better as a predictor of the global political scene, attracting criticism for being essentializing, racist, and unaware of the complex realities of a permeable world. But, while some westerners reject it, this particular grand theory is not unpopular among Chinese intellectuals, who are eager to compare their long-lived civilization to that of the west and to argue for the superiority of the former. Wen Yang 文扬 at the China Research Institute of Fudan University, and a supporter of Huntington's thesis, recently published a book entitled *The Logic of*

Civilizations (文明的逻辑 *Wenming de luoji*). In it he argued (with a startling degree of what might be called simplification) that "western civilization emerged as a new civilization founded by barbarians, and it is also the destroyer of ancient civilizations."[14] In contrast, China's civilization as been developing for 5,000 years—"Chinese civilization is the only one which has this 'eternality.' For this reason, Chinese civilization should be the yardstick against which other civilizations should be evaluated"—that is to say, the Chinese were and are continuing to do something right. They are also on their own land, unlike the wandering, warmongering barbarians. Now it is America and the west that are in decline as the international political and economic landscape is undergoing a seismic shift.[15]

Francis Fukuyama's views, on the other hand, have been much pilloried by the Chinese. The idea that western liberal democracy has established its superiority and brought about an "end of history" so that democratic government will be an eternal norm, is, in the Chinese view, patently countered by reality. Fukuyama's claim in his 1989 essay "The End of History?" was that:

> The triumph of the West, of the Western *idea* is evident first of all in the total exhaustion of viable systematic alternatives to Western liberalism. In the past decade, there have been particular period [*sic*] of postwar history, but the end of history as such: that is, the end point of mankind's ideological evolution and the universalization of Western liberal democracy as the final form of human government.[16]

Despite the fact that the piece was in review at the time of June 4, 1989, almost none of its reviewers mentioned Tiananmen Square.[17] But the Chinese clamp-down, just before the appearance of the article, must have led some to wonder about its prediction. To the satisfaction of the CCP, history has proven otherwise; China has surged economically and Xi Jinping has fastened his grip on termless power. For Fukuyama's Chinese critics, his views are characteristic of modern western arrogance and of democracy's inability to see beyond two brief golden moments—classical Athens and (at least until Trump) the American present. Fukuyama gravely underestimated the depth and strength of communist-Confucian ideology.

Fukuyama declared himself undaunted—he takes the long view—and developed his ideas into a 1992 book that repeated and expanded them, *The End of History and the Last Man*. Five years after that he wrote a further defense of his views, claiming that they were "normative" rather than empirical, and he continues to argue that he'll prove right in the end.[18] And yet scores, even hundreds, of articles in major Chinese newspapers, in scholarly journals, and on blog sites assert that either Fukuyama is visibly wrong, or he is backing down on his claims about the end of history.[19] The second of these treatments involves harmonizing the man somewhat. According to Chinese Wikipedia, Fukuyama had a change of heart due to the handling of the COVID pandemic: "In April 2020, the *Opinion News* interviewed his new views under the Coronavirus epidemic. Fukuyama basically admitted that neoliberalism is dead. In the future, most people in the world will recognize the necessity for a strong government."[20] On the side that simply finds him wrong, the language can wax stronger. Chen Guan's 2020 blog on Zhihu (a Chinese Q & A website modeled on Quora), entitled "The Embarrassment of Francis Fukuyama," opines that:

> After 30 years of turmoil, in 2020, Francis Fukuyama will usher in the biggest embarrassment in his theoretical sales career. He has overlooked one point: the human history of a

5,000-year evolution, rather than a half century of cause and effect . . . Faced with the results of the epidemic, in an interview with "Viewpoint," Fukuyama had begun to shift the subject ingeniously. Faced with the facts, he must be honest about China's outstanding performance in the epidemic, but he clearly left a retreat for his institutional doctrine.

Chen even critiques Fukuyama's latest book on dignity with an apposite mention of Aristotle: "The ancient Greek sage Aristotle said in the *Nicomachean Ethics* that 'for people of different natures, what is meant by "happiness" has different interpretations.' China, as a country with a long history and tradition, cannot be interpreted casually by Fukuyama."[21]

Zeng Zhaoming 曾昭明—if I have the right man, "Chairman of the Dapu County Committee of the Chinese People's Political Consultative Conference"—has a still harsher reaction in his *Up Media* column of November 20, 2016. In Zeng's view, what Fukuyama has predicted is a bestialization of the human race (!):

> Fukuyama has never changed his basic views . . . He is complacent that the liberal democratic system is the "end point" of human history, but he never realizes that the liberal democratic system will only breed animalized "last people"— therefore, it is better to say that the liberal democratic system is the "end of world history."

Not only is the United States no longer a symbol of democracy, but that democracy is no longer a symbol of human civilization. Trump's unsavory victory, the result of pandering to base instincts, illustrates the "superiority" of the "path with Chinese characteristics."[22] I find it hard to agree with this perspective, partly because I don't wish my inevitable fate to be bestialization unless I transplant myself across the Pacific, but also because it is another of the globalizing myths I am trying to discredit.

What such myths disregard—no matter who is generating them—is the actual complexity of moral values and their deep ties to local culture and context. The classics are deep enough to reflect such complexity—but sadly, probably never will where governments are concerned.

NOTES

Preface

1. There is fascinating comparative work being done with ancient Greece and ancient China by such prominent scholars as Haun Saussy, Zhang Longxi, Walter Scheidel, Lisa Raphals, Steven Shankman, Stephen Durrant, Zhou Yiqun, Alexander Beecroft, François Jullien, Wiebke Denecke, and the giant figure of Sir G.E.R. Lloyd.

2. Emphasis in original. Baker et al. (2019), 10.

3. In this case, transborder, transhistorical, and trans-discipline would just about cover it. For a survey of the possibilities, see Bromberg (2021). Fleming (2006) has a thoughtful essay on the terms "use" and "abuse" as modes of reception.

4. These "professional classicists," in China, still tend to be scattered across departments of history or philosophy. "Western classics" is usually not a field of its own.

5. For recent examples that ask whether comparison of Greek and Chinese ethical thought can be meaningful, see Lane (2009), Yu and Bunnin (2001), and Lloyd (much of his work since 1996, especially 2007, 2009, 2014, and 2017). Take the word "citizen," which cannot be translated without losing much of what we associate with it as a term in European and American culture. So, all translation, really, is a jump into a foreign context.

6. Let me just mention one of many reception situations that cannot fit in this framework, as noted by Pormann (2013). In his view, the "West" is a problematic category, because, Pormann argued, our classics are not really western anyhow. Egyptian scholars who had studied (western) "Classics" in western universities did not see them as alien but rather wanted to re-root the study of Greco-Roman Egypt in their own country and to globalize "classical philology" by applying it to Arabic texts.

7. How to even ensure that the studies I cite are in some way representative of broader sentiments than those of the authors in question? In my research I found that general patterns emerged even at random, but I also took pains to select from commonly cited articles in the Chinese database CNKI, both pre- and post-June 1989. In the case of the most visible intellectuals and influential intellectuals,

their work often appears in newspapers or blogs. All of this would be inaccessible to a reader without Mandarin.

8. Fällman (2014), 66; emphasis added. On why the US should care about Chinese philosophy, see Van Norden and Kwan (2019).

9. In commenting on our own limitations as the cost of progress, Alexander Beecroft wrote, "Is it necessary to demonstrate mastery of all fields touched on (in which case comparative work becomes next to impossible), and if not, how do we deal with the inevitable errors or imprecisions of comparative work? These are questions, one suspects, that Classics will need to address more openly in the years ahead, as the discipline evolves to reflect the world in which it is studied." Beecroft (2021).

10. For example, see Gan Yang's 2019 comments at https://www.thepaper.cn /newsDetail_forward_5384161.

Introduction: The Ancient Greeks in Modern China

1. Thank you to Zhang Longxi (in his email communication of November 2020) for his translation of this quotation from the *Shi-jing*. The Mandarin reads: 溥天之下, 莫非王土。率土之濱, 莫非王臣. The English term "subject" here does not refer to "peoples" as we might think, but rather to a court official—"your servant."

2. I focus on texts by these authors in this study, but the Chinese were also interested in poetry, drama, and much else in the classical tradition. The Chinese court's earlier contact with some of these texts during the Jesuit mission will be discussed in Chapter 1.

3. In this study, I use the unpopular binary terminology of "China and the west," knowing full well that this opposition is not only inadequate but also brings with it a host of political and ideological issues. Already in the 1930s Lei Haizong criticized the exclusion of Egypt from "the west," and the essentialization of history into three eras. Xin Fan (2018), 207–10. Today new complexities take the stage. For example, the view that "the Chinese government uses the essentialization of the west as a means for supporting a nationalism that effects the internal suppression of its own people"! Chen (1992), 688. I try to acknowledge this by avoiding capitalization for the proper noun "west" throughout this work. For further discussion of the problem of East/west, see, among others, Goody (1996), Lloyd (2007) and (2014); for discussion of linguistic commutability, Liu (1995). Unpacking this binary would be a book-length study in itself, and since the Chinese scholars I study continue to use it, I have followed suit.

4. Marx too was a westerner, of course—but he served CCP ideology and belonged to modernity, not antiquity.

5. For example, Professor Huang Yang in the History Department at Fudan University and Professor Leopold Leeb at Renmin.

6. On why the US should care about Chinese philosophy, see Van Norden and Kwan (2019).

7. The Chinese, of course, are no strangers to empire either, but they are not busy decrying its injustices.

8. Some of these texts, such as the *Book of Changes*, have sections dating back to the western Zhou period (c. 1045 BCE–771 BCE). The authenticity of these texts is the subject of some controversy due to the mass burning of Confucian texts in 213 BCE, but at least one school of thought believes that the Qin had a state academy that preserved Zhou culture, including oral traditions on Confucian texts.

9. Note, however, that the Chinese did not originally have a term that correlated with the western concept of philosophy. There is no single Chinese term for philosophy. Eventually they fixed on *zhexue*, a gloss imported from Japan in the late nineteenth century.

10. A second volume was published in 2018 with 148 more quotations from classical Chinese.

11. In a speech to Peking university students, for example, Xi cited the *Guanzi* in support of the four anchors of moral formation: "ritual propriety, rightness, honesty, and a sense of shame." For further examples see https://is.cuni.cz/studium /predmety/index.php?do=download&did=161464&kod=JPM323.

12. Confucius, *Analects* 13.6. Here, I have opted for the James Legge translation. "Confucius" is of course a shortcut for the teachings of Kongzi and the Confucian tradition until neo-Confucianism developed around 1000 CE.

13. In fact, the whole political system is most often represented as meritocratic in defenses directed at the west.

14. In *Federalist* No. 55. This work is published in a variety of online locations including the Library of Congress at https://guides.loc.gov/federalist-papers/text -51-60#s-lg-box-wrapper-25493431.

15. Paradoxically, the textbook also stresses some aspects of classical Athenian values that resemble the values of contemporary China: the control of "disrupters" of society by exile, the disappearance of class, the government by and of the "proletariat," and the importance of meritocracy. *Normal High School Curriculum Standardized Experimental Textbook* Vol. 1 [师范高中课程标准实验教材卷 *Shifan gaozhong kecheng biaozhun shiyan jiaocai juan 1*]. Changsha. 2012, 24–6.

16. *Normal High School Curriculum Standardized Experimental Textbook Vol. 1* [师范高中课程标准实验教材卷 *Shifan gaozhong kecheng biaozhun shiyan jiaocai juan 1*]. Changsha. 2012, 24. At https://bp.pep.com.cn/jc/, a website by the People's Education Press, one may find digital versions of all official textbooks from elementary school to high school. On page twenty-four of the Spring 2020 version of the History Vol. 1 textbook, under Unit 2 ("The Political Order of Ancient Greece and Rome"),

there is a similar quotation: "The theory and application of Athenian democracy laid the earliest foundation for the political order of the contemporary and modern west" (雅典民主的理论与实践，为近现代西方政治制度奠定了最初的基础).

17. But not for the first time. One of the slogans that followed the Reform Movement of 1898 was 中体西用 (zhong ti xi yong): to keep the Chinese spirit while using the west.

18. In fact, most of the articles in the sixteen issues that appeared before publication ceased were on Greek philosophical texts or other well-known works from antiquity. The journal is now offline, but the text of this statement may be found in the prefatory material of Issue 1, No. 1. The subsequent quotation also comes from this prefatory material.

19. Text edited slightly for idiomatic English usage.

20. To be sure, one might reasonably ask: to what extent can we make generalizations about Chinese culture at large on the basis of a journal which most Chinese have never heard of? This is a valid question, and I hope the subsequent chapters of this book will show that this journal echoes a much wider cultural sentiment about constructing China via some relationship to the west, whether emulative or oppositional, or, most likely, more complex than these binaries suggest.

21. Here and throughout this volume, I use modernity as a loose synonym for the past century rather than as the technical term(s) it has become in the humanities and social sciences. See, for example, the entry in the *Encyclopedia Britannica*, which points out *s.v.* that "To participate in *modernity* was to conceive of one's society as engaging in organizational and knowledge advances that make one's immediate predecessors appear antiquated or, at least, surpassed."

22. The former are at least as old as the fourth century BCE, the latter emerging by the sixth century BCE and blended with Confucian and Daoist ideas.

23. On the tradition of virtue politics, see Hankins (2019).

24. Which, of course, remains the name by which the Chinese people and nation refer to themselves, 中国 (Zhongguo).

25. Perhaps exaggerating the impact of the movement, in 1939 Mao Zedong himself wrote that the May 4th Movement "marked a new stage in China's bourgeois-democratic revolution against imperialism and feudalism" and argued that "a powerful camp made its appearance in the bourgeois-democratic revolution, a camp consisting of the working class, the student masses, and the new national bourgeoisie." See his essay "The May Fourth Movement" in *Selected Works of Mao Zedong* at https://www.marxists.org/reference/archive/mao/selected-works/volume-2/mswv2_13.htm.

26. See Gu (2001) for the impact of Rousseau on the reformers' understanding of democracy. As my research intern Henry Zhao pointed out (in an email

communication of 9/9/2020), it is interesting that this Aristotelian tenet at least partially concedes the more Confucian emphasis on general social embeddedness.

27. The chance of rising or falling through the three "natural classes" is extremely small.

28. See, e.g., Ames (1992), Deng (2011), Gernet (2010), Lloyd (2017), and Reding (2004).

29. Batnitzky (2016).

30. Such scenarios give us dangerous room for generalizations that may nonetheless contain a shred of truth. For example, the Chinese verb *xue* (to learn) originally meant to copy or imitate, a way of doing philosophy that is much emphasized in the *Analects*; as Zengzi says in *Analects* 1.4, "Each day I examine myself in three ways: in doing things for others, have I been disloyal? In my interactions with friends, have I been untrustworthy? Have not practiced what I have preached?"

31. I must end this introduction with an apology, then, to Chinese scholars who do traditional (European) philological and historical work for students of classics departments, because this book is not about them (I hope they will have their own book, since they are richly deserving). I address instead the fewer, but more prominent, Chinese classicists who form the "squeaky wheel" of classics interpretation in China. And the book is also about public opinion, editorials, and ideology, about blogs and Party statements. Apologies, then, to my colleagues in classical scholarship including Huang Yang, Nie Minli, Gao Fengfeng, Weng Leihua, Chen Jingling, Leopold Leeb, Zhang Longxi, Yiqun Zhou, Liang Zhonghe, the late Jiyuan Yu, and many others who have devoted themselves to the rigorous study of classical antiquity without a political agenda.

32. See Yu Ying (2015). Here and elsewhere, the paucity of women who study the western classics in China is curious. On this interview, see Zhou (2017). As she points out, it was first published February 6, 2015, in *Wenhui xueren* as "Various Controversies in Classical Studies in China" (*"Gudianxue zai Zhongguo de shishi feifei," Wenhui xueren*) but reprinted the next day in 2.7.15 *Pengpai xinwen*, an important web-based news media site, with the new title, "Classical Studies is Not the Way Liu Xiaofeng and his Associates Do It" (*Gudianxue bushi Liu Xiaofeng tamen gaode natao*, 古典学不是刘小枫他们搞的那套 *Pengpai xinwen*, February 7, 2015). One professor, Zhang Wei, even said "westerners do not speak of usefulness, their scientific spirit is to investigate the truth of nature itself. This belief comes from the Greeks." Yu Ying (2015).

33. Liu Xiaofeng is the former editor of *The Chinese Journal of Classical Studies*.

34. The interest and disagreement are, in the end, a bold compliment to these ancient texts: for there are by far fewer western scholars delving diligently into Confucian texts in order to make them relevant to US government in the twenty-first

century. But see the recent activity of Peter Bol and James Hankins, who hosted a conference on "Political Meritocracy in Comparative Historical Perspective" at the Edmund J. Safra Center for Ethics at Harvard University on November 1–2, 2018.

35. To ensure that the studies I cite are in some way representative of broader sentiments, I took pains to select from commonly cited articles on the Chinese database CNKI, both pre- and post-June 1989. I consulted Chinese colleagues at Chinese universities. Finally, in the case of the most visible intellectuals and influential intellectuals, their work often appears in newspapers or blogs, and as such I assume they are of interest to the general public.

Chapter One: Jesuits and Visionaries

1. Zhu Yijun, the fourteenth Emperor of the Ming dynasty, reigned until 1620. The Spanish Jesuit Francis Xavier attempted to reach China in 1552, but he died on Chinese island of Shangchuan off the mainland.

2. On Ricci, see, e.g., Fontana (2011), Hsia (2010), Mungello (1985), 44–71, and Spence (1985). For a general discussion of the advisors at the imperial court, see Spence (1969). Much has been published on the complex relationship that the missionaries (not all were Jesuits) had with this court and the next; see, e.g., Liu (2008) and (2014) and Mungello (1985).

3. On the interest that educated Europeans showed in news from China, see Statman (2019) and Wu (2017). Writes Statman of the Parisian savants: "They used their knowledge of China to address issues of world history to which Chinese texts were not necessarily, or even obviously, relevant. In this way, non-European culture permeated the ideas of the Enlightenment at a deeper level than often imagined." Statman (2019), 367. As Statman shows, the scholar de Guignes used Chinese sources to try to shed new light on the fall of the Roman Empire, while free thinkers used Chinese history to argue against a historical reading of the Old Testament.

4. The exiled Southern Ming court showed great favor to Catholicism and asked for help from the pope. The empress dowager and the crown prince were even baptized.

5. Many thanks to James Hankins for this anecdote!

6. There would be a second Jesuit mission starting in 1842.

7. As described by Spence (1985), Ricci used the mnemonic technique of a "memory palace" to remember the difficult Chinese characters.

8. Semedo (1996 [1667]), 216.

9. On the Jesuits' scientific contribution to the Ming and Qing courts, see Li Hui (2002), Spence (1985), and Xia (2002).

10. The Jesuit Ruggieri had written a catechism predating Ricci's writings entitled "The Nature of the Lord of Heaven." It covered Adam's fall, the immortality of the

soul, and then, briefly, the doctrines of incarnation and redemption in two pages. Ruggieri also used the virgin birth in the miraculous birth tradition of China. As Hsia points out, the Jesuit was not very successful. Hsia (2010), 145.

11. This gave rise to the famous "Rites Controversy:" was ancestor-worship religious or not? The Dominicans and Franciscans complained that it entailed the worship of demons, and Clement XI finally banned it in 1704. On the "Rites Controversy," see Mungello (1994).

12. This was also true for the missionaries' non-doctrinal texts. Ricci's 1595 publication *Ways of Friendship* (交友论, *Jiaoyou Lun*) absorbed many ideas from Aristotle's *Ethics*, including the famous tenet: "A friend of mine is not anybody else but a half of myself. In another way we can say, it is a second me. So we should treat friends just like we treat ourselves." Ricci, however, presented this as a quotation from St. Augustine's *Confessions*.

13. The Stoics' views on volition might have struck a common note with Buddhists, but not Confucians, however, the Jesuits were not interested in proselytizing to the former. (We should not confuse the Jesuit attempt to accommodate to Confucianism with finding common ground with all Chinese ethical traditions).

14. There were, however, several semi-divine figures who came to earth and benefited the people in the other traditions, such as the bodhisattva known as Guanyin in Chinese Buddhism, and many folk stories about humble people with spiritual gifts— Mazu for example. All of this the Jesuits excluded from their project, deliberately.

15. Spalatin (1975), 556.

16. This was particularly true of the neo-Confucian view that there was an interior heart/mind (*xin*) from which all action flowed.

17. It was the time of a Stoic revival in Europe as well, starting with Justus Lipsius's *De Constantia* (1583).

18. For a general overview of the Jesuit mission's use of Greek and Roman literature, see Müller-Lee (2018).

19. Some scholars feel that Confucius himself is more or less an invention of the Jesuits.

20. On the Jesuit's humanistic education see Garcia (2014), Kainulainen (2018), and Ranieri (2016). It is a large and complex topic.

21. See e.g., Goodman and Grafton (1990), Liu Yu (2008) and (2013).

22. Goodman and Grafton (1990), 104–105. See Liu Yu (2008).

23. For a general overview of the Jesuit mission's use of Greek and Roman literature, see Müller-Lee (2018).

24. Liu Yu (2013), 834. Standaert remarks that the Epictetan text was also an important component of Ricci's *Jiren Man* (1608). Standaert (2003), 367. For a collection of Chinese Christian texts, see Standaert and Dudink (2002). In 1636,

Vagnone published the *Da dao ji yan* (达道纪言), 355 gnomic statements culled from Greco-Roman sources and organized according to the principles of the five main relationships in Confucianism. See Standaert (2001), 607–8 and Müller-Lee (2018).

25. Seneca is claimed as the source of two very similar works by their authors: Giacomo Rho's *On the Works of Mercy* and Alfonso Vagnone's *Ten Consolations*. Both, however, treat very generic Stoic topics; see Fang (2019).

26. Ricci also refuted Nothingness and Emptiness, the Daoist and Buddhist explanations for the origin of the universe. Hsia (2010), 227.

27. On this, see Cawley (2013). The book was preceded by *The True Record of the Lord of Heaven* (天主实录 *Tianzhu Shilu*), which Michele Ruggieri (1543–1607), Ricci's companion on the trip to Guangdong Province in 1583, published in 1584 in Zhaoqing. Ricci left out many of the key Catholic doctrines that Ruggieri had included.

28. Hsia (2010), 2014.

29. Yu Liu (2014) argues that Ricci's claim of a monotheistic affinity between Catholicism and Confucianism in *Tianzhu Shiyi* was a tactical move. For a detailed discussion, see, among others, Cawley (2013), Yu (2008) and (2014). For the text, see Ricci (1985), 107.

30. *De Christiana Expeditione apud Sinas* (1615), I.10, 98. My thanks to Wentao Zhai for tracking down this reference!

31. Most notably by Pope Clement XI, but also by other Jesuits such as Niccolò Longobardi. In general, the Dominicans opposed accommodation altogether.

32. Mungello (1985), 18.

33. Gernet (2010), 25.

34. As Yu argues, Ricci's views were seen as useful for fighting against Buddhist influence at the imperial court. His separation of ancient Confucianism from neo-Confucianism, however, was not accepted by his Chinese peers. Yu (2008), 475–76.

35. Alexander appears also in, among other works, the *Alexander Romance* and the *Shahnameh*, adaptations of which were current in Mongolia and Tibet.

36. In Mandarin Chinese, multiple characters may convey the same sound and tone, so the transliteration of western words can vary until they are institutionalized.

37. See Müller-Lee (2018), 30–1.

38. On the spread of Aristotle's thought in China, see Mi (1995) and (1997). On Vagnone's accommodations, Meynard (2013).

39. Many scholars read Aristotle as a monarchist, including Giles of Rome, author of *De regimine principum*.

40. Ricci's 1602 map had China offset to one side—and was less popular.

41. Meynard (2013), 155.

42. See the discussion in Meynard (2013). On the treatment of other classical texts in the latter half of the mission, see Müller-Lee (2018) and Standaert (2003). The concept of the *junzi*—he who rules by virtue of his own goodness—is profoundly impactful in Chinese culture, but hard to translate. This aversion to bringing instrumental thought into the consideration of virtue is still relevant in the modern Chinese reception of classical texts, as we will see in Chapter 4.

43. Ricci, "Storia dell'Introduzione del Cristianesimo in Cina," I, 36.

44. As quoted in a 1584 letter by Pietro Tacchi Venturi, "Letter to Giambattista Roman . . ." II, 45. On this topic, see Hosne (2015).

45. *Novissima Sinica Historiam Nostri Temporis Illustrata*. Edente 1679, cited by Walker (1972), 198.

46. See the discussion in Walker (1972), 194–230 and Mori (2020).

47. Emperor Qianlong's letter to George III (1792), as found at http://marcuse .faculty.history.ucsb.edu/classes/2c/texts/1792QianlongLetterGeorgeIII.htm.

48. The Guangxu Emperor was Zaitian by name; he was the tenth emperor of the Qing dynasty. The Hundred-Day Reform was launched in 1898 by Chinese intellectuals who had won the support of the emperor. The reformers argued that what China needed most were not, say, military and scientific advances, but rather political, social, and institutional reforms. Gransow (2003).

49. Cixi herself is a complicated figure. She spearheaded many reforms for women's education, but she was ruthless in her pursuit of power. Her support of the Manchu leadership contributed to the fall of the Qing dynasty.

50. Sun Yat-sen (1866–1925) led a nationalist effort that aimed to transform Qing subjects into Chinese nationals whose culture was defined by anti-Manchuism. Other reformers were less racially motivated.

51. Pu-yi eventually become a puppet figure used by the Japanese, and then, under Mao, a member of a political advisory board to the CCP.

52. Dewey actually visited China in 1919–21 and delivered a well-received set of lectures. Above all, he argued that there could be no hasty political responses to the warlord government in Peking; what was needed was the slow change of Chinese institutions. The influence of his lectures cast a long shadow, but he was not taken up by the CCP. On Dewey's legacy in China, see Hoyt (2006).

53. Later, in the 1920s, Plato also became a subject of interest. Here I focus exclusively on figures who reacted to political and philosophical texts from (classical) antiquity. Others, like Zhou Zuoren (1885–1967), read, translated, and commented on ancient literature; he was an advocate of literary reform in the May 4th Movement. He idealized the beautiful spirit of the classics. The famous Hu Shi (1891–1962) likewise backed language reform and wrote on Chinese philosophy in a fashion

parallel to western treatments of classical philosophy. Luo Niansheng translated ancient Greek drama in the 1930s and produced an "Ancient Greek Chinese Dictionary."

54. Beecroft (2016), 11. Such as Zhou Zuoren "The Thought of Chinese Citizens" (中国的国民思想 *Zhongguo de guomin sixiang*) in his *Prose Writings, Arranged by Category* (文類編 *Zhou Zuoren wen leibian*), 1.085–171; Chen Duxiu in his 1940 "My Fundamental Opinions" (我的根本意見 *Wo de genben yijian*; my thanks to Haun Saussy for help with this reference); and, Liang Qichao in "On the Study of Ancient Greece" (論希臘古代學術 *Lun Xila gudai xueshu*) in Liang (1978). In his review of this manuscript for Princeton University Press, James Hankins observed that "I suspect that the rejection of Christianity as a cultural beacon can be explained by the saturation of China by missionary stations, schools, publishing houses, etc. It's normal to be suspicious of such force-feeding. When students went abroad, they were often surprised to learn how much smaller the footprint of churches was in European and American societies."

55. Kang Youwei 康有为 may have been influenced by Plato's *Republic* in writing a treatise entitled "Utopia" (*Da Tong shu* 大同书) that borrows much from Plato's thought; in contrast to Confucian teaching, Kang downplayed the five basic Confucian relationships and urged the abolition of the family and filial piety. Eugenics was part of the ideal society and the country was united under a single leader. He also published a periodical *Buren zazhi* 不忍雜誌 (*Journal of Irrepressible Sentiments*), which contained comparative studies of the cultural histories of Egypt, Persia, and India as well as of the Greeks and Romans.

56. For a summary, see Zhou (2017). On Liang in general, see Hao (1971) and Levenson (1953). For collections of his work, both in Chinese, see Liang (1978) and Liang (1999). I am surprised that so much of Liang's writing has gone untranslated.

57. See Vittinghoff (2002) for the explosion of the Chinese press market at the turn of the century.

58. The corresponding Chinese text is 亞氏 which is a respectful way of referring to Aristotle, by only using his "last name." Since Aristotle doesn't have a last name, Liang used the first character of the transliterated name 亞 instead. I'm rendering it as "Master Aristotle" only here.

59. Here, Liang first uses the English word "politics" and then translates it into Chinese, signifying that this may be an unfamiliar or novel term for the intended reader.

60. Liang (1999).

61. Aristotle, *Politics* 1.2.

62. Aristotle, *Politics* 1.2.

63. On Liang Qichao's introduction of *guomin*, see Lee (2007), Shen (2006), Shen and Chien (2006), and Zarrow (1997). Shen and Chien (2006) argue that the coinage was a result of Liang's exposure to western political thought in Japan; in fact, he borrowed the phrase from the Japanese, who had previously borrowed it from the Chinese. For a list of such terminology, see Chen et al. (2011), 312–15, 324–27. In his review of this manuscript for Princeton University Press, James Hankins remarked, "The more exact equivalent would have been *shimin* 市民 'city-dweller,' but cities did not have a distinctive political role in Chinese political imagination."

64. On Liang's influence in China's intellectual transition from empire, see Chang (1971)

65. On this idea of Aristotelian "citizens," see Lee (2007).

66. Sima Qian, "*Qin Shihuang benji*" (Annals of the Qin Shihuang) (1969), 245.

67. Shen and Chien (2006) single out the "political *guomin* of a state-nationalism" of Liang as one particular kind of nationalism, even if the term *guomin*, which consists of the two separate words, *guo* (国, "nation") and *min* (民, "people"), was not a coinage. It was Liang's usage that turned it into a key term in the discussions about citizenship.

68. Shen and Chien (2006), 5.

69. Shen and Chien (2006), 50. Xu Xiaoxu 徐晓旭 (2004) takes on the concept of "nation" in ancient Greece to show that it was a tribal affair, possibly based on ethnicity, thus destabilizing much of Liang Qichao's reception of Aristotle.

70. Liang (1978), volume 26, "Aristotle's Political Theory."

71. See Aristotle, *Politics* 6.1–4. Hansen (2006).

72. In his "Short Notes on Sparta," Liang also praised the martial spirit of the Spartans, over and against the feeble Chinese, as did the famous author Lu Xun 鲁迅 in his 1903 essay "The Spartan Soul" [斯巴达之魂 *Sibada zhi hun*]. See discussion in Huang (2018).

73. This first saw light as a series of articles published between 1902 and 1905 in the *Journal on the New Citizen*.

74. Cheek (2015), 34. For further studies of Chinese use of western terms, themselves usually borrowed from Japanese coinages, see also Lydia Liu (1995). On the effect of the May 4th Movement on the Chinese language itself, see Harbsmeier (2001). For the language of logic used in a seventeenth-century Chinese translation of Aristotle's *Categories*, see Wardy (2000).

75. That said, Liang still upheld certain Confucian ideas. Above all, self-cultivation was still important as a characteristic of the new citizen.

76. Liang (1999), vol. 1, 413–4, as cited and translated in Yang Xiao (2002), 20. On slaves versus citizens, see Shen and Chien (2006).

77. Liang (1978), vol. IV, 56.

78. The politician Cleisthenes famously eliminated traditional classifications and kin groups and created a new classification which distributed tribe members among the demes.

79. Liang, "On Political Ability" (1998), 153. Sun Yat-sen, by contrast, equated nationalism with racial purity, hoping to transform Qing subjects into Han Chinese who were defined by anti-Manchuism. On Bluntschli, see Chang (1971), 238–71 and Lee (2007). These ideas would come to fruition in his reading of the German philosopher Johann Bluntschli.

80. Zarrow (1997), 235. Liang, "On Public Morality" (1998), 12. One of Liang's critics, Wu Mi (1894–1978) studied comparative literature under Irving Babbitt at Harvard and cofounded *Xueheng* (*Critical Review*), a conservative pro-Confucian journal. Wu was critical of Liang for challenging Chinese culture. For Wu, "The western classics were valuable less as a series of clues to why the west had won the race to modernity, and more as a way of understanding the complexity of the west and its own conflicts between tradition and modernity"—as well of identifying shared transcendent values between Greek and Chinese antiquity. Beecroft (2016). On *Xueheng*, see especially, Hon (2015), Liu Jinyu (2018), and Saussy (2010).

81. Liang (1999), vol. 3, 1311. However, he was not a fan of the historical Athens, which Liang saw as an aristocratic slave state rather than a democracy. On this point (and on Liang's view of the undeveloped seeds of democracy in ancient China), see Liang (1999), vol. 1, 108. Nor did he advocate abolishing Confucian thought, as Hu Shi did.

82. Zhou (2017), 109–10. By the time of the May 4th Movement, however, Liang was souring on western values, having seen what they had wrought during WWI.

83. Zhou (2017), 106–29.

84. 新文化运动 *Xinwenhua Yundong*. On the May 4th Movement, see, e.g., Tang (1996), Chow (1960), Schwarcz (1986), Hao (1971), and Zhu (1999).

85. Aristotle was one in a western constellation of texts and ideas, of course—such as John Stuart Mill's *On Liberty*, also influential in Liang's thought.

86. For text and translation, see Mi (1997), 253.

87. The first complete Chinese edition of Aristotle did not appear until 1931; until then there were only summaries, mentions, and redactions.

88. As Edward X. Gu noted, Li followed Rousseau in suggesting that the citizens were simultaneously rulers and ruled, and that in such a democracy "coercive forces cannot work anymore." See Gu (2001), esp. 596–97. As Gu wrote, "Chen Duxiu, Gao Yihan, and Li Dazhao, three prominent representatives of New Culture intellectuals . . . showed little knowledge of the distinction between the Rousseauian and the Anglo-American notion of democracy." Li's article was published in *Baoli Yu Zhengzi* (暴力与政治 *Violence and Politics*), *Taipingyang* (太平洋 *The Pacific Ocean*) on

October 15, 1917. Shen Sungchiao wrote, "What resulted could only be the summoning of what Hobbes calls Leviathan." Shen (2006), 23.

89. Like Liang, Yan Fu was deeply impressed by Mill's *On Liberty*. It may have colored his appreciation of Aristotle.

90. Liang, despite shared interests with the May 4th generation, also had significant ideological differences. For example, Liang did not agree with the May 4th Movement's wholehearted attack on Confucianism, Buddhism, and Taoism.

91. Jin Guantao and Liu Qingfeng (1986), 74–80. Mohism was an exception, but not influential enough. See also Jin, Fan, and Liu (1996).

92. On Feng Youlan and philosophy, see Lomanov (1998) and Yu Jiyuan (2014).

93. As cited and quoted in Liu Yu (2014), 56.

94. Liu Yu (2014), 67.

95. During the period 1915–1918, just 青年.

96. As cited and quoted in Spence (1991), 315.

97. Chen Duxiu, "Xin qingnian zuian zhi dabianshu," as cited in Gu (2001), 589.

98. Chen (1916). Other intellectuals, such as Li Dazhao, Hu Shi, and Gao Yihan, also wanted a radical shift promoting the cultural and political change that had started with the efforts of the reformers at the turn of the century.

99. On the long-term impact of the reformers, see Fung (2010), Levenson (1953), Schwarz (1986), Wang Hui (1989), and Zhu (1999).

100. That said, the journal *Xueheng* (学衡 *Critical Review*) explored Greek philosophy and ethics in depth and tried to reconcile Confucian ideals such as *li* with western ideas, but the political content of such work was scanty. See Liu (2018). The first complete Chinese edition of Aristotle's *Politics* was published in Shanghai in 1931 (4 volumes). Translations from the English continued to appear until the Cultural Revolution of 1966–76.

101. Mao (1990), 5.

102. However, before the Anti-Rightist Campaign in 1957, ancient Greek philosophy was influential in the academic world, and the Commercial Press also produced a Chinese translation of the classic works in this area.

103. See the fascinating analysis of Mao's 1941 comments by Zhou Yiqun (2020), who sees ancient Greece as a cipher for Soviet communism.

104. Mao Zedong, "Reform Our Study" (*gaizao women de xuexi*), in *Selected Works of Mao Zedong*, vol. 3, as cited by Zhou (2022, forthcoming). Yiqun Zhou, who has written perceptively on Mao's 1941 speeches, notes that classical Greece at this point may simply be standing in for a disliked political "other." "In these passages, ancient Greece not only is identified with established authority, as had long been the usage in western history since the Renaissance, but it also stands for an *extraneous* source of authority that a foreign power and its Chinese adherents and agents attempted to

impose upon China with no regard for what she needs and what suits her specific circumstances"—that is, the followers of Soviet-style communism. Zhou Yiqun (2022, forthcoming).

105. Leighton (2015), 1.

106. Gu (1997), 230.

107. He was briefly rescued by the economist Sun Yefang, who arranged a research position for Gu in the Institute of Economics of the (Division of) Philosophy and Social Sciences (学部, *Xuebu*) of the Chinese Academy of Sciences (CAS).

108. On Gu Zhun's reading of Aristotle's *Politics*, see Zhang Longxi (2015), 13–4.

109. As quoted in Wang Hai (1999).

110. A modified version of *Politics* 1.2.

111. From Gu Zhun (1982), as cited in Zhang Longxi (2015), 12. Gu Zhun again quotes *Politics* 1.2 here.

112. Gu (1982).

113. The Pseudo-Xenophon *Constitution of Athens* likewise connects sea power and democracy, partly because of the benefit to the sailor class.

114. Gu Zhun, as cited in Wang (1999).

115. Gu Zhun, 希腊城邦制度 *Xila Chengbang Zhidu*, included in Gu (1999), *Gu Zhun's Collected Works* (顾准文集 *Gu Zhun Wenji*). In all this, Gu paid little attention to the political reforms carried out by aristocrats such as Solon and Cleisthenes, which could not be put to use for his theory about the connection of maritime trade to democracy. Gu also omitted any mention of the seafaring that went on in the Indian Ocean and Southeast Asia.

116. I am greatly indebted here to Zhou Yiqun's essay "Greek Antiquity, Chinese Modernity," delivered at a conference on the western classics in Modern China in Beijing, April 2012, for first bringing this series to my attention. Much of my original knowledge about the early-twentieth-century figures derived from her lecture, which has since been published as Zhou (2017). For further on *River Elegy* and what followed, see Chiou (1995), De Jong (1989), Lau Tuenyu and Lo Yuet-keung (1991), and Wu Zhiqiang 吴志强 (1991). On the decade leading up to it, see Chen Fong-Ching and Jin Guantao (1997).

117. Ironically, his work was most read during the brief Gu Zhun fever of the 1990s.

118. Su and Wang (1991), 209.

119. Su and Wang (1991), 257. Yan is cited for his belief that western ideas such as the social contract and the will to power could create vital cultural change.

120. Su and Wang (1991), 260–1.

121. Su and Wang (1991), 253.

122. Su and Wang (1991) 260–1.

123. Su and Wang (1991), 254.

124. Chen (1992), 699.

125. Su and Wang (1991), 255–6. Astonishingly, all six parts of the documentary are available on YouTube.

126. Chen (2002), 26. A summary of the critique of *Heshang*'s oversimplifications by figures such as Yan Tao, etc. is available in Chen (1992). He suggests that "The depiction in 'He Shang' of a problematic cultural past and a progressive Occidental Other are merely pretexts to debunk current official ideology." Chen (1992), 704. For further on *River Elegy*, see De Jong (1989), Gunn (1991), Lau Tuenyu and Lo Yuet-keung (1991), Liu Jun (2001). On its relationship to Tiananman Square, see Chen Fong-Ching and Jin Guantao (1997), Chiou (1995), Ma (1996), and Wu (1991). A transcript is supplied by Su and Wang (1991).

127. David Moser (2011). Available at https://digitalcommons.unl.edu/china beatarchive/904/.

128. Xu Jilin (2000), 173.

129. "Resolution on Certain Questions in the History of Our Party Since the Founding of the People's Republic of China," adopted by the Sixth Plenary Session of the Eleventh Central Committee of the Communist Party of China on June 27, 1981. *Resolution on CPC History (1949–81)*, (Beijing: Foreign Languages Press, 1981), 32.

130. Hu, the General Secretary of the CCP from 1980 to 1987, was handpicked by Deng to succeed him. Hu's support for this and earlier student movements, however, led to his removal from power.

131. However, most of the deaths occurred outside of the square, in the west of the city. Other parts of Beijing were also targeted, though not as infamously. For more on Tiananmen, see Zhang Liang (2001), Feng Congde (2013); and the Office of the Historian, the U.S. Department of State available at https://history.state.gov/milestones /1989-1992/tiananmen-square and The National Security Archive at GW University available at https://nsarchive2.gwu.edu/NSAEBB/NSAEBB16/#12-29.

132. Estimates of the death toll from martial law generally range around 1,000–3,000.

133. Huang Yang (2018) notes that the Chinese government blamed *River Elegy* for the uprising.

134. Although human rights are often bundled with these concepts, the ancient Greeks did not have a concept of human rights. See, for example, Samons (2004), 172–5.

Chapter Two: Classics after the Crackdown

1. As Stephen Veg put it, "They are *minjian*—unofficial, unaffiliated, and among the people." (The quotation is from the publisher's description.) On the role of the intellectual after Tiananmen, see also Cheek (2015), 244–331, Goldman (2002),

204 NOTES TO CHAPTER 2

Chang (1971), Zhang Shuang (2009), and Zhao (1997). On Su Shuangbi, Ru Xin, and Sing Bensi, reformers who recast their language to be acceptable to the CCP, see Cheek (2015), 249–52.

2. In 1999, Zhu Yong even published a book called *What are Intellectuals to Do?* (知识分子要干什么? *Zhishi fenzi yao gan shenme?*)

3. Zhao Suisheng (1997), 725.

4. Bandursky (2019).

5. Buckley (2019).

6. Classics as a topic of apolitical academic study is flourishing in many universities. This has been reflected in a striking increase in the publication and availability of classical texts in China over the past decades, as well as institutional changes that take western classics as an area of study. See, e.g., Huang (2018) and Mutschler (2018).

7. Zhao (1997), 732, adds that "Many liberal scholars, especially anti-traditionalist scholars, argued strongly against neo-authoritarianism by questioning the validity of the allegedly causal relationship between Confucianist authoritarianism and/or economic success."

8. Zhao (1997), 732.

9. Zhao (1997), 731–32.

10. A brief biography may be found at http://www.ted.com/speakers/eric_x_li .html.

11. Li (2012).

12. We are still waiting for our last president to be accountable for his actions.

13. Samons (2004), 6.

14. See Pan Yue (2020) and Pan Wei (2006).

15. Li Changlin (1984), 44.

16. Zhang (1982), 108.

17. Li (2012).

18. For a study of the question, see Taylor (2010).

19. Thucydides, *Peloponnesian War* 2.65.8.

20. Thucydides, *Peloponnesian War* 2.65.10–11. Cleon in particular, like Donald Trump the first prominent representative of the commercial class in Athenian politics, fares badly at Thucydides's hand—a man noted for his personal dishonesty in financial matters, his blustering in the assembly, and his warmongering rhetoric.

21. Li (2012). For a statement of similar views, see Brenner (2003).

22. Li (2012).

23. C.f. Pericles's funeral oration in Thucydides, *Peloponnesian War*, 2.35–46.

24. For a discussion of the clash between the Chinese and western political systems, see Metzger (2005).

25. Lin and Dong (2006). This piece was written in a Party journal, so its audience is not merely other academics.

26. Lin and Dong (2006).

27. Lin and Dong (2006). While not as dramatic, one could add that the new scholarship on Aristotle makes sure there's politics in Aristotle's *Politics*. See, e.g., Deng (2005), who argues that virtue is problematic in Aristotle because the state precedes individuals; Ding (2012), who asserts that the philosophy of praxis is the basis and prerequisite of philosophy of theory; and Liao (1999), who suggests that the first problem in creating a good city-state is to create a good citizen, which relies on friendship rather than ideology.

28. Thucydides, *Peloponnesian War*, 3.36–49. Lin and Dong (2006).

29. Lin and Dong (2006).

30. Wu Shuchen (1985). For example, Xu and Qian (1981) wrote, "the founder of politics of all exploiting classes," and Wu (1979) who wrote on the small number who qualified to vote.

31. Xu (1981) and Wang (1982).

32. As Xin Fan points out, classical antiquity was also equated with slave society in Chinese Marxist thought, and Marxist scholars such as Guo Moruo claimed in the 1930s that China likewise had an antiquity rooted in slavery. To claim (like Lei Haizong) that such parallels were faulty would undermine the applicability of Marxism to all societies, and undermine the ideology of the communist regime. Xin (2018), 203.

33. Technically, the Chinese emperors outlawed chattel slavery, though war criminals played this role and the peasantry lived in perpetual servitude.

34. Liu ends by arguing that Aristotle's corpus obscures the difference between the good person and the good citizen.

35. This has spurred attempts to create a uniquely Chinese ethico-political genealogy, as we shall see with Gan Yang's "three traditions" theory later in Chapter 5. Liu is echoed by many others, such as Wang Xu 王旭, faculty at Tianjin Normal University, who argues that "However, even the greatest thinker cannot escape the limitations of class and history. Aristotle's thinking is still the endorsement of the slave-owning class, advocating elite rule, and criticizing democratic systems." Wang Xu (2016). See likewise Liu, who appears to have been critical of Aristotle in the period before 1989; however, the essay ends with a call to action that he sees as Aristotelian. Criticizing the writer Lu Xun, Liu wrote, "It can be seen that man cannot be separated from society for a moment. In a society with class struggle, man cannot be separated from political struggle." Liu (1981).

36. See the critique by Xu (2001). Of these important scholars, Pan Wei, Bai Tongdong, Gan Yang, and Liu Xiaofeng are of the most relevance to this study. Cui

Zhiyuan 崔之元 and Wang Hui 汪晖 are both faculty at Tsinghua University. Cui Zhiyuan's work on alternatives to neo-liberal capitalism and his work on property rights mark him out as part of the Chinese New Left, while Wang's research focuses on Chinese literature and intellectual history. The latter was co-editor of magazine *Dushu* from 1996 to 2007. Foreign Policy named him as one of the top 100 public intellectuals in the world in May 2008. I do not address either figure because western antiquity does not play a large role in their thought. Liu Xiaofeng will appear principally in Chapter 5 on the influence of Leo Strauss.

37. *Sina*, November 11, 2017, available at http://news.sina.com.cn/c/nd/2017-11 -18/doc-ifynwnty4741795.shtml. See also Fang (2009).

38. *Sina*, November 11, 2017, available at http://news.sina.com.cn/c/nd/2017-11 -18/doc-ifynwnty4741795.shtml.

39. See Article 111 in the 2004 revision of the Constitution.

40. Fang (2009).

41. As reported by Keith Bradsher and Steven Lee Myers in a *New York Times* column of December 8, 2021, A6 available at https://www.nytimes.com/2021/12/07 /world/asia/china-biden-democracy-summit.html.

42. Bradsher and Myers (2021).

43. *Sina*, November 11, 2017, available at http://news.sina.com.cn/c/nd/2017-11 -18/doc-ifynwnty4741795.shtml.

44. Lu (2012) suggests that this view of China as essentially democratic explains the joint fact of Chinese citizens' support for their one-party system and their positive view of democracy.

45. For a reception study of this idea in China, see Chen (2000). As far as I know, Hansen and Nielsen's 2004 study of ancient poleis has not been addressed by this group.

46. Xin (2018), 215. In an earlier version of this argument, Xu (1998) took a related but different tack in claiming that ancient Greece had no city-states as traditionally understood.

47. Ironically, these claims were plagiarized from the Russian scholar Anatoly Fomenko. See, http://chronologia.org/en/.

48. He (2013), available at http://blog.sina.com.cn/s/blog_4b712d230102e7a3 .html. All of the subsequent quotations from He Xin are from this blogpost.

49. To my astonishment, it appears that long before He Xin, the French Jesuit Jean Hardouin (1646–1729) claimed that the classics (except Homer, Herodotus, Cicero, the *Natural History* of Pliny, the *Georgics* of Virgil, and Horace) were invented by thirteenth-century monks. Many thanks to James Hankins for this tidbit!

50. For a Chinese critique of He Xin's theory, see e.g., Wu (2020) and the comments at Google's cache originally at http://www.bbglobe.com/Article/Default.aspx

?aid=111426. This is a snapshot of the page as it appeared on 2 Aug 2020 11:29:19 GMT but has since disappeared.

51. Bernal rejects the common view that Greek civilization was founded by Indo-European settlers from Central Europe, and charges classicists with underrepresenting Egyptian and Phoenician influences on ancient Greece.

52. Who's calling who a barbarian now, eh?

53. He (2013), available at http://blog.sina.com.cn/s/blog_4b712d230102e7a3 .html.

54. For further details, see He's two volumes (2013 and 2015). Most Chinese scholars, after a few attempts at rebuttal, have essentially ignored him.

55. My colleague Haun Saussy describes this as a discussion board with a public that includes some serious and seriously educated people, and others all the way down to high schoolers trying to prep for an exam.

56. This usage is not unlike the "superstition of rationality" attacked by Gan Yang and others, the subject of Chapter 4.

57. But, of course, so do western authors: the same fact seems good to one man, bad to another, to paraphrase Protagoras. Pan's views feel off to me because he's not in my ideological camp on ancient Greece, and I feel like "an outsider" is "distorting ancient Greece." But if I press myself, I wonder: how strongly can I really claim he is "wrong"? How much of my view is based on the institutions in which I learned it?

58. Pan Wei (2006). All subsequent quotations are from this source.

59. In *Apology* 24a, Socrates says, "The cause of my unpopularity was my parrhesia"—that is, my free speech. Again, a possible but not convincing reason to lay all the causes of his death at the door of democracy.

60. The main players were the Euboeans (eighth century BCE) followed by Corinth, Miletus, Megara, and Phaocaea in the seventh century BCE.

61. Pan Wei is quoting *Richard II*, act 2, scene 1.

62. Pan Yue (2020).

63. A close reading of the Confucian scholar Xunzi that I am not qualified to evaluate follows, based on history, philosophy, and Xunzi's unification of Confucianism and Legalism. This, says Pan, created a unified national structure throughout East Asia that was unknown to westerners. Pan also discusses Liang Qichao's understanding of Xunzi's dictate that human nature is evil. Pan (2020).

64. Pan Yue makes some very interesting observations about Aristotle's "absolute kingship."

65. Bell has penned a polite disagreement: "With regard to the West, I am not convinced by [the representation] of ancient Greek-style foreign policy, i.e., the naked exploitation of resources from abroad for the benefit of the country, or their assumption that foreign people are inhuman 'barbarians' who can be exploited and

enslaved ... And China for all its talk of unity should learn to value diversity." Bell (2020).

66. Bell (2020).

67. Wang Huaiyu (2009). Readers interested in Augustine's views on this very special erectile dysfunction may consult his "On Marriage and Concupiscence."

68. Wang Huaiyu (2009).

69. Wang Huaiyu (2009).

70. Xunzi, himself a Confucian philosopher, argued in chapter 23 of his eponymous work that human nature (性xing) is naturally bad.

71. I should also point out that most writers avoid the political citizen in Aristotle today. For example, see Ding (2012) in his discussion of western philosophy asserts that philosophy of praxis is the basis and prerequisite of philosophy of theory, like Bai's defense of Confucianism; Liao (1999) who argues that the first problem in creating a good city-state is to create a good citizen, one maintained by friendships; and Deng (2005) who argues that virtue is problematic in Aristotle, because the state takes precedence over individuals.

72. See Chapter 4 on Plato's "Noble Lie."

73. Wang Huaiyu (2009).

74. See Gao and Walayat (2021), He (2012), Kim (2017), Xu (2006), and many others.

75. Hu (2020).

76. In the Chinese context, this means socialism with Chinese characteristics.

77. Nie (2017).

Chapter Three: Thinking with Plato's "Noble Lie"

A version of this chapter was originally published in *KNOW*. Many thanks to the audience of my second Martin lecture at Oberlin College in October 2018 for their feedback and suggestions, and to my colleague Haun Saussy in particular for his helpful guidance on many issues.

1. Whitehead (1979), 39.

2. On this topic, see Chapter 5.

3. Weng (2015a), 313.

4. A lucky few may enjoy mobility between these ranks of merit, but it is not the rule.

5. See discussion in Chapter 6.

6. Contrast Rawls (1999), for whom justice requires that any inequalities must benefit all citizens and is based on a principle of fairness. Dombrowski notes, "The ideal of democratic citizenship, enhanced by the objectivity provided by Rawls's

original position, is built on the shared reason of citizens, a sharing that involves publicity at several levels." Dombrowski (1997), 578.

7. See Lane (2009), 585–60. As she remarks, this switch from "ordinary justice" to "Platonic justice" does not elide the former, since a person who is platonically just will be just in everyday life as well.

8. Plato, *Republic*, 442d.

9. Parallels to this idea of the multi-part soul can be drawn in specific Confucian philosophers. See, for example, Lorenz on Mencius and Plato, who both set up a thinking part against a desiring part of the soul. Lorenz (2004), 83–116. But of course, the Chinese word *xin* (heart/mind) can hardly be translated as the Platonic *logistikon*; nor do the emotions carry the same negative connotation. For Confucius, humans are superior to animals not because of their ability to reason so much as the depth of their emotions, which stem from within the soul, take shape externally, and are the source of rites and music.

10. Plato, *Republic*, 590d.

11. Plato, *Republic*, 2.372c–373d.

12. As Haun Saussy pointed out to me (email message to the author, November 15, 2018), "The theory of the separation of powers (prominent in all the eighteenth-century theorists that the American Founders read) is also a kind of mapping of the faculties of the mind (will, judgment, and reason) onto three branches of government (executive, judicial, and legislative) that must be kept from overwhelming each other if the whole is to be balanced and healthy."

13. For an interesting consideration of what "rational" means in this context, see Gabriela Palavicini Corona, "Political Rationality: The Democratic Challenge," a paper delivered at the 2006 Fukuoka's IPSA Congress.

14. Consider Thucydides's description of Pericles, for example, at *History of the Peloponnesian War* 2.65. There are many other features of the *Republic* that would have seemed far stranger, such as the arrangement of special "mating festivals" organized by class, but there is no space to discuss them here.

15. On the Athenian attitude toward deception, especially in oratory, see Hesk (2000). For a treatment of Strauss's reading of Platonic ideas about deception, see Moore (2009).

16. The translation of this term can be complicated: is it a fiction about the well-born, a myth about origin, a falsehood that has medical value for the soul, or something else entirely?

17. Plato, *Republic*, 414e. In Kallipolis, gold class children do not grow up with their parents, so the familial ties that would cause them to balk still further at the Lie do not exist.

18. Plato, *Republic*, 415d.

19. Plato, *Republic*, 459d, 460b–c.

20. Popper (1970). For a critique of the extreme position, see Dombrowski (1997), 565–78.

21. *Thomas Jefferson*, "To John Adams, Monticello, July 5, 1814," Available at http://www.let.rug.nl/usa/presidents/thomas-jefferson/letters-of-thomas-jefferson/jefl231.php.

22. Lee, trans., ed. *Plato: The Republic* (2003), 177.

23. In defense of this view, Lee points out that Socrates would have the philosopher-kings believe the Noble Lie as well, if possible. C.f., Plato, *Republic*, 414b–c.

24. Rowett (2016), 68.

25. Rowett (2016), 86.

26. Kasimis (2016), 339.

27. Kasimis (2016), 339.

28. As Kasimis points out, Athens's founding myth was itself one of autochthony, birth from mother earth—a discourse meant to forge ideological support for the democracy by naturalizing the political equality of the citizens. Furthermore, in 451 BCE Pericles's citizenship law turned all of Athens into one genos, or kind, when it required double Athenian parentage for citizenship status—thus strengthening an essentially exclusionary politics. For a slightly different approach, see Nails (2012), 1–23, who concentrates on the political background of the *Republic* to argue that Socrates's description of Kallipolis is meant to be a counter-weight to Athens, not an ideal in and of itself.

29. Plato, *Republic*, 389b–c.

30. A much less common defense is to agree with the fundamentals of what Plato says; see e.g., the article "In Defense of Plato's *Republic*," by Joseph Trabbic (2017), published in the official journal of the conservative think tank Witherspoon Institute in Public Discourse, available at http://www.thepublicdiscourse.com/2017/03/18512/. Trabbic wrote, "For Socrates, its [the Noble Lie's] purpose is to make sure that people do the work that they're suited to. It is crucial to a well-ordered city that the citizens are employed according to their competence: people who aren't skilled at farming shouldn't farm; people who would make poor soldiers shouldn't be guardians; and people who don't have the good of the city at heart shouldn't rule."

31. Pan (2006).

32. Song (1988), 41. Wang Cenggu 全增嘏, ed. (1983). *A History of Western Philosophy* (Shanghai People's Press), 159.

33. Song (1988), 41.

34. Xiao (1980), 71.

35. Chen (1986), 20.

36. Hu (1985), 100.

37. This is suspiciously close to an opiate for the masses.

38. Cheng (2005), 86–8. It is worth noting that Cheng received his PhD from Sun Yat-sen University under the supervision of the Straussian scholar Liu Xiaofeng, who has influenced many of China's young classicists. This would be a factor shaping his viewpoint.

39. Zhang (2013).

40. Luo (2012), 30–5. Qing (2006).

41. Wang Wenhu (2009). In the *Zhejiang Daily*, Gong Weibin (2010) and Li Peilin (2005) argue in favor of both hierarchy and social mobility. There is further discussion in Li Qiang (2003), endorsing Deng Xiaoping's idea of "letting some people get rich first" and claiming social stratification promotes social harmony.

42. Chen (2006). The essay was published on the Chinese cultural commentary site Douban, which distinguishes itself from other social media platforms (like Weibo, the Chinese Twitter) by its intellectual bent.

43. Chen (2006).

44. Li Yongcheng (2017).

45. Li Yongcheng (2017). And lest we think Noble Lies play no role in our past in the US, we need just remind ourselves of Manifest Destiny.

46. Edmund Burke, (January 19, 1791) "A Letter from Mr. Burke to a Member of the National Assembly; In Answer to Some Objections to his Book on French Affairs," 3rd edition (Paris, Printed, and London, Re-printed for J. Dodsley, 1791), available at http://metaphors.iath.virginia.edu/metaphors/20164.

47. Jefferson—and many high school students—aside, however, most of the world seems to have taken Plato's puerilities seriously, even as they reread them and changed their understanding of them in the course of time.

48. "Thomas Jefferson to John Adams, 5 July 1814," *Founders Online*, National Archives, https://founders.archives.gov/documents/Jefferson/03-07-02-0341. [Original source: *The Papers of Thomas Jefferson*, Retirement Series, Vol. 7, *28 November 1813 to 30 September 1814*, ed. J. Jefferson Looney. Princeton, NJ: Princeton University Press, 2010, 451–5.] We are in trouble if college students get wind of this view.

49. Confucius, *Analects* 2.21. For Plato, it's the just soul writ large. Nonetheless, the emphasis in both is precisely the importance of everyone knowing their own place in the hierarchy.

50. Xunzi, "On the Regulations of a King," as quoted in Wang (2015), 96.

51. I thank Wentao Zhai for pointing this out to me. For a discussion of this aspect of Confucius's thought, see Yong (2011). Of course, these are only two ways of representing Confucian thought; there are many scholars who would emphasize other key aspects of such a long and shifting tradition.

52. See Tao Wang (2012a) and (2012b) for a discussion of the many ways in which Strauss has influenced Chinese readers.

53. See Strauss (1964) 60–1, 98–9, 102–3, 124–5.

54. Dombrowski (1997), 571–2.

55. A reminder: from 1988 to 1991, Hu Ping was Chairman of the China Democratic Solidarity Alliance. He has presided over the magazines *Chinese Spring* and *Beijing Spring*. Today he is the Honorary Editor-in-Chief of *Beijing Spring*, Executive Director of China Human Rights, and Honorary Director of Independent Chinese PEN.

56. Hu Ping (2017).

57. Hu Ping occasionally claims he is only talking about feudal China, not contemporary China. And yet, Xi Jinping *is* the philosopher-king of China: the general secretary of the Communist Party of China, the holder of an ex-officio seat on the Politburo standing Committee, the president of the People's Republic of China, and the chairman of the Central Military Commission. On top of this, in 2016 the CPC officially gave Xi Jinping the title of "core leader." He is, in effect, China's ruler—a ruler for whom the term limits in effect since Mao's death have been eliminated.

58. Qiang (2005).

59. Hu Ping (2017).

60. Plato said little explicitly about harmony in the *Republic*, which has not stopped Chinese scholars essentially redefining justice as harmony to make Plato produce a thumbs-up on Chinese political "harmony."

61. Moak (2018).

62. As quoted in Osnos (2008), 37. On this generation of Chinese thinkers, see also Cheek (2015), 154–72.

Chapter Four: Rationality and Its Discontents

1. Simultaneously, in Meiji Japan, Ernest Fenollosa was using the same duality (though with its application reversed) even as he urged for a fusion of western and eastern values: "If we compare the two civilizations in their best types, we shall find that, while the strength of the Western has tended to lie in a knowledge of *means*, the strength of the Eastern has tended to lie in a knowledge of *ends*." Fenellosa (2009), 164. Emphasis in original. Many thanks to Haun Saussy for this observation.

2. Doan (2011), 188.

3. The linking of capitalism and rationality is, of course, western as well, but usually in a positive sense. Charles P. Webel claims "that the ideal model of rationality is economic in structure, that facts and values are absolutely distinct, and that the growth and extension of scientific knowledge and technology are 'apolitical' and 'nonideological.'" Webel (2014), 8.

4. At the end of 2019, a search on CNKI turned up 6,338 articles on instrumental rationality. Most of these articles appear in journals published by specific university departments. Many are very sophisticated, discussing thinkers from Quassim Cassam to F. A. Hayek. In some cases, the authors seek to unite the two forms of rationality but generally the approach to instrumental reason is critical.

5. There has been some pushback. See e.g., Liu (2005). Liu (1998) offers a positive view of Plato's "rational reflection" on the Greek city-state crisis, without turning to the critique of rationality that is the subject of Chapter 4.

6. As Zhang (1997) points out, contemporary Chinese scholars use Weberian terms to criticize the same Enlightenment notions of reason and rationality that westerners (like Weber) have themselves already critiqued.

7. Weber (1978).

8. Hindess (1992), 224. Jürgen Habermas would identify multiple stages within instrumental rationality alone, and Weber speaks elsewhere of a third category, formal rationality, i.e., a value-neutral calculation of the best means.

9. Max Weber's theory of bureaucracy, also known as the "rational-legal" model, defines bureaucracy in rational terms and argues that it is "based on the general principle of precisely defined and organized across-the-board competencies of the various offices" which are "underpinned by rules, laws, or administrative regulation."

10. Gerth and Mills (1970), 155. See also Liu Dong (2003); Mommsen (2006); Schechter (2010); Schluchter (1981); and Whimster and Lash (2006), 1–8; For pushback against a simple treatment of Weber's views on disenchantment, see Albrow (2006).

11. Note that rationalization, as a social process, is not the same as instrumental rationality, which is but one of its tools. All religions, for example, contain some degree of rationalization, the most rational response to a given understanding of the world. In his later works such as *Economy and Society*, Weber would argue that "Confucianism was the most rational form of adjustment to the world, Protestantism the most rational form of domination of the world, and Indian salvation religions the most rational form of world—flight." As quoted in, Whimster and Lash (2006), 16.

12. Weber (1958), 182. On the limited scope for human rights in Weber's sociology of law, see Turner (2002).

13. Liu Dong (2003), 197–8. Emphasis added.

14. Weber used other terminology as well—for example, *formal* rationality. But I am focusing on what one set of Chinese scholars have taken from him. Ren (2004) distinguishes between three forms of western rationalism: political, philosophical ("British"), and neoliberal. From his point of view, we are discussing only the first here.

15. Other scholars have argued that Roman law had a far bigger footprint.

16. Webel (2014), 8, 11. See also Goody (1993), 9–10: "The sociological tradition identifies a special form of rationality as enabling the west to take the lead in the economic or intellectual developments seen as associated with the modern world."

17. Glover (2000), 6–7.

18. Glover (2000), 310.

19. For more on this topic, see Zhang (1997).

20. Lang (1990), 168.

21. Bauman (1989), 13. In this way, these contemporary Chinese scholars are in line with a series of western thinkers who also traced the degeneration of west back to the general concept of enlightenment from ancient Greece (epitomized by the cunning bourgeois hero Odysseus) to twentieth-century fascism.

22. For a critique of generalizations about the Enlightenment, see Schmidt (2000) and the essays in Wilson (1970).

23. Selby-Bigge (1962), 172.

24. de Condillac (1754). Available in *Condillac's treatise on the sensations*, trans. Geraldine Carr (London: Favil Press, 1930).

25. Given their use of a priori principles, the rationalists of the period all failed to fulfill their claims to rationalist metaphysics anyhow, as with Descartes's foundationalist and subject-centered conception of reason. For a good introduction, see the *Stanford Encyclopedia of Philosophy*, s.v. Enlightenment.

26. Tu (2003), 164. Of course, this claim does not fit well with the thinking of the Enlightenment critics.

27. Zhang Longxi (1998), 204.

28. On this, see, for example, Dirlik (1995), 229–73, and Chen (1992), the latter of whom wrote that "Orientalism is quintessentially reflected . . . in Chinese appropriations of the idea of history as progress and teleology, notions derived from the western Enlightenment and from various schools of western utopian thinking." Chen (1992), 687.

29. Kant (1991), 54. Emphasis in original.

30. Honneth (1987), 692–3.

31. Lao Ji's blog, 2018-6-24, available at http://www.oscclub.com/home.php?mod=space&uid=23&do=blog&id=7025.

32. Halberstam (1988), 44–5.

33. Halberstam (1988), 45.

34. "For Kant this dignity rests on the autonomy of each human being's reason, while for Confucius it is dependent upon our interconnection with each other, demanding ongoing self-extension." Froese (2008), 258.

35. This is, of course, because in the *Republic* Plato ascribes different amounts of reason to different kinds of people, while for Kant it's simply a unique human trait.

36. Honneth (1987), 695–6.

37. Gan (2012).

38. Sprenger comments, "It is deplorable that modern Chinese thinkers have not or only superficially looked at this phenomenon. Since the May 4th Movement they have concentrated on the study of western science and technology but ignored or even rejected the spiritual-religious tradition of the west." Sprenger (1991), 4.

39. Gan (2012). The claim is made by others as well. Liu (2006), for instance, links Aristotelian rationality to modern science, albeit through no fault of Aristotle's. Liu claims that the "science" of the modern scientific worldview has lost its classical meaning; it is more regarded as a Weberian "technology" than as reason, and is more and more reduced to "instrumental rationality." The deadly arrogance of the west "lies in the fact that science believes that what it has studied is universally applicable truth." Liu (2006).

40. Gan (2012). Note that in "Science as a Vocation" Weber argues that knowledge of even the Platonic Forms is instrumental rather than value laden (despite Plato's moralizing) because Plato himself used them to make political claims for the superiority of philosopher-kings as rulers and of his own thought-system. Weber (2004), 1–31.

41. For a version of the essay without the photo of the Nazi rally, see http://www.xinfajia.net/9404.html.

42. Gan (2012). No mention is made in this particular line of argumentation (at least among the Chinese authors) of the millions who died under Mao's Great Leap Forward (1958–62).

43. Gerth and Mills (1970), 141. As Stephen Turner remarks, for Weber "the Platonic idea of knowledge of the forms as the highest and controlling form of knowledge is a model of possible expertise, which happens to have been based on epistemic error." This interpretation "would help Weber preserve his image of rationality as distinctly western." Turner (2008), 129.

44. In Weber's view, the factors which produced capitalism were "the rational permanent enterprise, rational accounting, rational technology and rational law, but again not these alone. Necessary complementary factors were the rational spirit, the rationalization of the conduct of life in general, and a rationalistic economic ethic." Weber (1961), 260. If readers wonder how this vision of Plato as the pre-Enlightenment source of "rationality gone mad" dovetails with the Plato whose Noble Lie seems to be endorsed by some contemporary Chinese thinkers, I can only note that these different approaches arise out of different intellectual camps and trying to reconcile them may cause noticeable cerebral damage.

45. Zhang Xudong protests against this flat-handed treatment of the west as well: "Tradition, reduced to 'culture' as an immanent pattern, is unconditionally subject

to a universal 'scientific' measure, which is itself a ruthless reduction of the west, whose own historical, ideological contradictions are left out of the picture altogether." Zhang (1997), 40.

46. The fact that Weber's own views on China were somewhat insulting does not seem to have affected his popularity or the prevalence of his terminology.

47. Liu Dong (2003), 212. Contrast this treatment of instrumental rationality to that of earlier days. As Tran Van Doan writes of Dr. Y.B. Tsai, chancellor of the National University of Peking in the 1920s, "Tsai transformed the university into a locus of research with mottos like 'not to the preservation of national quintessence but to its reevaluation by scientific methods' . . . or absolute academic freedom, free expression of all theories and viewpoints on rational ground," Doan (2001), 188. Liu Dong is an interesting figure. One of the *minjian* intellectuals in the early 1990s, his focus is on reviving national scholarship; he currently edits the journal *China Scholarship* (*Zhongguo xueshu*).

48. Christianity is a different story, but at least in the work I've encountered, the Chinese seem to think that the west is more the product of antiquity than Christianity.

49. Li Jin (2003), 146.

50. See Mencius, *Mencius* 1B.15 and Zisi, *Zhongyong* 20. Also, Ames and Hall (1998), 114.

51. See the argument of Ames and Rosemont (1998), 48. Under "Chinese Ethics," the *Stanford Encyclopedia of Philosophy* includes: "*The Analects*, in fact, has been read as a record of how a group of men gathered around a teacher with the power to elevate, and as a record of how this group created a culture in which goals of self-transformation were treated as collaborative projects. These people not only discussed the nature of self-cultivation but enacted it as a relational process in which they supported one another, reinforced their common goals, and served as checks on each other in case they went off the path, the dao." This entry is available at https://plato.stanford.edu/entries/ethics-chinese/.

52. Confucius, *Analects* 13.13; see also, 12.19 and 12.17.

53. Is there then no strain in Chinese philosophy in which logic and deductive thought are privileged? There is one—the Logicians' School, a branch of Mohism that was developed by scholars who studied the ancient Chinese philosopher Mozi. In some ways, the questions of logic and inference in these texts resemble the work of the Sophists. Mohist logic declined by the end of the Han dynasty, and modern scholars are divided as to its significance.

54. Ni (2011), 2.

55. Of course, it would be impossible for reasoning to have no relationship to an ideal like *ren*; *Mencius* 1A describes its utility for the good ruler.

56. Confucius, *Analects* 2.12. *Ren* also merges considerations of interpersonal respect with the health of the state, effectively making the western concept of a separation of church and state untenable.

57. Not to be confused with the atypical use of the term in Fang (2011) and in the work of Peng and Nisbett generally.

58. In his fascinating *Cognitive Development: Its Cultural and Social Foundations,* Alexander Luria describes a Soviet peasant's reaction to a syllogism: "Q: All bears are white where there is always snow; in Zovaya Zemlya there is always snow; what color are the bears there? A: I have seen only black bears and I do not talk of what I have not seen." Luria (1976), 108–9. See also Soles (1995), 250 on the critiques of Confucius as lacking rationality.

59. Confucius, *Analects* 15.27.

60. Ironically, he also attempted to point out a logical fallacy in his interlocutor Hui Shi's arguments, in a famous discussion about the happiness of fishes (*Zhuangzi* 17)!

61. It must be noted that Confucian thought was never identified as a "philosophy" by the Chinese themselves, for whom the word 哲学 *zhexue* was the translation of a word coined by the Japanese Nishi Amane and promoted by Meiji period thinkers, and then translated into Chinese by Huang Zunxian (1848–1905), a Chinese diplomat in Japan.

62. Wong (2019).

63. Hall and Ames (1998), 54–5.

64. Waley (1979). Nisbett (2003). In such conversations, the scarcity of formal deductive arguments in the Confucian tradition as well as the presence of explicit statements criticizing the utility of rational deduction as a philosophical tool are both stressed.

65. Graham (1967); see Wong (2019). Rational argument is very present in some forms of Buddhist philosophy, where debates were a frequent social rite.

66. Confucius, *Analects* 1.4. See further, Fang (2011); Peng and Nisbett (1999), 743; Graham (2000).

67. Fang (2011), 25.

68. See especially P. P. Li (2008).

69. Lam Chi-Ming concedes that the analogical mode of argumentation is dominant in Chinese philosophy, especially in pre-Qin (before 221 BCE) Confucianism, but points out that analogies also depend on rational considerations, again privileging the view that rational deduction is an important element in philosophy. Confucius "encourages his followers to think for themselves and draw their own inferences about other cases from one instance." Lam (2014). See also Bai (2020), 11–2 on the notion of the "argumentation sketch" in which many of the

steps are simply left out—making it more, not less, challenging for the reader to understand.

70. Here *li* is the dynamic ordering pattern of the world. The most eminent Neo-Confucianist was Zhu Xi, a brilliant synthesizer of prior traditions.

71. Moody (2008), 95, 96.

72. Hansen (1983), 15. The Daoist Zhuangzi, meanwhile, often relied on rational argument precisely to confound the dictates of logic.

73. The Jesuit Verbiest was not allowed to print his *Studies to Fathom Principles* in China because the emperor felt that learning through inference, as taught by Aristotle, was inappropriate for Chinese learning!

74. Hansen emphasizes the grammar of Classical Mandarin in explaining these differences, especially the apparent absence of abstractions. Hansen (1983), 30–54. His argument has been criticized as being excessively Whorfian. Jean-Paul Reding, in a not dissimilar vein as Hansen, attributes the fascination with such issues as ontology or unchanging Platonic ideas to the fact that the Greek verb for "to be" can have an existential function and can also give rise to the abstract noun "being." The Chinese copula *shi* 是, however, cannot be used existentially; it also cannot be turned into an abstract noun. See Reding (2004), 167–94. For further exposition of Confucian rationality, see Chen (1998). Jullien (2002) opposes "wisdom" to a truth that exists only if the opposite party is forced to agree.

75. In fact, there exists scholarship likening Kant's thought to Confucius's. See here Wawrytko (1982). Wang (2000) emphasizes the rational human in both philosophies.

76. The chain of causality here is more than tenuous. As the *Stanford Encyclopedia of Philosophy* points out *s.v.* Enlightenment, "The changes in our understanding of nature and cosmology, effected by modern natural science, make recourse to the systems of Plato and Aristotle problematic. The Platonic identification of the good with the real and the Aristotelian teleological understand of natural things are both difficult to square with the Enlightenment concept of nature." This entry is available at https://plato.stanford.edu/entries/enlightenment/.

77. For a fuller explanation of "the irrational," see Dodds (1951), especially his chapter six on the way Plato goes beyond rationalism—for example, by mixing it with reincarnation. Socrates's daimonion also eludes rational explanation. Lane remarks, "Philosophies (or again, at least ancient, political, and moral philosophies) are more like religions than like competing accounts of symbolic logic." Lane (2009), 592. The papers in Buxton (1999) challenge the developmental picture of rationality in ancient Greece.

78. Wu Jia (2013), 12, 9.

79. A view shared by some Chinese; see e.g., Ju and Xing (2005).

80. Lloyd (2017), 93.

81. Lloyd (2017), 19. For an early rejection of "rationality" as sufficient to guide the judgments of mankind, see John Henry Newman's 1870 "Grammar of Assent."

82. Scholars such as Ben Xu, Zhang Longxi, G. E. R. Lloyd, Arif Dirlik, Liu Dong, and others have already started to do this.

Chapter Five: A Straussian Interlude

1. See e.g., Jiang (2014); Lilla (2010); Wang (2012a) and (2012b); Tao (2012); Shaw (2017); Bai and Xiao (2008); and Weng (2010), (2015a), and (2015b). Liu and Chen (2018); Marchal and Shaw (2017); Nadon (2017), etc. The Committee on Social Thought at the University of Chicago is a rare Straussian hotbed.

2. Carl Schmitt is also popular among this circle, but less relevant to this discussion of reception of antiquity in China. On Schmitt in China, see the essays in Marchal and Shaw (2017). The chapters by Shaw, Marchal, and Nadon are especially helpful in clarifying the Schmittians and Straussians in China. Habermas has also been influential in Chinese academia; see Davies and Davis (2007).

3. For Chinese studies of Strauss's influence in China, see Gao Shankui (2013) and Zhang Xudong (2010).

4. Their interpretations of Strauss's work are not identical, and Gan is moving away from Strauss towards a new overarching theory of how China should construe its own tradition, as presented in his new book *Tongsantong*.

5. This transformation is obviously a response to the crackdown, though all these intellectuals will deny it. On the phenomenon, see Zhao (1997). Gan's career trajectory has been criticized by Wu Guanjun (2014).

6. All titles originally in Chinese, of course. For Gan Yang's introduction to *Natural Right and History*, see http://www.aisixiang.com/data/16179.html. Other known Chinese Straussians include the nationalist Zhang Zhiyang, professor of Philosophy at Hainan University in Haikou, and a scattered group including Chen Jiaying, Zhang Bobo, Xu Jian, Chen Jianhong, Hai Yi, Lin Guohua, Wu Fei, Zhang Hui, Zhang Ming, and Lin Guorong. Of these, Zhang Hui, Lin Guohua, and Wu Fei used Strauss's translation of Plato's *Apology* while studying at Harvard and worked with the Straussians Seth Benardete and Stanley Rosen. For still further Strauss-influenced scholars, see Marchal (2017), 178.

7. On the Straussian bent of this series, see Chen Dandan (2015), with analysis of several of the volumes it contains. Another influential Straussian is the Korean scholar Jug Kyeok Kwak at Sun Yat-sen University, Zhuhai campus, who received his PhD from the University of Chicago's Committee on Social Thought in 2002.

8. Zhao (1997), 725.

9. Sun (2018). For a detailed description of the cultural fever of the 1980s, see Wu (1988). Also, see Zhang (2001) and http://www.communistchina.org/June_4th_massacre.html. For the recollections of one of the protest's leaders, see Feng Congde (2013).

10. Gan (1985), 25. On Gan Yang's thinking in the 1980s, see Wu Guanjun (2014), 127–33. Xu Jilin (2000), 179, notes of the journal editors that "Their particular interest was in introducing western humanist thought from its earliest classical origins up to the modern period."

11. Li Junpeng (2017), 55. "From the mid-1980s to the end of the 1980s, Gan Yang consistently lamented that China's failure in the twentieth century was a result of the intellectuals' overemphasis on social responsibility and national interest at the expense of individual freedom."

12. Gan Yang (1990), 108.

13. Gan (1997) and (1998), 52.

14. On Liu's career trajectory, see esp. Jiang (2014), 12–36; Nadon (2017); Fällman (2014); and Sprenger (1991).

15. For commentary, see Marchal (2017) and Leeb's introduction to his 2015 translation of Liu's *Sino-Theology*. (Leiden: Brill). Leeb also discusses the context of Christian studies in China.

16. See Weng (2010), 64–5; Sprenger (1991).

17. The second edition of *Delivering and Dallying*, published in 2001, was much less aggressive in its views.

18. Liu Xiaofeng (2002b) "Preface to 'the Docility of the Hedgehog'" [刺猬的温顺序言 *Ciwei de wenshun xuyan*]. As cited by Jiang (2014), 18. For a review of Liu's views on Christianity, see He Guanghu (1989).

19. The most notable translation of Plato in the early 1990s was Liu Xiaofeng's translation of the *Symposium* (*Huiyin*), which later was incorporated as the first publication in the Hermes series. Gan Yang likewise created a new version of his former series, still titled "Culture: China and the World" but with the addition of "New Series," in 2007. See Weng (2015a).

20. Weng (2015b), 316.

21. Liu Xiaofeng (2002b).

22. Gan (2002), ii.

23. As Chen Dandan explains, "Liu's emphasis on the issue of morality instead of the relationship between revelation and reason (or Jerusalem and Athens) has its background in the history of post-socialist China. First, the tension between Jerusalem and Athens is rooted primarily in concerns of the western tradition; second, China's socialist revolutions have destroyed most theological elements in its political culture and social life."

24. Leihua Weng (2010), 18.

25. For Chinese criticism of the Chinese Straussians, see Bai and Xiao (2008) and Deng (2013).

26. Liu (2009a).

27. Shaw describes the Straussians as "Chinese looking for China-based historical and cultural universalism that opposes western modernity and its elevation of democracy and human rights into universal values." Shaw (2017), 45.

28. Tang (2011), 101.

29. Liu (2013), 337.

30. If only Donald Trump had known!

31. Liu (2013), 50. See Weng (2015a), 322. Shaw elaborates on the idea: "Liu presents 'a life-and-death historical choice' for the Chinese intellectuals: either 'learning the modern western mode of enlightenment and corrupting themselves' or 'accepting the Platonic mode of the Socratic Enlightenment, and cultivating themselves.'" Shaw (2017), 50.

32. See Weng (2015b), 329. Gao Shankui writes, "Strauss's study of western ancient ideas unveils a different western world to Chinese scholars . . . showing us that the modern west is full of flaws because she has refused and forgotten the ancient knowledge." Gao (2013), 54.

33. C.f., Strauss (1941), 34.

34. For a critique of Strauss on the *Republic*, much of it in *The City and Man*, see e.g., Klosko (1986); for a defense, Ferrari (1997).

35. Cheng (2005).

36. Wang Jin (2016). A Straussian (Mei Hao Lan, also known as Jacob Howland) who published a book in the Hermes series called *The Paradox of Political Philosophy: Socrates' Philosophic Trial* (2012) was excoriated by a western reviewer as having no argument at all, only Straussian pick-and-choose.

37. Zhang (2016).

38. The western Straussian Eve Adler's book on the *Aeneid*, *Vergil's Empire: Political Thought in the Aeneid* (2003) takes a similar tack but did not find wide readership in the west.

39. See similarly the Straussian readings of classical texts by Wang Jin (2016), Li Mingkun (2012), and Dai (2016), all in *Gudian Yanjiu*.

40. See Weng (2010), 21 for the citation and translation. For Strauss's own treatment of the *Symposium*, see Sharpe (2013).

41. For an excellent analysis of this text, see Weng (2015b). For a critique, see Zhang (2015), 14–5. *Huiyin* includes interpretative essays on *Symposium* by three Straussians—Allan Bloom's "Plato's 'Ladder of Love;'" an essay by Seth Bernadete; and another one by Karl Heinrich Meier, author of *Carl Schmitt and Leo Strauss: The Hidden Dialogue*.

42. Liu Xiaofeng (2013), 34–60. Discussed in Marchal (2017), 181–2 and Jiang (2014), 19–20.

43. For a (non-Straussian) comparison of Socrates's position to Confucius, see Bai (2010).

44. Personal email communication to the author, January 2021.

45. See the discussion in Moore (2009). For one, Strauss argued that Thrasymachus's argument that Justice is "the interest of the stronger" was in fact a truth that Socrates told him off stage, but asked him (apparently without success) not to bring up in public.

46. Liu (2009b), 145. "L'impératif 'classique' qui charactérize la philosophie politique promue par Strauss n'est pas autre chose que le rejet fondamental de cetter modernité enthousiaste et aveugle . . . La première raison pour la quelle nou nou intéressons à Strauss en Chine est qu'il nous permet de nous defair d'un siècle de quête continue des different '-ismes,' enthousiastes et aveugles, venus de l'Occident."

47. Liu (2009a).

48. Liu (2009a). Liu also claims that using Strauss as a lens is akin to reading these texts for their own sake.

49. "The Han Confucians used the 'tiny words and big meanings' method to explain Confucius' compilation 'The Spring and Autumn' and other historical works. They then explained the meaning of many sages such as Confucius who had not stated [them] clearly." See "Small Words are Righteous" in the *Daily Headlines* [每日頭條] 微言有大, 2019-04-01. Available at https://kknews.cc/history/3q8k4x8 .html. Liu is continuing, in his own way, the Gongyang School's emphasis on exoteric reading in its treatment. Liu also pointed out sentences in the *Analects* showing that Confucius had said the truth was not for everyone: "The Master said, 'When a person should be spoken with, and you don't speak with them, you lose them. When a person shouldn't be spoken with and you speak to them, you waste your words. The wise do not lose people, nor do they waste their words.'" Liu renders this differently as "The wise err neither in regard to their man nor to their words of Confucian classics." *Analects* 15.8.

50. As ably demonstrated by Melzer (2014).

51. Shadia Drury complains of "contradictions, principles frequently stated but silently contradicted by upholding incompatible views, inexact repetitions, pseudonyms, strange expressions, a frequent use of technical language, ambiguity of expression, and other infelicities of style." Drury (2005), 25.

52. Smith (2006), 7, 37. Frazer (2006) suggests that maybe we should read Strauss's comments on esoterism esoterically!

53. Carl Shaw is critical about their degree of proximity: "A genuine Straussian liberal education would require understanding the classical texts as the authors themselves did, and entail 'listening to the conversation among the great minds' so as to understand human greatness. By contrast Gan's ultimate goal is . . . an appropriation of the classical tradition for the use of the present age." Shaw (2017), 53–4.

54. See also Strauss (1941), 24–5. As Batnitzky notes, "Esotericism is a means toward preserving the limits of philosophy and revelation (or law) vis-à-vis one another. The law comes up against its own limitations in the quest to articulate the philosophical foundations of the law. But at the same time, philosophy comes up against its own limits in recognizing that the philosopher is always already within society (or the law) and for this reason dependent upon the law." Batnitzky (2006).

55. Wang (2012b), available at https://claremontreviewofbooks.com/leo-strauss-in-china/.

56. As Nadon summarizes Strauss's view, the imperfection of any political regime necessitates esoterism—philosophy is the attempt to replace opinion with knowledge, but the knowledge it offers is corrosive and cannot be shared with the public. Nadon (2017), 157.

57. Along with Karl Schmitt, whom I cannot consider here.

58. Marchal (2017), 180. For a Chinese view of the Chinese reception of Strauss before 2003, see Zhang Xu (2010). See also Weng (2015a), 317: "[I]nstead of remaining 'academic,' Chinese Platonists are prone to be 'politically' active, in the sense that they are immensely interested in investigating modern Chinese history and positively re-valuating the Maoist political heritage, especially Mao's third-world theory against the American hegemony in the 1950s."

59. That Liu would like to be seen as an influential voice in the regime is clear from many of his lectures and articles. My own comments here were gently corrected by a western-educated scholar of the classics who will remain anonymous, but told me: "You used the term 'public intellectual' for Liu and Gan, but to my knowledge, which is heavily biased, they are often sarcastically called 'state counselors' [国师 guoshi]. . . . It seems like their influence is waning, partly because they have too few followers who have serious academic output, whereas the 'classicist' camp is growing." Email communication to author, January 4, 2021.

60. See, Liu Xiaofeng, "The Republic: China's Burden of a Century" [共和,中国 的百年之累 Gonghe: Zhongguo de bai nian zhilei], talk at Phoenix TV Reading Session 凤凰读书会, April 19, 2013, CUPSL, Beijing.

61. Fällman (2014). The term guofu is also commonly used for George Washington (!).

62. Weng (2010), 81. Wang rejects the idea that the interest in Strauss is due to Chinese nationalism. Instead, it is "because Strauss sparked Chinese scholars to realize the internal problems of modern rationalism, to research the attitude towards ancient Chinese thinking since early modern China, and because Strauss's ideas enabled some Chinese scholars to overcome the modern division of knowledge and realize the limitation of all kinds of modern doctrines." Wang (2012a), 78. However, to my mind, the view of Osnos (2008) that links Straussianism to nationalism is likely correct.

63. See Marchal (2017), 189–90.

64. See https://cul.qq.com/a/20171205/024104.htm for the whole text. The author's name is 叙拉古之惑, *Confused One from Syracuse*, presumably a reference to Plato's visit to Dionysus II. Wentao Zhai, email communication to author, January 2021.

65. I take this description from David Ownby's introduction to Gan Yang's lecture *"Unifying the Three Traditions" in the New Era: The Merging of Three Chinese Traditions* [*sic*] at Tsinghua University, May 12, 2005, available at https://www.readingthechina dream.com/gan-yang-tongsantong-chapter-1.html. This trio omits the legalist/bureaucratic tradition that maintained the state apparatus in dynastic China. On *Tongsantong*, see e.g., Weng (2015a), 325 and (2010), 65. On western classics and the spirit of nationalism among the young generation in China see Lilla (2010) and Osnos (2008). On the intersection of Deng's philosophy with Confucian thought, see Yang and Stening. "The distinct lines drawn by Mao (as a Marxist) between socialism and capitalism are distinctly blurred in modern China," Yang and Stening (2013), 433.

66. See the lecture version at Gan (2005).

67. Thus, one critique of Gan Yang's use of Strauss is that "Gan did not mention that the philosopher was actually the most self-sufficient man who lived on the margin of the political community and only had a minimum attachment with his fellow citizens. He [Gan] intentionally diluted the aspect of the philosopher's detachment from politics and portrayed him as an active political actor." Weng (2010), 51. On their differences see, Jiang (2014).

68. Li (2019).

69. See Yu Ying (2015).

70. Of course, I agree with Nie Minli's commitment not to distort the original texts. I too strive for this. But it's never that easy to read texts with a mind as uninfluenced as a tabula rasa.

Chapter Six: Harmony for the World

1. As quoted and cited in Delury (2008).

2. Delury (2008). On the "pseudo-Confucianization of the CCP" and the changing nuances of the terms used for "harmony," see Delury (2008). He adds, "To gentle critics of the Hu-Wen administration, "harmonious society" is a shibboleth signaling that the author is willing to work for reform within the ideological framework provided by the state."

3. Jiang Yi-huah (2018), 69–70. All subsequent quotations in this paragraph are from this source.

4. See, e.g., Jian (2018).

5. For a deeper study of Mao's complicated relationship to Confucian thought, see Boer (no year). See also "Confucianism during the Mao Era" (2021), available at https://factsanddetails.com/china/cat3/sub9/entry-4319.html#chapter-4. The quotation is from "Confucianism during the Mao Era."

6. As quoted in "Confucianism during the Mao Era" (2021), available at https://factsanddetails.com/china/cat3/sub9/entry-4319.html. For the complexity of Mao's relationship to ancient Chinese culture, see Perelomov (1977).

7. Fan (2006).

8. As cited in Fan (2006). See, for example, Xia (2018), who wrote, "Instead of focusing on individuals and personal interest, which are upheld by the western world, Chinese culture emphasizes the idea of 'people as the basis of society' and 'the world community is equally shared by all.'"

9. On *hexie*, see Fan (2006) and Delury (2008). There is a general perception that Hu's initiative did not do much. For example, "Hu's gravest pitfall lies in the failure of his mandate for a harmonious society. His rhetoric on the harmonious society resonates poorly—and ironically—as the country's spending on internal public security has skyrocketed in recent years, overtaking spending on national defense in 2010 and totaling $84 billion." Li and Cary (2011).

10. Li Jianhui (September 15, 2010), *News Center-China Net*, last accessed November 2021 at http://www.china.com.cn/news/zhuanti/gjhx/2010-09/15/content_20937824.htm. This no longer appears to be online, but the sentiments are echoed in many op-eds and articles of the period; see e.g. https://baike.baidu.com/item/和谐社会本质上是法治社会/23279877.

11. On the influence of the historical concept of the "Great Unity" on Chinese political thought, see Pines (2000).

12. Delury (2008).

13. Year 20 of the Duke of Zhao in the *Zuozhuan*. Similarly, so in chapter Zhouyu B of the *Guoyu*, a text most likely from the Warring States period associated with the Confucian tradition.

14. As cited in Perris (1983), 12.

15. *Analects* 8.8.

16. The *Book of Rites* from Zehou, 19. trans. Kirkendall (2017). Further on the musical analogy, see Whimster and Lash (2006), 15–6. For a comparison of music in the *Analects* to music in the *Republic*, see Lin (2003).

17. One of the four books of Confucianism—the *Doctrine of the Mean* (*Zhongyong*) attributed to Zisi, one of Confucius's grandsons—is devoted to the topic of the harmony and balance of the soul. According to the work, this was achieved by observing moderation, rectitude, sincerity, honesty, and other qualities such as respecting the ministers, but not giving too much importance to any one

goal. A friend should be neither too close nor too remote, grief and joy should be moderated. Such behavior marked out the "superior individual" (*junzi*).

18. Confucius, *Analects* 13.23.

19. *Chunqiu Zuozhuan*, Chapter Zhaogong Year 20. Most scholars now feel that the *Zuozhuan* was composed as an independent work that was later rearranged into a commentary.

20. Confucius, *Analects* 13.15.

21. *The Book of Rites* lists the situations in which *yayue* might be performed, such as ceremonies in honor of Heaven and Earth, the gods, or the ancestors.

22. Plato, *Republic* 424b–c; quotation from Homer, *Odyssey* 1.351.

23. Plato, *Laws* 800a.

24. For example, we read in the *Republic* that the philosopher "should come to resemble that with which it delights him to associate. . . . Hence the philosopher through the association with what is divine and orderly (*kosmios*) becomes divine and orderly (*kosmios*) insofar as a man may." Plato, *Republic* 500c.

25. Plato, *Republic* 443c–d.

26. Plato, *Phaedo* 92 contains discussion of soul as a harmony—but it's a denial, a response to the argument of *Phaedo* 86. Many thanks to my colleagues Agnes Callard and Gabriel Richards for their help on this topic.

27. Plato, *Laws* 822a, 812a–e. See discussion in Naddaf (2000). Fascinatingly, "according to Pseudo-Plutarch musical compositions were originally called *nomoi* because it was not permitted to deviate from the tuning established as canonical for each of them." Naddaf (2000), 3.

28. Confucius, *Analects* 2.3.

29. Whimster and Lash (2006), 15–6.

30. In *The Book of Rites*, Confucius also spoke about an internal harmony—produced by the unification of plurality! For further information on the role of music in Confucianism, see Kirkendall (2017) and Lin (2003).

31. Schluchter (1981), 94.

32. Most western scholars have not paid attention to Platonic *harmonia* (a word that the philosopher uses differently in different contexts). For a recent treatment and summary of the scholarship, see Chaturvedi, who concludes in fact that "even though most contemporary studies of Plato's thought fail to study this notion in any detail, it nonetheless plays an important role in many of his central doctrines" Chaturvedi (2018), v.

33. Wang Yong (2012). All subsequent quotations in this paragraph come from this source.

34. As Wang continues, he argues that for both Plato and Confucius, violating the principle of "each to his own rank" will mean the destruction of the country, which will become unjust *and* disharmonious.

35. A common move; see e.g., Wang (2011), Yang (2001) and the scholarly conferences discussed later in this chapter.

36. Hou (2005).

37. Wen (2006).

38. Rong (2013).

39. Zhang Xiaomei (2009). For a study that keeps the two systems separate, see Li and Gao (2005). Cheng (2006), whom we have met before as the Director of the Center for Classical Studies at Southwest University of Political Science and Law, concludes that Kallipolis is not a blueprint for human life, while Qiu (2004) thinks Kallipolis refers to Sparta.

40. Wang (2003). See also Zhang Jian (2007), Zhang Xiaomei (2009).

41. Henry Liu (2003).

42. This was first used by Hu Jintao in his 2012 Party Congress Report.

43. International Conference in Honor of the 2,570th Anniversary of Confucius and Sixth Congress of the International Confucian Committee, Beijing, November 2019. For further information see, https://www.rujiazg.com/article/17758.

44. Even the Belt and Road initiative is "justified" by judicious use of Confucian writings, especially 和 而 不同, 和而不同, 達則兼濟天下, and 四海之內皆兄弟. My thanks to Hansong Li for this point, who notes the existence of "mythologies/Zhou accounts of Xia division of the world space" and suggests that Belt and Road is a Hang-Tang reimagination. Personal communication, November 2021.

45. Chinese President Xi Jinping's 2014 comments at the 60th anniversary of the Chinese People's Association for Friendship with Foreign Countries (CPAFFC). On the Thucydides Trap, see Chapters 6 and 7.

46. Mardell (2017). Every Chinese friend I have claims that it's the Chinese who are the real cynics.

47. Roland (2018).

48. On neo-Confucianism today, see Feng (2014), Makeham (2012), Schneider (2010), Cha (2003), and Dirlik (1995). Note that this is not the same as the neo-Confucianism of the Song and Ming dynasties. For a comparative approach, see Liu Hanzhen (2015).

49. Cheek notes that Chinese theorists are using Confucius to promote ideas of "a new Chinese Universalism, a new *tianxia*." Cheek (2015), 23. Thus Joseph Levenson's contrast between empire and nation has been muddied by this return of Confucius. On the history of Chinese nationalism, see Carl (2002). On Chinese nationalism today, see Fitzgerald and Chien (2006), Liu Jun (2001), Shen and Chien (2006), and Tang (1996). See Zhao (1997) on the different schools in the anti-western movement, including one that blames monotheism for war and competition.

50. Boer (2012).

51. "The CCP has turned to . . . the promotion of a selective interpretation of the Confucian tradition." Dotson (2011), 3.

52. Dotson (2011), 3.

53. Already in 1989, some scholars were arguing for an authoritarian Confucian state. For one systematical analysis of neo-conservatism, see Fewsmith (1995).

54. Dotson (2011) discusses the uses of Confucius in Party propaganda.

55. These views on nature and technology are more in line with Daoism; the Zhuangzi has text similar to that of the "Deinos Ode" of Sophocles's Antigone.

56. Tu (2010). The text of his speech was available at http://tuweiming.net/2017/01/12/april-2010-the-global-significance-of-concrete-humanity-essays-on-the-confucian-discourse-in-cultural-china/ but I have not been able to link to it since November 2021. On this phenomenon, see Xu (2006). Fan Ruiping, a professor at the City University of Hong Kong, also writes about the relationship between man and nature in his book Reconstructionist Confucianism (2010).

57. For further discussion, see Xuyang (2013).

58. As quoted in Xuyang (2013).

59. Some prominent names from the twentieth century are Tang Junyi, Xu Fuguan, and Mou Zongsan. Mou even argued for a rapprochement between Confucius and Kant. They contributed to the 1958 New Confucian Manifesto which outlined their beliefs. In Hong Kong there are many professors of philosophy whose work touches on the classics, such as Zhang Longxi, Jiwei Ci, Sungmoon Kim, and Joseph Chan. Up to quite recently, their work tended to interpret Confucian thought as compatible with western humanism, e.g., Chan (2014). For discussions of the development of the New Confucianism, see Jiang (2018) and Chang (1976).

60. I have not capitalized neo here to distinguish this group from the historical Neo-Confucians.

61. Dirlik (1995).

62. This is actually a topic of controversy IN China, as Anna Sun analyses in her 2013 study. Some contemporary Confucians such as Tu Wei-ming argue that Confucianism is, fundamentally, a religion, and so did Weber.

63. Cohen (2018). And it's true that the Legalists are a grim lot. The foundational text Shang jun shu contains such wisdom as the following: "The people's intrinsic selfishness constantly endangers social order; and to safeguard this order, the ruler should resolutely rein in his subjects through the law [fa 法 in this context refers primarily to punitive laws]. The state should tightly control its subjects: the system of mandatory registration of the population and creation of mutual responsibility groups among the populace will ensure that every crime is denounced and the criminal—particularly those who abscond from the battlefield—will know that there is no place to flee from the army ranks, and migrants can find no refuge." (Shang

jun shu 18: 108; *Shang jun shu* 18.3). From *s.v.* "Legalism in Chinese Philosophy," *Stanford Encyclopedia of Philosophy*, available at https://plato.stanford.edu/entries/chinese-legalism/.

64. Their proximity in time makes them appealing figures for cross-cultural comparison, never mind that "Confucius" is largely a back projection of the Han dynasty and that we know both Socrates and Confucius only through their texts. At this conference, even their "biographies" were found to be alike.

65. Is comparison itself too problematic? Sometimes the case for incommensurability is made by pointing to the pervasive and central presence of a term in one tradition for which no equivalent term can be found in another tradition. This is the stance taken by Gernet in (2010), 17–31. See also Lloyd (2017), 1–7. For further comparative views, see the essays in Wilson (1970), most of which deal with the topic with special reference to the sociology of religion.

66. Chen et al. (2011), 14.

67. Chen et al. (2011), 15. One may be surprised to hear that Socrates expected a great harmony of human beings (perhaps Chen was thinking of the Kallipolis of Plato's *Republic*?)

68. Vergil, *Aeneid* 1.278–9.

69. Chen (2011), 80–8.

70. Plato, *Republic*, 508e2–3.

71. Chen et al. (2011), 84.

72. Chen et al. (2011), 85, 86.

73. Chen et al. (2011), 86.

74. Chen et al. (2011), 100.

75. Chen et al. (2011), 308.

76. Chen et al. (2011), 125.

77. References to Hesiod's golden age do appear in the *Cratylus*, and to an age of Kronos in the *Statesman* and *Laws*, but the usage is highly ironic.

78. Chen et al. (2011), 43.

79. Much published work also follows this trend, see e.g., Wang Yang (2014); Hou (2005), who wrote, "The establishment of a well-ordered harmonious society is the ultimate goal of Plato's "Utopia;" Wen (2006), who commented, "Plato exchanges the freedom of the citizens for stability and harmony;" and dozens more. Many studies also praise Plato for his vision of a "communist" state. Of course, the most qualified Chinese and American scholars have produced comparative studies of key concepts in both thinkers that do not seek either to rank or to harmonize them.

80. Greek *harmonia* had its origins in joining or jointing, especially ship-building, but was also applied to music. To the best of my knowledge, it does not appear in any other sense in Plato's opus.

81. Sometimes comparisons are simply impossible; see, for example, Murphy and Weber (2010), who point out that the voluntarism and rationalism stipulated by the *Euthyphro* dilemma are simply absent in Confucianism.

82. Confucius, *Analects*, 7.1. Chen et al. (2011), 30.

83. Chen et al. (2011), 142.

84. The earliest dialogues are held to be closest to historical Socrates's method and they are aporetic.

85. Tu Wei-ming at https://gallery.its.unimelb.edu.au/imu/imu.php?request =multimedia&irn=129600. Date unclear.

86. See Yu (1998), (2004), (2005), and (2014).

87. Yu (2005), 185.

88. Chen et al. (2011), 17.

89. And also in academic literature sometimes, see e.g., Jin Nan (2010), where all we need is love.

90. See e.g., Shun (2004b).

91. "The Enlightenment Daily," but not the same word as the western Enlightenment that is so often criticized—that is *qimeng*.

92. Zheng and Zheng (2010).

93. On political Confucianism see Hankins (2017).

94. For English-language studies, see Bell (2015), Bell and Wang (2020). These categories tend to get blurry around the edges; Jiang (2018) suggests that there are more intermediary positions.

95. Bell's books include *Just Hierarchy: Why Social Hierarchies Matter in China and the Rest of the World* (with Wang Pei, 2020); *The China Model: Political Meritocracy and the Limits of Democracy* (2016); and *China's New Confucianism: Politics and Everyday Life in a Changing Society* (2010).

96. Bai was a former Berggruen Fellow at the Edmond J. Safra Center for Ethics at Harvard. According to its website, the Berggruen Institute, "was established in 2010 to develop foundational ideas about how to reshape political and social institutions in the face of these great transformations. We work across cultures, disciplines and political boundaries, engaging great thinkers to develop and promote long-term answers to the biggest challenges of the 21st Century." See https://www.berggruen .org/about/.

97. A different sort of public servant exam exists to this day.

98. Bai (2020), 99. In an earlier book, *China: The Political System of the Middle Kingdom* (2012), Bai argued that China in the Spring and Autumn and the Warring States period (771–221 BCE) was socially and politically akin to early modernity in Europe, at least in the emergence of a populous, mobile, and non-feudal population.

99. Bai quotes Rawl's 1993 book *Political Liberalism*, xliv, as follows: "Citizens are reasonable when, viewing one another as free and equal in a system of social

cooperation over generations, they are prepared to offer one another fair terms of social cooperation . . . and they agree to act on those terms, even at the cost of their own interests in particular situations, provided that others also accept them."

100. Bai (2020), 94.

101. Bai (2020), 65.

102. For similar critique, see Ma and Zhang (2021).

103. Mencius 125 draws on Confucius, *Analects* 1.2 to suggest that one eventually treat others as family. Christianity is constantly being elided in these discourses about the west's lack of meaning. So, for example, Bai can say that the "form of the good" is too vague to help the west, but then does not mention religious values.

104. Bai (2020), 263.

105. See e.g., Menn (1992).

106. C.f., Confucius, *Analects* 12.22.

107. Plato, *Republic*, 508a–c.

108. Bai (2020), 161, referring to Plato, *Republic*, 419a. The criticism is repeated by Aristotle at *Politics* 1264b.

109. Bai (2020), 162.

110. See Bell (2015) for similar arguments.

111. Hankins (2020), 160–1. Emphasis in original.

112. Bai (2020), 96.

113. Note the animus against the so-called Confucius Institutes in the US.

114. See e.g., Moore (2009), 110: "In the course of pursuing the enlightened good of the state, the philosopher-statesman [according to Strauss] may be required to present a fictional version of events to *hoi polloi* in order to justify the undertaking of some action deemed necessary from their enlightened perspective."

115. Suskind (2004).

116. George (2005), 174.

117. Further on *hexie*, see Choukrone and Garapon (2007), Rošker (2013), and Wang et al. (2020). On the internet, the homonym "river crab" has been used (*héxiè* instead of *héxié*) to refer to "harmony" as the government uses it. As Wang Xuan et al. write, netizens use this word to "voice criticism of claims that state-imposed censorship is the means to build a 'harmonious society.'" Wang et al. (2016), 310.

Chapter Seven: Thoughts for the Present

1. For an excellent discussion of many of the issues and individuals I have discussed in this book, but without the Greek classics as a lens, see Leonard (2008).

2. This has spurred attempts to create a uniquely Chinese ethico-political genealogy, as we see with Gan Yang's "three traditions" theory.

3. For a critique of this reductionism, which is deleterious to both sides of the comparison, see Zhang (1996), 137–41. For more on the revival of Confucianism in contemporary China, see Chapter 5.

4. Thucydides, *Peloponnesian War* 1.23.

5. There is also a "Tacitus Trap," the situation of a government in which the public no longer believes in anything done or said by the leadership but sees deceit everywhere. The phrase was coined in 2007 by Pan Zhichang at Nanjing University, who quoted Tacitus to the effect that "When a government is unpopular, both good and bad policies tell against the government itself." C.f., Tacitus *Histories* 1.7. Xi Jinping used the term at the meeting of the Party's Lankao County Committee in 2014 and has noted that the Party "urgently needs to face up to the impact and challenge of the 'Tacitus Trap' phenomenon on social governance and to reshape the government's credibility in an all-round way." Some Chinese say it is the Chinese themselves. For further information see, http://cpc.people.com.cn/xuexi/n1/2016/0518/c385474 -28359130.html. My thanks to Neville Morley for drawing my attention to this "trap"!

6. For example, Jin Canrong 金灿荣 and Zhao Yuanliang 赵远良 (2014).

7. Guo Jiping (2019).

8. Guo Jiping (2019).

9. That analogy has been made in the context of Athenian and American foreign policy (the latter during the Cold War) by Harding (1995).

10. Bowers (2017).

11. See Plutarch, *Lycurgus*, 18.1.

12. Palmer (2020).

13. The theory was developed in a 1993 *Foreign Affairs* article titled "The Clash of Civilizations?" and later expanded into *The Clash of Civilizations and the Remaking of World Order* in 1996.

14. My thanks to Tuvia Gering for bringing Wen Yang to my attention, on Twitter of all media!

15. See Wen Yang's 2021 interview on his recent book, *The Logic of Civilization*, at https://www.guancha.cn/WenYang/2021_11_04_613483_s.shtml.

16. Fukuyama (1989), 3. Emphasis in original.

17. See the discussion in Menand (2018).

18. Fukuyama's latest book is *Identity: The Demand for Dignity and the Politics of Resentment* (2018). Interestingly, his undergraduate degree at Cornell was in classics.

19. As a simple search for "Francis Fukuyama, end of history" on the Wangfang database will show.

20. See, https://zh.wikipedia.org/wiki/弗朗西斯·福山.

21. Chen (2020).

22. Zeng (2016).

BIBLIOGRAPHY

For Chinese authors I have maintained the traditional order of last name followed by first name with no intervening comma. In the case of Chinese-origin authors writing in English, however, I have followed the usual Anglicized practice of last name, comma, first name.

Albrow, Martin (2006). "The Application of the Weberian Concept of Rationalization to Contemporary Conditions." In Whimster and Lash, eds. *Max Weber, Rationality and Modernity*, 164–83.

Ames, Roger T. (1992). "Chinese rationality: An oxymoron?" *Journal of Indian Council of Philosophical Research* 9: 95–119.

Ames, Roger T. and Henry Rosemont, Jr. (1998). *The Analects of Confucius: A Philosophical Translation*. New York: The Random House Publishing Group.

Ames, Roger T. and David L. Hall. (1998). *Thinking from the Han: Self, Truth, and Transcendence in Chinese and Western Culture*. Albany, NY: State University of New York Press.

Bai Tongdong. 白彤东. (2010). "What to Do in an Unjust State? On Confucius's and Socrates's Views on Political Duty." *Dao* 9: 375–390.

———. (2019). "The Private and the Public in the *Republic* and in the *Analects*." In *Confucius and Cicero*. Edited by Andrea Balbo and Jaewon Ahn. 29–42. Berlin and Boston: De Gruyter.

———. (2012) *China: The Political System of the Middle Kingdom*. London and New York: Zed Books.

———. (2020). *Against Political Equality: The Confucian Case*. Princeton, NJ: Princeton University Press.

Bai Tongdong 白彤东 and Xiao Jianqiu 肖涧秋. (2008). "The Path to the Destruction of Classical Philosophy?" [走向毁灭经典哲学之路? *Zouxiang huimie jingdian zhexue zhilu?*]. *World Philosophy* 世界哲学. 1: 56–59.

Baker, Patrick et al. eds. (2019). *Beyond Reception: Renaissance Humanism and the Transformation of Classical Antiquity*. Berlin: De Gruyter.

Bandursky, David. (2019). "Burying 'Mr. Democracy.'" *China Media Project* (5/3/19). https://u.osu.edu/mclc/2019/05/11/burying-mr-democracy/

Barnes, Jonathan. (2003). "Review of *The Way and the Word: Science and Medicine in Early China and Greece* by Geoffrey Lloyd and Nathan Sivin." *The Guardian.* Available at www.theguardian.com/books/2003/nov/03/londonreviewofbooks.

Bartsch, Shadi. (2018a). "The Ancient Greeks in Modern China: History and Metamorphosis." In *Receptions of Greek and Roman Antiquity in East Asia.* Edited by Almut-Barbara Renger and Xin Fan. 237–257. Leiden: Brill.

———. (2018b). "The Wisdom of Fools: Christianity and the Classical Tradition" (傻瓜的智慧": 基督教和古典传统 *Shagua de zhihui": Jidujiao he gudian chuantong). China Scholarship* (2018c): 59–65.

———. (2019). "Plato's *Republic* in the People's Republic of China." *KNOW* 3: 167–91.

———. (2020). "The Rationality Wars: The Ancient Greeks and the Counter-Enlightenment in Contemporary China." *History and Theory* 58: 127–143.

Batnitzky, Leora. (2016). "Leo Strauss." In *The Stanford Encyclopedia of Philosophy* (Summer 2016 Edition). Edited by Edward N. Zalta. Available at https://plato.stanford.edu/entries/strauss-leo/.

Bauman, Zygmunt. (1989). *Modernity and the Holocaust.* Ithaca, NY: Cornell University Press.

Beecroft, Alexander. (2016). "Comparisons of Greece and China." In *Oxford Handbooks Online: Classical Studies, Classical Reception.* Available at https://www.oxfordhandbooks.com/view/10.1093/oxfordhb/9780199935390.001.0001/oxfordhb-9780199935390-e-14.

———. (2021). "Review of Murray, *China from the ruins of Athens and Rome: Classics, Sinology, and Romanticism, 1793–1939.*" *Bryn Mawr Classical Review* 2021.11.02.

Bell, Daniel A. (2010). *China's New Confucianism: Politics and Everyday Life in a Changing Society.* Princeton, NJ: Princeton University Press.

———. (2015). *The China Model. Political Meritocracy and the Limits of Democracy.* Princeton, NJ: Princeton University Press.

———. (2020). Review of Pan Yue (2020). "Chinese leaders need to explain their traditional thinking again—Comments on Pan Yue's 'Warring States and Greece.'" [中国领导人需要再解释其传统思想— 评潘岳"战国与希腊 *Zhōngguó lǐngdǎo rén xūyào zài jiěshì qí chuántǒng sīxiǎng—píng pānyuè "zhànguó yǔ xīlà).* Available at https://www.rujiazg.com/article/18755.

Bell, Daniel A. and Wang Pei. (2020). *Just Hierarchy: Why Social Hierarchies Matter in China and the Rest of the World.* Princeton, NJ: Princeton University Press.

Berggruen, Nicholas and Nathan Gardels. (2012). *Intelligent Governance for the 21st Century. A Middle Way between West and East.* New York, NY: Polity.

Berryman, Silvia. (2015). "Ideology, Inquiry, and Antiquity: A Critical Notice of Lloyd's *The Ideals of Inquiry: An Ancient History.*" *Canadian Journal of Philosophy* 45: 242–256.

Blumenthal, Dan. (2020). "China's Steps Backward Began Under Hu Jintao." *Foreign Policy*. June 4, 2020.

Boer, Roland. (No year). "Confucius and Chairman Mao: Towards a Study of Religion and Chinese Marxism." *Crisis and Critique* 2: 37–55. Available at http://crisiscritique.org/uploads-new/BOER.pdf.

Bowers, Jack. (2017). "Are China and the US Destined for War?" https://theconversation.com/are-china-and-the-us-destined-for-war-78035.

Brenner, Eliot. (2003). "The Violent Teacher." *The Ethical Spectacle*. https://www.spectacle.org/0203/brenner.html.

Bromberg, Jacques A. (2021). *Global Classics*. London: Routledge.

Buckley, Chris. (2013). "China Takes Aim at western Ideas." *The New York Times*. August 19, 2013.

Buxton, Richard, ed. (1999). *From Myth to Reason? Studies in the Development of Greek Thought*. New York, NY: Oxford University Press.

Carl, Rebecca. (2002). *Staging the World: Chinese Nationalism at the Turn of the Twentieth Century*. Durham, NC: Duke University Press.

Carmola, Kateri. (2003). "Noble Lying: Justice and Intergenerational Tension in Plato's *Republic.*" *Political Theory* 31: 39–62.

Cawley, Kevin N. (2013). "De-constructing the name(s) of God: Matteo Ricci's translational apostolate." *Translation Studies* 6: 293–308.

Cha, Seong Hwan. (2003). "Modern Chinese Confucianism: The Contemporary Neo-Confucian Movement and its Cultural Significance." *Social Compass* 50: 481–91.

Chan, Joseph. (2014). *Confucian Perfectionism: A Political Philosophy for Modern Times*. Princeton, NJ: Princeton University Press.

Chang Hao 張灝. (1971). *Liang Ch'i-ch'ao and Intellectual Transition in China, 1890–1907*. Cambridge, MA: Harvard University Press.

———. (1976). "New Confucianism and the Intellectual Crisis of Modern China." In *The Limits of Change: Essays on Conservative Alternatives in Republican China*. Edited by Charlotte Furth. 276–303. Cambridge, MA: Harvard University Press.

Chaturvedi, Aditi. (2018). "On the Role of Harmonia in Plato's Philosophy." Publicly Accessible Penn Dissertations. 2800.

Cheek, Timothy. (2015). *The Intellectual in Modern Chinese History*. Cambridge, UK: Cambridge University Press.

Chen Dandan. (2015). "The Spread of Leo Strauss's Thought and the Flowering of Classical Political Philosophy in Post-Socialist China." *Intertexts* 19: 39–65.

Chen Dezheng 陈德正. (2000). "Discussions of Ancient City-State Issues in Chinese and Foreign Academic Circles in the 20th Century" [20世纪中外学术界对古代城邦问题的讨论 20 Shiji zhongwai xueshu jie dui gudai chengbang wenti de taolun]. Journal of Binzhou Education College 滨州教育学院学报 1: 40–43.

———. (2009). "Liang Qichao's Introduction and Dissemination of Greek and Roman History" [梁启超对希腊, 罗马史的引介和传播 Liang qichao dui xila, luoma shi de yinjie he chuanbo]. Shandong Normal University Journal. 山东师范大学学报 54: 73–76.

Chen Duxiu 陳獨秀. (1915). "The Fundamental Difference between the Intellectual Traditions of Eastern and Western Peoples" [东西民族根本思想之差异 Dongxi minzu genben sixiang zhi chayi]. New Youth 新青年 1: 283–87.

———. (1916). "A Refutation of Kang Youwei's Letter to the President and Prime Minister" [驳康有为致总统总理书 Bo Kang Youwei Zhi Zongtong he Zongli Shu]. Available at https://zh.m.wikisource.org/zh/驳康有為致總統和總理書.

Chen Fong-Ching 陳方正 and Jin Guantao 金观涛. (1997). From Youthful Manuscripts to River Elegy: The Chinese Popular Cultural Movement and Political Transformation 1979–1989. Hong Kong: Chinese University Press.

Chen Guan 琛观. (2020). "The Embarrassment of Francis Fukuyama" [弗朗西斯·福山的尴尬 Fulangxisi-fushan de ganga]. Available at https://zhuanlan.zhihu.com/p/139462107.

Chen Guanghua 陈光华. (1986). "On the Role of Division of Labor in Plato's Republic" [试论分工在'理想国'中的地位 Shilun fengong zai 'lixiang guo' zhong de diwei]. Journal of Shangrao Normal University Social Sciences Edition [上饶师范学院学报, 社会科学版], 2: 15–20.

Chen Haosu et al. eds. (2011). Confucius-Socrates. Proceedings of Three Conferences on Chinese and Greek Philosophy. Beijing: Embassy of Greece.

Chen Hongyi 陈弘毅. (2001). "Mediation, Litigation and Justice—Reflection on Modern Free Society and Confucian Tradition" [调解、诉讼与公正— 对现代自由社会和儒家传统的反思 Tiaojie, susong yu gongzheng—dui xiandai ziyou shehui he rujia chuantong de fansi]. Modern Law. 现代法学 3: 3–14.

Chen Jianhong 陈建洪. (2008). "On Leo Strauss's Political Philosophy and his Doctrine of Esotericism." [论施特劳斯的政治哲学及其隐微论 Lun shitelaosi de zhengzhi zhexue jiqi yinwei lun]." Seeking Truth [求是学刊] 35.6: 41–44.

———. (2015). On Strauss [论施特劳斯 Lun shitlaosi]. Shanghai: East China Normal University Press.

———. (2016). "Strauss on Ancient and Modern Political Philosophy and their Ideals of Civilization" [施特劳斯论古今政治哲学及其文明理想 Shitelaosi lun gujin zhengzhi zhexue jiqi wenming lixiang]. Political Philosophy 政治哲学 25th Aug.: 51–55.1.

Chen Jiaying 陈嘉映. (2015). *The Good Life.* ["何为良好生活" *He wei liang hao shenghuo*]. Shanghai: Chinese Literature and Art Publishing House.

Chen Kuide 陳奎德. (2000). "The cultural fever: background, ideology and two tendencies" [文化热: 背景, 思潮及两种倾向*Wenhua re: beijing, sichao ji liangzhong qingxiang*]. In *Contemporary Cultural Changes in Mainland China* [中国大陆当代文化变迁*Zhongguo dalu dangdai wenhua bianqian*]. Edited by Chen Kuide. 37–61. Taipei: Guigan chubanshe.

Chen Xiaomei 陳小眉. (1992). "Occidentalism as Counterdiscourse: 'He Shang' in Post-Mao China." *Critical Inquiry* 18: 686–712.

_____. (2002). *Occidentalism: A Theory of Counter-discourse in Post-Mao China.* New York, NY: Rowman & Littlefield.

Chen Xunwu. (1998). "A rethinking of Confucian rationality." *Journal of Chinese Philosophy* 25: 483–504.

Chen Yan 陈彦. (2006). "Thinking about 'Noble Lies'" [思索 '高贵的谎言 *Sisuo 'gaogui de huangyan'*]. *Douban.* Available at https://www.douban.com/group/topic/1095343/.

Cheng Ling 程岭. (2014). "The Pedagogical Implication of Western Rationalism and the Enlightenment" [西方理性主义的发展及其对教学的启示 *Xifang lixing zhuyi de fa zhan ji qi dui jiaoxue de qishi*]. *Contemporary Education and Culture* [当代教育与文化 *Dāngdài jiàoyù yǔ wénhuà*] 6: 48–53.

Cheng Zhimin 程志敏. (2005). "Looking at the Relationship Between Philosophers and City-states from the Perspective of the 'Noble Lie.'" [从'高贵的谎言'看哲人与城邦的关系 *Cong 'gaogui de huangyan' kan zheren yu chengbang de guanxi*]. *Zhejiang Academic Journal* 浙江学刊1: 86–90.

———. (2006). "The Correction of Plato's Utopia." [柏拉图"理想国"辨正 *Bolatu 'lixiang guo' bianzheng*]. *Zhejiang Academic Journal* [浙江学刊] 3. Available at https://d-wanfangdata-com-cn.proxy.uchicago.edu/periodical/zjxk200603020.

Chiou, C.L. (1995). "The 'River Elegy' and the 4 June Tiananmen Massacre." In *Democratizing Oriental Despotism.* C.L. Chiou. 52–72. Palgrave Macmillan: London.

Choukrone, Leila and Antoine Garapon. 2007. "The Norms of Chinese Harmony: Disciplinary Rules as Social Stabiliser." *China Perspectives* 3: 36–49.

Chow Tse-Tung 周策纵. (1960). *The May Fourth Movement: Intellectual Revolution in Modern China.* Cambridge, MA: Harvard University Press.

Cohen, Jerome. (2018). "Xi Jinping sees some pushback against his iron-fisted rule." *Washington Post*, August 2, 2018. Available at https://www.washingtonpost.com/news/global-opinions/wp/2018/08/02/xi-jinping-sees-some-pushback-against-his-iron-fisted-rule/.

Cooper, John M., ed. (1997). *Plato's Complete Works.* Indianapolis, IN: Hacket.

Copenhaven, Brian. (2019). *Magic and the Dignity of Man: Pico della Mirandola and His Oration in Modern Memory.* Cambridge, MA: Harvard University Press.

Dai Xiaoguang 戴晓光. (2016). "An Interpretation of the 'Theuth mythos' in Plato's *Phaedrus.*" [斐德若中的 '忒伍特神話'(274c–5276a 解析 *Feideruo zhong de 'tewute shenhua' jiexi*]. *The Chinese Journal of Classical Studies* [古典研究*Gudian Yanjiu*] 25: 1–17.

Davies, Gloria. (2009). *Worrying about China: The Language of Chinese Critical Inquiry.* Cambridge, MA: Harvard University Press.

Davies, Gloria and Gloria Davis. (2007). "Habermas in China: Theory as Catalyst." *The China Journal* 57: 61–85.

De Jong, Alice. (1989). "The Demise of the Dragon: Backgrounds to the Chinese Film 'River Elegy.'" *China Information* 4: 28–43.

Delury, John. (2008). "'Harmonious' in China." *Policy Review,* Monday, March 31, 2008. Available at https://www.hoover.org/research/harmonious-china.

Deng Anqing 邓安庆. (2005). "Tracing the Origin of Concepts in Western Ethics: An Existentialist Interpretation of Aristotle's Ethical Concepts." [西方伦理学概念溯源— 亚里士多德伦理学概念的实存论阐释 *Xifang lunli xue gainian suyuan—Yalishiduo de lunli xue gainian de shi cun lun chanshi*]. *Social Sciences in China.* 中国社会科学 4: 73–82.

Deng Feihuang 邓飞黄. (1922). "The Origin and Impact of Individualism" [個人主義的由來及其影響*Gerenzhuyi de youlai jiqi yingxiang*]. *Eastern Magazine* 东方杂志19: 35–46.

Deng Xiaomang 邓晓芒. (2011). "Rationality and Irrationality in the History of western Philosophy." [西方哲学史中的理性主义和非理性主义*Xifang zhexue shi zhong de lixing zhuyi he fei lixing zhuyi*]. *Modern Philosophy* 现代哲学 3: 46–48.

———. (2013). "On Liu Xiaofeng's 'Scholarship.'" [评刘小枫的"学理*Ping Liu Xiaofeng de 'xuili'*]. *Xiaomang's Campus* 晓芒学园. Available at http://www.xiaomang.net/forum.php?%20mod=viewthread&tid=297.

Ding Liqun 丁立群. (2012). "Philosophy of Theory and Philosophy of Praxis: Which is the First?" [理论哲学与实践哲学：孰为第一哲学? *Lilun zhexue yu shijian zhexue: Shu wei di yi zhexue?*]. *Philosophical Researches* 哲学研究 1: 78–84.

Dirlik, Arif. (1995). "Confucius in the borderlands: Global capitalism and the reinvention of Confucianism." *Boundary2* 2.22: 229–273.

Doan, John B. Tran Van(1997). "The Crisis of Rationality and Confucian Reasonableness." Available at https://vntaiwan.catholic.org.tw/theology/crisis.htm.

Doan, Tran Van. 陳文團. (2001). *Reason, Rationality, and Reasonableness.* Vietnamese Philosophical Studies. Vol 1. Washington, DC: Council for Research in Values & Philosophy.

Dodds, E. R. (1951). *The Greeks and the Irrational*. Berkeley, CA: University of California Press.

Dombrowski, Daniel. (1997). "Plato's 'Noble' Lie." *History of Political Thought* 18: 565–578.

Dotson, John. (2011). "The Confucian Revival in the Propaganda Narratives of the Chinese Government." *U.S.-China Economic and Security Review Commission Staff Research Report*, July 20th, 2011. 1–22.

Drury, Shadia. (2005). *The Political Ideas of Leo Strauss*. New York, NY: Palgrave MacMillan.

Du Zhengshen 杜正勝. (1986). "A Survey of State Form in Zhou Dynasty A Preliminary Opinion on the 'Feudal City-State.'" [關於周代國家形態的蠡測 —「封建城邦」說芻議 *Guanyu zhoudai guojia xingtai de li ce yi 'fengjian chengbang' shuo chuyi*]. *History and Philosophy Collection* [史語所集刊] 58(3): 465–500. Available at http://www2.ihp.sinica.edu.tw/file/3461nKELmku.pdf.

Elstein, D. (2014). "Reviewed Work: *China: The Political Philosophy of the Middle Kingdom* by Bai Tongdong." *Philosophy East and West* 64: 513–515.

Fällman, Fredrik. (2014). "Enlightened or not? Notes on Liu Xiaofeng and the 'Father of the Nation.'" *Orientaliska Studier* 138: 64–72.

Fan, Maureen. (2006). "China's Party Leadership Declares New Priority: 'Harmonious Society.'" *The Washington Post*. October 12, 2006.

Fang Kaicheng. (2019). "'There was a Western sage named Seneca:' Seneca's Consolations in seventeenth-century China." [Typescript].

Fang Ning 房寧. (2009). "The People's Congress System is a Concentrated Embodiment of China's Democratic Politics." [人民代表大會制度是中國民主政治的集中體現 *Renmin daibiao dahui zhidu shi Zhongguo minzhu zhengzhi de jizhong tixian*]. *Guangming Daily* 光明日報. April 7, 2009, 3.

Fang, Tony. (2011). "Yin Yang: A New Perspective on Culture." *Management and Organization Review* 8: 25–50.

Fenellosa, Ernest. (2009). "The Coming Fusion of East and West." In *The Chinese Written Character as a Medium for Poetry: A Critical Edition*. Edited by Haun Saussy. 153–65. New York, NY: Fordham University Press.

Feng Congde 封從德. (2013). *A Tiananmen Journal* [六四日記 增訂版 *Liusi riji zengding ban*]. Hong Kong: Hong Kong Standard Press.

Feng Deping 封德平. (2014). "The Contemporary Significance of Confucianism and Its Modern Transformation." [儒家思想的当代意义及其现代性转化 *Rujia sixiang di dang dai yiyi ji qi xiandai xing zhuang hua*]. *Theoretical Review* [理论导刊] 12: 37–41.

Feng Lulu 冯璐璐. (2013). "A Personalization of the Crisis of Rationalism in Western Europe—A Study of Max Weber's Life and His Theoretical System." [西欧理性

主义危机的人格化体现: 马克斯·韦伯生平及其思想理论体系研究之一 *Xiou lixing zhuyi weiji de rengehua tixian—Makesi weibo shengping ji qi sixiang lilun tixi yanjiu zhi yi*]. *Journal of Shenyang University (Social Science Edition)* [沈阳大学学报(社会科学版)] 15: 645–650.

Ferguson, Niall. (2011). *Civilization: The West and the Rest.* London: Penguin Group.

Ferrari, G.R.F. (1997). "Strauss's Plato." *Arion: A Journal of Humanities and the Classics* 5: 36–65.

Fewsmith, Joseph. (1995). "Neoconservatism and the End of the Dengist Era." *Asian Survey* 35: 635–651.

———. (2001). *China Since Tiananmen: The Politics of Transition.* Cambridge, UK: Cambridge University Press.

Fitzgerald, John and Sechin Y.S. Chien, eds. (2006). *The Dignity of Nations: Equality, Competition, and Honor in East Asian Nationalism.* Hong Kong: Hong Kong University Press.

Fleming, Katie. (2006). "The Use and Abuse of Antiquity: The Politics and Morality of Appropriation." In *Classics and the Uses of Reception.* Edited by Charles Martindale and Richard F. Thomas. 127–37. Malden, MA, and Oxford, UK: Blackwell Publishing.

Fogel, Joshua A. and Peter Zarrow, eds. (1997). *Imagining the People: Chinese Intellectuals and the Concept of Citizenship, 1890–1920.* Armonk, NY: M.E. Sharpe, Inc.

Fontana, Michela. (2011). *Matteo Ricci: A Jesuit in the Ming Court.* Lanham, MD: Rowman & Littlefield.

Frazer, Michael L. (2006). "Esotericism Ancient and Modern: Strauss Contra Straussianism on the Art of Political Philosophical Writing." *Political Theory* 34: 33–61.

Froese, Katrin. (2008). "The Art of Becoming Human: Morality in Kant and Confucius." *Dao: A Journal of Comparative Philosophy* 7: 257–268.

Fu Qilin 傅其林. (2015). "The Reception of Mao's 'Talks at the Yan'an Forum on Literature and Art' in English-language Scholarship." *Comparative Literature and Culture* 17.12 http://docs.lib.purdue.edu/clcweb/vol17/iss1/12.

Fukuyama, Francis. (1989). "The End of History?" *The National Interest* 16: 3–18.

———. (1992). *The End of History and the Last Man.* New York, NY, and London: Free Press.

Fung, Edmund. (2010). *The Intellectual Foundations of Chinese Modernity: Cultural and Political Thought in the Republican Era.* New York, NY, and Cambridge, UK: Cambridge University Press.

Gan Yang 甘阳. (1990). "The Ideal of Freedom: Negative Aspects of the May Fourth Tradition" [自由的理念: 五四传统之阙失面 *Ziyou de linian: Wusi chuantong zhi queshi mian*]. In *Reverberations of History* [歷史的反響 *Lishi de fanxiang*]. Edited by Liu Qingfeng 刘青峰. 135–153. Hong Kong: 三联书店San-lian Press.

———. (1997). "Anti-democratic liberalism or democratic liberalism?" [反民主的自由主义还是民主的自由主义 *Fan mínzhu de ziyou zhuyi haishi minzhu de ziyou zhuyi?*]. *Twenty-First Century* [二十一世纪] 2: 4–17.

———. (2002). "Strauss as a Political Philosopher: The Revival of Classical Conservative Political Philosophy" [政治哲人施特劳斯*Zhengzhi zheren shitelaosi*]. In the introduction to *Leo Strauss, Natural Right and History* (Chinese Version). ii–xx. Hong Kong: University of Oxford Press.

———. (2003). *The Political Philosopher Leo Strauss*. [政治哲人施特劳斯 *Zhengzhi zheren Shitelaosi*]. Hong Kong: Niujin University Press.

———. (2005). "Unifying the Three Traditions." In *New Era: The Merging of Three Chinese Traditions*. Lecture presented at Tsinghua University on May 12, 2005. Introduction and Translation by David Ownby. Available at https://www.readingthechinadream.com/gan-yang-tongsantong-chapter-1.html.

———. (2007). *Inheritance of Three Traditions* [通三统*Tong San Tong*]. Beijing: Sanlian Press.

———. (2012). "Freed from Western Superstition" [从西方迷信中解放出来 *Cong xifang mixin zhong jiefang chulai*]. Available at http://www.xinfajia.net/9404.html.

———, ed. (2014). *Strauss and Classical Studies* [施特劳斯与古典研究 *Shitelaosi yu gudian yanjiu*]. Beijing: Sanlian Press.

Gan Yang and Liu Xiaofeng. (2014). "The Cultural Positioning and Self-Betrayal of Peking University." Introduction and Translation by Matthew Dean. Available at https://www.readingthechinadream.com/gan-yang-and-liu-xiaofeng-on-yenching-academy.html.

Gan Yang, Liu Xiaofeng, and Zhang Zhilin. (2012b). "Classical Western studies in China." Trans. Michael Chang. *Chinese Cross Currents*. 9: 98–114.

Gan Yang. (1998). "A Critique of Chinese Conservatism in the 1990s." Translated by Xudong Zhang. *Social Text* 55: 45–66.

Gao Shankui高山奎. (2013). "Strauss and Chinese Problems." [施特劳斯与中国问题 *Shitelaosi yǔ zhōngguó wèntí*]. *Theoretical Investigations* [理论探讨 *Lilun Tantao*]. 2: 54–58.

Gao, S. and A. J. Walayat. (2021). "Confucianism and Democracy: Four Models of Compatibility." *Journal of Chinese Humanities* 6: 213–234.

Garcia, B. (2014). "Aristotle Among the Jesuits: A Note Concerning a Recent Publication." *Rivista Di Filosofia Neo-Scolastica* 106: 177–194.

George, J. (2005). "Leo Strauss, Neoconservatism and US Foreign Policy: Esoteric Nihilism and the Bush Doctrine." *International Politics* 42: 174–202.

Gernet, Jacques. (2010). "Language, Mathematics, Rationality. Categories or Functions Concerning China and Our Age-Old Traditions." *Chinese Studies in History* 43: 17–31.

Gerth, H. H. and C. Wright Mills, eds. (2012). *Max Weber: Essays in Sociology*. London: Ulan Press. 1970.

Ghils, Paul. (2013). "The Essential Tension: Rational and Reasonable in Science and Philosophy." *Transdisciplinary Journal of Engineering & Science* 4: 40–56.

Glover, Jonathan. (2000). *Humanity: A Moral History of the Twentieth Century*. New Haven, CT: Yale University Press.

Goldman, Merle, ed. (2002). *An Intellectual History of Modern China*. Cambridge, UK: Cambridge University Press.

Gong Weibin 龔維斌. (2010). "Promoting Full Social Mobility and Forming Reasonable Social Stratification." [促進充分社會流動, 形成合理社會分層 Cùjìn chōngfèn shèhuì liúdòng, xíngchéng hélǐ shèhuì fēncéng]. *Zhejiang Daily* [浙江日報]. August 30, 2010. 7th edition.

Goodman, Howard L. and Anthony Grafton. (1990). "Ricci, the Chinese, and the Toolkits of Textualists." *Asia Major* 3: 95–148.

Goody, Jack. (1993). "East and West: Rationality in Review." *Ethnos: Journal of Anthropology* 58: 6–36.

———. (1996). *The East in the West*. Cambridge, UK: Cambridge University Press.

Gould, R. (2014). "Conservative in Form, Revolutionary in Content: Rethinking World Literary Canons in an Age of Globalization." *Canadian Review of Comparative Literature* 41: 270–66.

Graham, Angus. (1965). "'Being' in Linguistics and Philosophy: A Preliminary Inquiry." *Foundations of Language* 1: 223–231.

———. (1967). "Chinese Logic." *Encylopedia.com*. Available at https://www.encyclopedia.com/humanities/encyclopedias-almanacs-transcripts-and-maps/chinese-logic.

———. (1989). *Disputers of the Tao*. La Salle, IL: Open Court.

———. (2000). "The Place of Reason in the Chinese Philosophical Tradition." In *The Legacy of China*. Edited by R. Dawson. 28–56. Oxford: Oxford University Press.

Gransow, Bettina. (2003). "The Social Sciences in China." In *The Cambridge History of Science*. Volume 7: *The Modern Social Sciences*. Edited by Theodore M. Porter and Dorothy Ross. 498–514. Cambridge, UK: Cambridge University Press.

Gu Zhun 顾准. (1981). "Christianity, Greek Thought and Historian Culture" [基督教、希腊思想和史官文化 Jidujiao, xila sixiang he shiguan wenhua]. *Academic Journal of Jinyang* [晋阳学刊] 4: 10–19.

———. (1982). *The City-state Constitution of Greece* [希腊城邦制度 Xila chengbang zhidu]. Beijing: China Social Sciences Press. Available at http://www.aisixiang.com/data/97562-2.html.

————. (1994). *Collected Works* [顾准全集 *Gu Zhun quanji*]. Guiyang: Guizhou People's Press.

————. (1997). *Diary of Gu Zhun* [顾准日记 *Gu Zhun riji*]. Beijing: China Social Sciences Press.

Gu, Edward X. (2001). "Who Was Mr. Democracy? The May Fourth Discourse of Populist Democracy and the Radicalization of Chinese Intellectuals (1915–1922)." *Modern Asian Studies* 35: 589–621.

Gunn, Edward. (1991). "The Rhetoric of *He Shang*: From Cultural Criticism to Social Act." *Bulletin of Concerned Asian Scholars* 23: 14–22.

Guo Chongchen 郭冲辰, Chen Fan 陈凡, and Fan Chunfa 樊春华. (2001). "The Expansion of Instrumental Rationality and the Absence of Value Rationality—A Philosophical Review of American Hegemonism" [工具理性的膨胀与价值理性的缺失— 关于美国霸权主义的哲学审视 *Gongju lixing de pengzhang yu jiazhi lixing de queshi—guanyu meiguo baquan zhuyi de zhexue shenshi*]. *Journal of Northeastern University, Social Science Edition* [东北大学学报, 社会科学版] 4: 235–237.

Guo Jiping 国纪平. (2019). "There is no 'Thucydides trap' in the world. Comment on the danger of some Americans' strategic misunderstanding" [世上本无"修昔底德陷阱"— 评美国一些人战略迷误的危险 *Shishang ben wu "xiusidide xianjing"—ping Meiguo yixie ren zhanlue miwu de weixian*]. *People's Daily*. June 18, 2019. Available at http://www.xinhuanet.com/2019-06/17/c_112463 5884.htm.

Guo Shengming. 郭圣铭. (1980). "The Historical Heritage of Ancient Greece (Part 2)" [古希腊的史学遗产(下) *Gu xila de shixue yichan (xia)*]. *Journal of East China Normal University, Natural Science Edition.* [华东师范大学学报, 自然科学版] 4: 76–80.

Halberstam, J. (1988). "From Kant to Auschwitz." *Social Theory and Practice* 14: 41–54.

Han Xuebing 韩薛兵. (2012). "Discussion and Reflection on the Economic Attributes of Athens in the Classical Period in Academic Circles." [学术界关于古典时期雅典经济属性的探讨及反思 *Xueshu jie guanyu gudian shiqi yadian jingji shuxing de tantao ji fansi*]. Master's Thesis, Liaocheng University.

Hankins, James. (2017). "Reforming Elites the Confucian Way." *American Affairs* 1: 45–57.

————. (2019). *Virtue Politics: Soulcraft and Statecraft in Renaissance Italy.* Cambridge, MA: Harvard University Press.

————. (2020). "Regime Change with Chinese Characteristics." *American Affairs* 6: 149–66.

Hansen, Chad. (1983). *Language and Logic in Ancient China.* Ann Arbor, MI: University of Michigan Press.

Hansen, Mogens H. (2006). "Review of Loren J. Samons, *What's Wrong with Democracy?: From Athenian Practice to American Worship* (Berkeley: University of California Press, 2004)." In *Bryn Mawr Classical Review.* Available at https://bmcr.brynmawr.edu/2006/2006.01.32/.

Hansen, Mogens H. and Thomas Heine Nielsen. (2004). *An Inventory of Archaic and Classical Poleis.* Oxford, UK: Oxford University Press.

Hao Chang. (1971). *Liang Ch'i-ch'ao and Intellectual Transition in China, 1890–1907.* Cambridge, MA: Harvard University Press.

Hao Yuan 郝苑 and Meng Jianwei 孟建伟. (2012). "Logos and Nous: Two Origins of Western Scientific Culture." [逻各斯与努斯：西方科学文化的两个原点 *Luogesi yu nusi: Xifang kexue wenhua de liang ge yuandian*]. *Journal of Renmin University of China* [中国人民大学 学报] 2: 124–131.

Harbsmeier, Christoph. (2001). "May Fourth Linguistic Orthodoxy and Rhetoric: Some Informal Comparative Notes." In *New Terms for New Ideas: Western Knowledge & Lexical change in Late Imperial China.* Edited by Michael Lacknerm, Iwo Amelung, and Joachim Kurtz. 373–410. Leiden: Brill Academic Publishers.

Harding, Phillip. (1995). "Athenian Foreign Policy in the Fourth Century." *Klio* 77: 105–125.

Hardwick, Lorna and Carol Gillespie. (2007). *Classics in Post-Colonial Worlds.* Oxford: Oxford University Press.

Harrison, Thomas. (2007). "Religion and the Rationality of the Greek city." In *Rethinking Revolutions in Ancient Greece.* Edited by Simon Goldhill and Robin Osborne. 124–140. Cambridge, UK: Cambridge University Press.

He Baogang. (2012). "Four Models of the Relationship Between Confucianism and Democracy." In *Contemporary Chinese Political Thought.* Edited by Fred Dallmayr and Tingyang Zhao. 131–151. Lexington, KY: University Press of Kentucky.

He Guanghu 何光沪. (1989). "Love is What This World Needs Most—Reading Liu Xiaofeng's 'Salvation and Happiness.'" [这个世界最需要爱— 读刘小枫《拯救与逍遥》 *Zhege shijie zui xuyao ai: du liu xiaofeng "zhengjiu yu xiaoyao"*]. In *Du Shu* 6: 5–17.

He Xin 何新. (2013). *Greek Pseudo-History.* [希腊伪史考 *Xila wei shi kao*]. Tongxin: Tongxin Publishing House.

———. (2015). *A Continuation of Greek Pseudo-History.* [希腊伪史续考 *Xila wei shi xu kao*]. Yanshi: Yanshi Publishing House.

He Yinan. (2020). "China's Political Trajectory and Foreign Relations under the Influence of National Identity." *The ASAN Forum.* July–August 2020. 8(4). Available at https://theasanforum.org/chinas-political-trajectory-and-foreign-relations-under-the-influence-of-national-identity/.

Heinaman, Robert. (1988). "Eudaimonia and Self-Sufficiency in the Nicomachean Ethics." *Phronesis* 33:31–53.

Hesk, Jon. (2000). *Deception and Democracy in Classical Athens.* Cambridge, UK: Cambridge University Press.

Hindess, Barry. (1992). "Rationality and Modern Society." *Sociological Theory* 9: 216–27.

Hon Tze-Ki. (2015). *The Allure of the Nation: The Cultural and Historical Debates in Late Qing and Republican China. Ideas, History, and Modern China.* Boston, MA: Brill.

Honneth, Axel. (1987). "Enlightenment and Rationality." Translated by Jeremy Gaines. *The Journal of Philosophy* 84: 692–699.

Horkheimer, Max, and Theodor W Adorno. (2002). *Dialectic of Enlightenment: Philosophical Fragments.* Edited by Gunzelin Schmid Noerr and translated by Edmund Jephcott. Stanford, CA: Stanford University Press.

Hosne, Ana Carolina. (2015). "Jesuit Reflections on their Overseas Missions." *ReVista (Cambridge)* 14: 56–57.

Hou Dianqin 侯典芹. (2005). "On the Concept of Harmonious Society in Plato's 'Utopia.'" [论柏拉图《理想国》的和谐社会思想 *Lun Bolatu "Lixiangguo" de hexie shesui sixiang*]. *Journal of Inner Mongolia University for Nationalities, Social Science Edition* [内蒙古民族大学学报社会科学版] 5.

Hoyt, Mei Wu. (2006). "John Dewey's legacy to China and the problems in Chinese society." *Transnational Curriculum Inquiry* 3: 12–25.

Hsia, Ronnie Po-chia. (2010). *A Jesuit in the Forbidden City: Matteo Ricci, 1552–1610.* Oxford, UK: Oxford University Press.

Hu Ping 胡平. (2017)."'The Best Possibility' and 'The Most Possibly Good'—Plato's 'Republic' and Aristotle's 'Politics.'" ['最好的可能'与'最可能的好'— 柏拉图理想国与亚里士多德政治学 *"Zui hao de keneng" yu "zui keneng de hao"—bolatu "lixiang guo" yu Yalishiduo de "zhengzhi xue"*]. Independent Chinese PEN Center. Available at https://www.chinesepen.org/blog/archives/79970.

Hu Zhongping 扈中平. (1985). "Plato's Educational Ideal as Harmonious Development—Notes on the *Republic.*" [柏拉图和谐发展的教育思想—读理想国札记 *Bolatu hexie fazhan de jiaoyu sixiang—du lixiang guo zhaji*]. *Journal of Social Science of Hunan Normal University* [湖南师范大学社会科学学报] 2: 98–101.

Huang Yang 黄洋. (1995). "The Establishment of Private Ownership of Ancient Greek Land and the Formation of City-State System." [古代希腊土地私有制的确立与城邦制度的形成 *Gudai xila tudi siyouzhi di queli yu chengbang zhidu de xingcheng*]. *Fudan University Journal, Social Science Edition.* [复旦学报(社会科学版)] 1: 46–51.

———. (2009). "Classical Greek Idealization as a Cultural Phenomenon." [古典希腊理想化: 作为一种文化现象的 "Hellenism," *Gudian xila lixiang hua: Zuowei*

yi zhong wenhua xianxiang de Hellenism]. *Chinese Social Science* [中国社会科学]
2: 52–67.

———. (2018). "Classical Studies in China." In *Receptions of Greek and Roman Antiquity in East Asia*. Edited by Almut-Barbara Renger and Xin Fan. 363–75. Leiden: Brill.

Hui, Keith. (2014). "Could Plato's *Republic* Work in China?" *Philosophy Now* 101: 14–15.

Humphreys, Sarah C. and Rudolf G. Wagner, eds. (2013). *Modernity's Classics: Ruptures and Reconfigurations*. Heidelberg: Springer Nature.

Jiang Dongxian. (2014). "Searching for Chinese Autonomy: Leo Strauss in the Chinese Context." Masters Dissertation, Duke University.

Jiang Qing. (2003). *Political Confucianism: The Shift, Character and Development of Contemporary Confucianism* [政治儒学：当代儒学的转向、特指与发展 *Zhengzhi ruxue: dangdai ruxue de zhuanxiang tezhi yu fazhan*]. New Taipei City: Yangzhengtang Wenhua.

Jiang Yi-Huah. (2018). "Confucian Political Theory in Contemporary China." *Annual Review of Political Science* 21: 155–73.

Jin Canrong 金灿荣 and ZhaoYuanliang 赵远良. (2014). "Exploring and Taking Advantage of Favorable Conditions to Establish a New Model of Major-Country Relations between China and the United States." [构建中美轩型大国关系的条件採余 *Goujian zhong mei xuan xing daguo guanxi de tiaojian cai yu*]. *World Economics and Politics* [世界经济与政治] 3: 50–68.

Jin Guantao, Fan Hongye, and Liu Qingfeng. (1996). *Chinese Studies in the History and Philosophy of Science and Technology*. Dordrecht: Kluwer Academic.

Jin Guantao 金观涛 and Liu Qingfeng 刘青峰. (1986). "Why didn't the ancient Chinese philosophers discover the syllogism? A Comparative Study of Aristotle and Ancient Chinese Philosophers." [为什么中国古代哲学家没有发现三段论—亚里士多德和中国古代哲学家的比较研究 *Weishenme zhongguo gudai zhexue jia meiyou faxian sanduanlun—yalishiduo de he zhongguo gudai zhexue jia de bijiao yanjiu*]. *Researches in Dialectics of Nature* [自然辩证法研究] 18: 74–80.

———. (2005) "From 'Republicanism' to 'Democracy': China's Selective Adoption and Reconstruction of Modern Western Political Concepts (1840–1924)." *History of Political Thought* 26: 467–501.

Jin Nan 晋楠. (2010). "The Pursuit of Order and Harmony—A Comparison of the Concepts of Harmonious Society in Confucius and Plato." [秩序与和谐的追寻—孔子与柏拉图和谐社会构想之比较 *Zhixu yu hexie de zhuixun—kongzi yu bolatu hexie shehui gouxiang zhi bijiao*]. Master's degree at Hunan University.

Ju Naiqi 巨乃岐 and Xing Runchuan 邢润川. (2005). "On Technical Rationality and Its Criticism." [试论技术理性及其批判 *Shilun jishu lixing ji qi pipan*]. *Journal of*

Northeastern University, Social Science Edition [东北大学学报, 社会科学版] 7(3): 172–175.

Jullien, François. (2002). "Did Philosophers Have to Become Fixated on Truth?" Translated by Jane Lloyd. *Critical Inquiry* 28: 803–824.

Kainulainen, J. (2018). "Virtue and Civic Values in Early Modern Jesuit Education." *Journal of Jesuit Studies* 5: 530–548.

Kant, Immanuel. (1964). *Critique of Practical Reason*. Translated by H. J. Paton. New York, NY: Harper and Row.

———. (1991). "An Answer to the Question: 'What is Enlightenment?'" In *Kant: Political Writings*. Edited by H.S. Reiss. 54–60. Cambridge, UK: Cambridge University Press.

———. (2017). *Kant: The Metaphysics of Morals*. United Kingdom: Cambridge University Press.

Kasimis, Demetra. (2016). "Plato's Open Secret." *Contemporary Political Theory* 15: 339–357.

Kaufman, Alison A. (2007). "One Nation Among Many: Foreign Models in the Constitutional Thought of Liang Qichao." PhD Dissertation, University of California, Berkeley.

Kim, Sungmoon. (2017) "Pragmatic Confucian Democracy: Rethinking the Value of Democracy in East Asia." *Journal of Politics* 79: 237–49.

Kirkendall, J.A. (2017). "The Well-Ordered Heart: Confucius on Harmony, Music, and Ritual." Unpublished paper. Available at https://s3.wp.wsu.edu/uploads/sites/998/2018/11/JensenKirkendall-TheWellOrderedHeart.pdf.

Klosko, G. (1986). "The 'Straussian' Interpretation of Plato's 'Republic.'" *History of Political Thought* 7: 275–293.

Knight, Nick. (2006). *Marxist Philosophy in China: From Qu Qiubai to Mao Zedong, 1923–1945*. Dordrecht, Netherlands: Springer.

Kristoff, Nicholas D. (1989). "China Calls TV Tale Subversive." *New York Times*. October 2, 1989. 13.

Kuhn, Thomas S. (1970). "Notes on Lakatos." *PSA 1970* [*sic*]. 137–146.

Laks, André. (2013). "Phenomenon and Reference: Revisiting Parmenides, Empedocles, and the Problem of Rationalization," in *Modernity's Classics: Ruptures and Reconfigurations*. Edited by Sarah C. Humphreys and Rudolph G. Wagner. 165–86. Heidelberg: Springer Nature.

Lam Chi-ming. 林志明. (2014). "Confucian Rationalism." *Educational Philosophy and Theory* 46: 1450–1461.

Lane, Melissa. (2009). "Comparing Greek and Chinese Political Thought: The Case of Plato's *Republic*." *Journal of Chinese Philosophy* 36: 585–601.

Lang, Berel. (1990). *Act and Idea in the Nazi Genocide.* Chicago, IL: University of Chicago Press.

Lash, Scott. (2009). "Afterword: In Praise of the A Posteriori: Sociology and the Empirical." *European Journal of Social Theory* 12: 175–187.

Lau Tuenyu and Lo Yuet-keung. (1991). "*Heshang* (River Elegy) A Television Orchestration of a New Ideology in China." *Asian Journal of Communication* 1: 73–102.

Lear, Jonathan. (2017). *Wisdom Won from Illness.* Cambridge, MA: Harvard University Press.

Lee, Desmond, trans. & ed. (2003). *Plato: The Republic.* London, UK: Penguin Classics.

Lee, Theresa. (2007). "Liang Qichao and the Meaning of Citizenship: Then and Now." *History of Political Thought* 28: 305–327.

Leighton, Christopher. (2015). "Venture Communist: Gu Zhun in Shanghai, 1949–1952." In *The Capitalist Dilemma in China's Communist Revolution.* Edited by Sherman Cochran. 119–147. Ithaca, NY: Cornell East Asia Program.

Leonard, Mark. (2008). *What does China Think?* New York, NY: Public Affairs.

Levenson, Joseph R. (1953). *Liang Ch'i Ch'ao and the Mind of Modern China.* Cambridge, MA: Harvard University Press.

Li Baibai 李白白. (2007). "On the Separation and Integration of Instrumental Reason and Value Reason." [论工具理性和价值理性的分疏和整合 *Lun gongju lixing he jiazhi lixing de fen shu he zhenghe*]. *Journal of Xinyang Normal University, Philosophy and Social Sciences Edition* [信阳师范学院学报, 哲学社会科学版] 27: 30–32.

Li Changlin 李长林. (1984a). "Thucydides and the 'History of the Peloponnesian War'" [修昔底德和伯罗奔尼撒战争史 *Xiuxidide he boluobennisa zhanzheng shi*]. *History Teaching* [历史教学] 1: 44–47.

———. (1984b). "Two Issues Concerning the Evaluation of Thucydides's View of History" [关于修昔底德历史观评价的两个问题 *Guanyu xiuxidide lishi guan pingjia de liangge wenti*]. *Journal of Historiography* [史学史研究] 3: 51–54.

Li Cheng and Eve Cary. (2011). "The Last Year of Hu's Leadership: Hu's to Blame?" *Jamestown Foundation: China Brief* 11(23). December 20, 2011. Available at: https://jamestown.org/program/the-last-year-of-hus-leadership-hus-to-blame/.

Li Chengwei 李长伟. (2008). "The Educational Truth in 'Noble Lies'" ['高贵谎言' 中的教育真相 *Gaogui huangyan' zhong de jiaoyu zhenxiang*]. *Journal of Educational Studies* [教育学报] 4: 80–87.

Li Chengyang. (2006). "The Confucian Ideal of Harmony." *Philosophy East and West* 56: 583–603.

Li Hui. (2002). "Jesuit Missionaries and the Transmission of Christianity and European Knowledge in China." *Emory Endeavors in World History* 4. Available at http://history.emory.edu/home/undergraduate/endeavors-journal/volume-4.html.

Li Jianming 李剑鸣. (2011). "Between Athens and Rome: Classical Tradition and the Establishment of the American Republic" [在雅典和罗马之间: 古典传统与美利坚共和国的创建 *Zai yadian he luoma zhi jian: Gudian chuantong yu meilijian gongheguo de chuangjian*]. *Journal of Historical Science* [史学月刊] 9: 108–124.

Li Jin. (2003). "The Core of Confucian Learning." *American Psychologist* 58: 146–47.

Li Junpeng. (2017). "The Making of Liberal Intellectuals in Post-Tiananmen China." PhD Dissertation, Columbia University.

Li Junyin. 李骏寅. (2019). "On Leo Strauss's Classical Rationalism." [论列奥. 施特劳斯的古典理性主义 *Lun lieao shitelaosi de gudian lixing zhuyi*]. Master's Thesis, Sociology, Habin Engineering University.

Li Mingkun. (2012). "The Quarrel of Revelation and Philosophy in Leo Strauss's *Natural Right and History*." [自然權利和歷史中的啟示與哲學之爭 *Ziran quanli he lishi zhong de qishi yu zhexue zhizheng*]. *The Chinese Journal of Classical Studies* [古典研究 *Gudian Yanjiu*] 3(1): 69–88.

Li, P. P. (2008). "Toward a geocentric framework of trust: An application to organizational trust." *Management and Organization Review* 4: 413–439.

Li Peilin 李培林. (2005). "Talking about Social Stratification." [話說社會分層 *Huashuo shehui fenceng*]. *Zhejiang Daily* [浙江日報]. April 11, 2005.

Li Qiang 李强. (2003). "Does Social Stratification Do More Harm than Good?" [社會分層弊大于利嗎? *Shehui fenceng bi dayu li ma?*]. *Development Herald* [發展導報]. April 11, 2003.

Li Wuzhuang 李武裝 and Liu Shuguang 刘曙光. (2013). "The Critical Logic of Western Philosophy and the Rationalism of the Human Spirit." [西方哲学的理性主义批判逻辑与人类精神的理性主义优位诉求 *Xifang zhexue de lixing zhuyi pipan luoji yu renlei jingshen de lixing zhuyi you wei suqiu*]. *Journal of Huaqiao University, Philosophy & Social Sciences* [华侨大学学报, 哲学社会科学版] 3: 82–90.

Li Yongcheng 李永成. (2017). "Domestic Politics, Foreign Policy and American Diplomatic Lies—Some Issues Concerning the Development of Sino-US Relations" [国内政治、对外政策与美国外交谎言—兼及发展中美关系的若干问题 *Guonei zhengzhi, duiwai zhengce yu meiguo waijiao huangyan—jian ji fazhan zhong mei guanxi de ruogan wenti*]. *Sohu*. Available at https://www.sohu.com/a/132195362_618422.

Li Yongyi. (2014). "A New Incarnation of Latin in China." *Amphora* 11. Available at https://classicalstudies.org/amphora/new-incarnation-latin-china-yongyi-li.

Li Yunqin 李韵琴. (1989). "Analysis of the Main Reasons of Greek Colonial Movement in the Eighth-Sixth Century BC World History." [试析公元前八—六世纪希腊殖民运动的主要原因 *Shi xi gongyuan qian ba—liu shiji xila zhimin yundong de zhuyao yuanyin*]. *World History* [世界历史] 4: 112–121.

Li Zhiyuan 李致远. (2010). "The Prelude to the Gorgias." [高尔吉亚的开场 *Gaoerjiya de kaichang*]. *The Chinese Journal of Classical Studies* [古典研究 *Gudian Yanjiu*] 1: 15–28.

Li, Eric X. (2012). "Why China's Political Model Is Superior." *New York Times*. https://www.nytimes.com/2012/02/16/opinion/why-chinas-political-model-is-superior.html.

Li Hao and Gao Mingming. (2005). "Benevolence and Justice: A Comparison of the *Analects* of Confucius and the Republic of China." *Journal of Wuyi University (Social Science Edition)*, 1.

Li, S. (2009). "The Art of Misreading: An Analysis of the Jesuit 'Fables' in Late Ming China." In *Translating China*. Edited by Xuanmin Luo and Yuanjian He. 71–94. Bristol, UK: Multilingual Matters.

Liang Qichao 梁启超. (1978). *Collected Essays from the Ice-drinker's Studio*. [飲冰室合集. *Yin bing shi heji*]. Taipei: Zhonghua Press.

———. (1998). *Discourse on the New Citizen*. [新民说 *Xinmin shuo*]. Zhongzhou: Zhongzhou Ancient Books Publishing House.

———. (1999). *Collected Works of Liang Qichao*. [梁启超全集 *Liang Qichao Quanji*]. Beijing: Beijing Publishing House.

Liao Shenbai 廖申白. (1999). "The Position of Fraternity in Aristotle's *Ethics*." [友爱在亚里士多德伦理学中的地位 *You'ai zai Yalishiduo de lunli xue hong di diwei*]. *Philosophical Researches* [哲学研究] 5: 55–61.

Lilla, Mark. (2010). "Reading Leo Strauss in Beijing." *The New Republic*. Available https://newrepublic.com/article/79747/reading-leo-strauss-in-beijing-china-marx.

Lin Da 林达. (2003). "A Comparison of Musical Thoughts in *The Republic* and the *Analects* of Confucius." ["理想国"和"论语"中的音乐思想之比较 *'Lixiangguo' he 'Lunyu' zhong de yinyue sixiangzhi bijiao*]. *Symphony: Journal of Xi'an Conservatory of Music* [交响-西安音乐学院学报] 4.

Lin Qifu 林奇富 and Dong Cunsheng 董存胜. (2006). "Rethinking the Limitations of Classical Democracy—Analysis of the City-State Democracy of Ancient Athens." [反思古典民主的局限性—以古雅典的城邦民主为分析对象 *Fansi gudian minzhu de juxian xing—yi gu yadian de chengbang minzhu wei fenxi duixiang*]. *Journal of Fujian Provincial Committee Party School of CPC* [中共福建省委党校学报] 12: 23–25.

Liu Chenguang 劉晨光. (2006). "Aristotle's Political Science." [亞里士多德的「政治科學」 *Yalishiduo de de 'zhengzhi kexue'*]. *21st Century Online Edition* [二十一世紀] 2006.4.29. Available at https://www.cuhk.edu.hk/ics/21c/media/online /0511039.pdf.

Liu Dong. 刘 东. (2003). "The Weberian View and Confucianism." Translated by Gloria Davies. *East Asian History* 25–26: 194–99.

Liu Hanzhen. (2015). "Contemporary New Confucianism and the Ancient European Philosophy: Analysis and Comparison." *Studia Europejskie-Studies in European Affairs* 73: 115–136.

Liu Huiyang 刘辉扬. (1981). "'Man is Born a Political Animal'—Review of Aristotle's Political Thought." [人天生是政治的动物'亚里士多德政治思想述评*Ren tiansheng shi zhengzhi de dongwu; Yalishiduo de zhengzhi sixiang shuping*]. *Journal of Yangzhou Teachers College, Social Science Edition* [扬州师院学报, 社会科学版] 2: 91–95.

Liu Jinyu 刘津瑜. (2018). "Translating and Rewriting Western Classics in China (1920s–1930s): The Case of the Xueheng Journal." In *Receptions of Greek and Roman Antiquity in East Asia*. Edited by Almut-Barbara Renger and Xin Fan. 91–111. Leiden: Brill.

Liu Jun. 刘军. (2001). "Restless Chinese Nationalist Currents in the 1980s and the 1990s: A Comparative Reading of River Elegy and China Can Say No." In *Chinese Nationalism in Perspective: Historical and Recent Cases*. Edited by C.X. George Wei and Xiaoyuan Liu. 205–231. Westport, CT: Praeger.

Liu Kejie 刘柯杰. (2001). "Review and Prospect of Western Rationalism." [西方理性主义的回顾和展望 *Xifang lixing zhuyi de huigu he zhanwang*]. *Journal of Tianjin University of Commerce* [天津商学院学报] 5: 10–12.

Liu Qingping 刘清平. (2005). "Do we need 'instrumental rationality criticism'?" [我们需要的是"工具理性批判"吗? *Women xuyao de shi 'gongju lixing pipan' ma?*]. *Gansu Social Sciences* [甘肃社会科学] 4: 22–24.

Liu Wentai. (1998). "Rational Thinking in the City-State Crisis: A Review of Plato's 'Utopia.'" [城邦危机中的理性思考— 评柏拉图的"理想国" *Chengbang weiji zhong de lixing sikao—ping Bolatu de "lixiang gua"*]. *Academic Forum of Nan Du (Philosophy and Social Science Edition)* [南都学坛哲学社会科学版] 18.4.

Liu Xiaofeng 刘小枫, ed. (2002a). *Strauss and Ancient Political Philosophy*. [施特劳斯与古典政治哲学 *Shitelaosi yu gudian zhengzhi zhexue*]. Shanghai, Shanghai SDX Press.

———, trans. (2003). *Plato's Symposium*. [会饮 *Huiyin*]. Beijing: Huaxia Press.

———. (2000a). "An Esoteric and Exoteric Reading of Nietzsche." [尼采的微言大义 *Nícai de weiyan dayi*]. Available at https://www.aisixiang.com/data/15745 .html.

———. (2000b). "Intellectuals' Cat Walk." [知識份子的貓步 Zhishi fenzi de maobu]. Available at http://reading.cersp.com/DeepRead/Learning/200511/87.html.

———. (2002b). *The Docility of the Hedgehog.* [刺猬的溫順 Ciwei de wenshun]. Shanghai, Shanghai Literature and Art Press.

———. (2007). "The Vain Tranquility of the Sage." [圣人的虚静 Shengren de xujing]. In his *Pick up the Cold Branches* [捡尽寒枝]. 219–254. Beijing: Huaxia Publishing House.

———. (2009a). "Strauss and China: Encounter of Two Classics." [施特劳斯与中国：古典心性的相逢 Shitelaosi yu Zhongguo: Gudian Xinxing de Xiangfeng]. *The Ideological Front* [思想战线] 35: 59–65. Available at https://www.aisixiang .com/data/26462.html.

———. (2009b). "Leo Strauss et la Chine: une recontre author de l'ethos classique." Translated by Joël Thoraval. *Extrême Orient, Extrême Occident*, 31: 141–54.

———. (2009c). "Strauss and the Philosophy of Enlightenment." [施特劳斯与启蒙哲学 (上) Shitelaosi yu qiméng zhexue shang]." *Journal of NorthWestern Normal University* [西北师范大学学报] 46.3: 1–9.

———. (2013). *Strauss's Pathmark.* [施特劳斯的路标 Shitelaosi de lubiao: Leo Strauss als Wegmarke]. Beijing: Huxia Publishing House.

———. (2015a). *Sino-Theology and the Philosophy of History: A Collection of Essays.* Translated by Leopold Leeb. Leiden: Brill.

———. (2015b). "Which Tradition of Classical Studies?" [古典学的何种传统 Gudianxue de hezhong chuantong]. *Critical News* [批评新闻] December 13, 2015. Available at https://www.thepaper.cn/newsDetail_forward_1303406.

Liu Xiaofeng 刘小枫 and Chen Guangchen 陳廣琛. (2018). "Leo Strauss and the Rebirth of Classics in China." In *Receptions of Greek and Roman Antiquity in East Asia.* Edited by Almut-Barbara Renger and Xin Fan. 219–236. Leiden: Brill.

Liu Xiaofeng 刘小枫, Gan Yang 甘阳, and Zhang Zhilin 张志林. (2012). "Classical Western Studies in China." [古典西学在中国 Gudian xixue zai zhongguo]. Translated by Michael Chang. *Chinese Cross Currents* [神州交流] 3: 98–114.

Liu Yi 刘怡. (2011). "Penetrating the 'Noble Lie.'" [刺破 '高贵的谎言' Cipo 'gaogui de huangyan']. *World Vision* [世界博览] 2. Available at https://www.xzbu.com /1/view-195983.htm.

Liu Yu. (2008). "The Intricacies of Accommodation: The Proselytizing Strategy of Matteo Ricci." *Journal of World History* 19: 465–87.

———. (2013). "The Complexities of a Stoic Breakthrough: Matteo Ricci's 'Ershiwu Yan' (Twenty-five Paragraphs)." *Journal of World History* 24: 823–47.

———. (2014). "Adapting Catholicism to Confucianism: Matteo Ricci's *Tianzhu Shiyi.*" *The European Legacy* 19: 43–59.

Liu Zehua and Liu Jianqing. (1996). "Civic Associations, Political Parties, and the Cultivation of Citizenship Consciousness in Modern China." *Chinese Studies in History* 29: 8–35.

Liu Zhen 刘臻. (2010). "A Classical Conception of Rational Englightenment—A Modern Interpretation of Plato's Allegory of the Cave and the Line" [一种古典的理性启蒙观— 对柏拉图"洞喻"和"线喻"的现代解读 *Yi zhong gudian de lixing qimeng guan—dui bolatu 'dongyu' he 'xianyu' de xiandai jiedu*]. *Journal of Shihezi University* [石河子大学学报] 24 (6): 69–71.

Liu, Henry C.K. (2003). "The Abduction of Modernity Part 3: Rule of law vs Confucianism." *The Asia Times*. July 24 2003. Available at http://large.stanford.edu /history/kaist/references/confucius/liu3/.

Liu, Lydia H. (1995). *Translingual Practice: Literature, National Culture, and Translated Modernity: China, 1900–1937*. Stanford, CA: Stanford University Press.

———. (1996). "Translingual Practice: The Discourse of Individualism between China and the West." In *Narratives of Agency: Self-making in China, India, and Japan*. Edited by Wimal Dissanayake. 1–35. Minneapolis, MN: University of Minnesota Press.

Lloyd, G.E.R. (1990). *Demystifying Mentalities*. Cambridge, UK: Cambridge University Press.

———. (2007). *Cognitive Variations: Reflections on the Unity and Diversity of the Human Mind*. New York, NY: Oxford University Press.

———. (2009). *Disciplines in the Making: Cross-Cultural Perspectives on Elites, Learning, and Innovation*. Oxford, UK: Oxford University Press.

———. (2014). *The Ideals of Inquiry: An Ancient History*. New York, NY: Oxford University Press.

———. (2017). *The Ambivalences of Rationality: Ancient and Modern Cross-Cultural Explorations*. Cambridge, UK: Cambridge University Press.

Lomanov, Alexander. (1998). "Religion and Rationalism in the Philosophy of Feng Youlan." *Monumenta Serica* 46: 323–41.

Lorenz, Hendrik. (2004). "Desire and Reason in Plato's *Republic*." *Oxford Studies in Ancient Philosophy* 27: 83–116.

Lu Jie 吕杰. (2012). "Democratic Conceptions and Regime Support among Chinese Citizens." *Asian Barometer* 66. Available at http://www.asianbarometer.org/pub lications//0709f5e8329f872c6d593f09ea5698ae.pdf.

Luo Xinggang 罗兴刚. (2012). "An Education of Love: Behind the 'Noble Lie'— Political Philosophy as the Original Ethics." [爱的教育: '高贵的谎言'背后— 政治哲学如何作为原初的伦理学 *Ai de jiaoyu: 'Gaogui de huangyan' beihou— zhengzhi zhexue ruhe zuowei yuanchu de lunli xue*]. *The Journal of Humanities* [人文杂志] 4: 35–40.

Luria, Alexander. (1976). *Cognitive Development: Its Cultural and Social Foundations.* Cambridge, MA: Harvard University Press.

Ma Chun-ling 马春玲 and Zhang Xiao-mi 张晓密. (2009). "The Origin of the Attention to Rationality and Emotion." [对理性和情感关注的起源 *Dui lixing he qinggan guanzhu de qiyuan*]. *Journal of Harbin University* [哈尔滨学院学报] 30: 15–19.

Ma Jinchen 马金辰 and Zhang Nan 张楠. (2021). "On the injustice in the ruling thought of Plato's Philosopher King." [论柏拉图哲学王统治思想中的非正义性]. *Journal of Inner Mongolia Electric University* [内蒙古电大学刊] 5.

Ma Shuyun 马树人. (1996). "The Role of Power Struggle and Economic Changes in the 'Heshang Phenomenon' in China." *Modern Asian Studies* 30: 29–50.

Mashaal, Samantha. (2019). "Plato's Party-State: Evaluating China's Political System through the Framework of the Republic." *Penn Journal of Philosophy, Politics & Economics* 14 (1): 6. Available at https://repository.upenn.edu/spice/vol14/iss1/6.

Mahood, G.H. (1971). "Socrates and Confucius: Moral Agents or Moral Philosophers?" *Philosophy East and West* 21: 177–188.

Makeham, John. (2003). "The Retrospective Creation of New Confucianism." In *New Confucianism: A Critical Examination.* Edited by John Makeham. 25–53. New York, NY: Palgrave Macmillan.

———. (2012). "Disciplining Tradition in Modern China: Two Case Studies." *History and Theory* 51: 89–104.

Mao Zedong. (1990). *Mao Zedong's early writings: 1912.6–1920.11.* [毛泽东早期文稿 *Mao Zedong zaoqi wengao*]. Zhangsha: Human Press.

———. (2005). *Mao Zedong on Dialectical Materialism: Writings on Philosophy, 1937.* Edited by Nick Knight. Armonk, NY: M.E. Sharpe, Inc.

Marchal, Kai. (2017). "Modernity, Tyranny, and Crisis: Leo Strauss in China." In *Carl Schmitt and Leo Strauss in the Chinese-Speaking World.* Edited by Marchal and Shaw. 173–96. Lanham, MD: Lexington Books.

Marchal, Kai and Carl K. Y. Shaw, eds. (2017). *Carl Schmitt and Leo Strauss in the Chinese-speaking World: Reorienting the Political.* Lanham, MD: Lexington Books.

Mardell, Jacob. (2017). "The 'Community of Common Destiny' in Xi Jinping's New Era. Building a 'community of common destiny' is the motivating force behind China's future foreign policy." *The Diplomat* Oct. 25, 2017. Available at https://thediplomat.com/2017/10/the-community-of-common-destiny-in-xi-jinpings-new-era/.

McDaniel, R. (1998). "The Nature of Inequality: Uncovering the Modern in Leo Strauss's Idealist Ethics." *Political Theory* 26: 317–345.

Melzer, Arthur M. (2014). *Philosophy Between the Lines: The Lost History of Esoteric Writing.* Chicago, IL: The University of Chicago Press.

Menand, Louis. (2018). "Francis Fukuyama Postpones the End of History." *The New Yorker* September 3, 2018.

Meng Xianping 孟宪清. (2011). "The Development and Substantive Tendency of Western Traditional Rationalism." [西方传统理性主义的发展和实体性倾向 Xifang chuantong lixing zhuyi de fa zhan he shiti xing qingxiang]. Journal of Yunnan University, Social Sciences Edition [云南大学学报, 社会科学版] 3: 35–41.

Menn, Stephen. (1992). "Aristotle and Plato on God as Nous and as the Good." The Review of Metaphysics 45: 543–573.

Metzger, T.A. (2005). A Cloud Across the Pacific: Essays on the Clash Between Chinese and Western Political Theories Today. Hong Kong: Chinese University Press.

Meynard, Thierry. (2013). "Aristotelian Ethics in the Land of Confucius: A Study of Vagnone's Western Learning on Personal Cultivation." Antiquorum Philosophia 7: 145–169.

Mi Chenfeng 米辰肇. (1995). "The Spread of Aristotle's Political Theory in China." Rivista Di Cultura Classica e Medioevale 37: 243–257.

Mi, Michael C. (1997). "The Spread of Aristotle's Political Theory in China." Political Theory 25: 249–257.

Moak, Ken. (2018). "Why China prefers its own ideology to US-style democracy." Asia Times April 4, 2018. Available at https://asiatimes.com/2018/04/china-prefers-ideology-us-style-democracy/.

Mommsen, Wolfgang. (2006). "Personal Conduct and Societal Change." In Max Weber, Rationality and Modernity. Edited by Sam Whimster and Scott Lash. 35–51. London and New York, NY: Routledge

Moody, P. R. (2008). "Rational Choice Analysis in Classical Chinese Political Thought: The 'Han Feizi.'" Polity 40: 95–119.

Moore, Kenneth R. (2009). "Platonic Myths and Straussian Lies: The Logic of Persuasion." Polis 26: 89–115.

Mori, Giuliano. (2020). "Natural theology and ancient theology in the Jesuit China mission." Intellectual History Review 30: 187–208.

Moss, Stephen. (2014). "Francis Fukuyama: 'Americans are not very good at nation-building.'" The Guardian October 14, 2014. Available at https://www.theguardian.com/books/2011/may/23/francis-fukuyama-americans-not-good-nation-building.

Müller-Lee, Andreas. (2018). "The Jesuit Mission to China and the Reception of Ancient Greek and Roman Culture in China and Korea." In Receptions of Greek and Roman Antiquity in East Asia. Edited by Almut-Barbara Renger and Xin Fan. 19–49. Leiden: Brill.

Mungello, David E. (1985). Curious Land: Jesuit Accommodation and the Origins of Sinology. Honolulu, HI: University of Hawaii Press.

———. (1994). The Chinese Rites Controversy: Its History and Meaning. Monumenta Serica 123. Beijing: Institut Monumenta Serica.

———. (2005). *The Great Encounter of China and the West, 1500–1800*. Lanham, MD: Rowman & Littlefield.

Murphy, Tim and Ralph Weber. (2010). "Confucianizing Socrates and Socratizing Confucius: On Comparing *Analects* 13:18 and the *Euthyphro*." *Philosophy East and West* 60.2: 187–206.

Mutschler, Fritz-Heiner. (2018). "Western Classics at Chinese Universities—and Beyond: Some Subjective Observations." In *Receptions of Greek and Roman Antiquity in East Asia*. Edited by Almut-Barbara Renger and Xin Fan. 430–444. Leiden: Brill.

Naddaf, Gerard. (2000). "Literary and Poetic Performance in Plato's Laws." *The Society for Ancient Greek Philosophy Newsletter* 312. Available at https://orb.binghamton.edu/sagp/312.

Nadon, Christopher. (2017). "Leo Strauss' Critique of the Political in a Sinophone Context." In *Carl Schmitt and Leo Strauss in the Chinese-Speaking World*. Edited by Marchal and Shaw. 151–172. Lanham, MD: Lexington Books.

Nails, Debra. (2012). "Plato's "Republic" in its Athenian Context." *History of Political Thought* 33: 1–23.

Ni, Peiman. (2011). "Classical Confucianism I: Confucius." In *The Oxford Handbook of World Philosophy*. Edited by Jay L. Garfield and William Edelglass. Oxford, UK: Oxford University Press.

Nie Minli 聂敏里. (2017). "The New Life of Classics: Political Imagination or Historical Critique?" [古典学的新生: 政治的想象, 抑或历史的批判? *Gudian xue de xinsheng: Zhengzhi de xiangxiang, yihuo lishi de pipan?*]. *Tsinghua Studies in Western Philosophy* [清华西方哲学研究] 1: 272–295.

Nisbett, R. E. (2003). *The geography of thought: How Asians and Westerners think differently . . . and why*. New York, NY: Free Press.

Norden, Bryan W. Van. (2004). "Review of Jean-Paul Reding, *Comparative Essays in Early Greek and Chinese Rational Thinking*." *Notre Dame Philosophical Reviews* Available at https://ndpr.nd.edu/news/comparative-essays-in-early-greek-and-chinese-rational-thinking/.

Osnos, Evan. (2008). "Angry Youth: The New Generation's Neocon Nationalists." *New Yorker* July 28, 2008. 28–37.

Page, Carl. (1991). "The Truth about Lies in Plato's Republic." *Ancient Philosophy* 1: 1–33.

Palmer, James. (2020). "Oh God, Not the Peloponnesian War Again." *Foreign Policy* July 28, 2020. Available at https://foreignpolicy.com/2020/07/28/oh-god-not-the-peloponnesian-war-again/.

Pan Honglin 潘洪林. (2000). "Why Scientific Reason Oversteps Value Reason—Another Criticism of Western Scientific Reason." [科学理性何以僭越价值理性—对西方科学理性的另一种批判 *Kexue lixing heyi jianyue jiazhi lixing—dui xifang kexue lixing de ling yi zhong pipan*]. *Ningxia Social Science* [宁夏社会科学] 6: 7–10.

Pan Wei 潘维. (2003). *The Rule of Law and "Democratic Superstition."* [法治与"民主迷信" *Fazhi yu "minzhu mixin"*]. Hong Kong: Hong Kong Social Sciences Press.

———. (2006). "Ancient Greece and Democracy." [古希腊与民主制度 *Gu xila yu minzhu zhidu*]. http://www.aisixiang.com/data/12365.html.

Pan Yue. (2020). "A Serious Misunderstanding of the 'Roots' of Civilization is the Biggest Issue in Today's Dispute Between China and the West." *The Paper, Cultural Aspects* [澎湃号 > 文化纵横] June 3, 2020. Available at https://www.sohu.com/a/400767099_788167.

Pangle, Thomas. (1983). "The Roots of Contemporary Nihilism and Its Political Consequences According to Nietzsche." *The Review of Politics* 45: 45–70.

Pei Wen 裴雯. (1998). "The Economic Characteristics of Athens in the Classical Period." [古典时期雅典的经济特征 *Gudian shiqi yadian de jingji tezheng*]. *Journal of Fudan University, Social Science Edition* [复旦学报, 社会科学版] 5: 130–34.

Peng Gonglian 彭公亮. (2001). "The Original Mission of Greek Philosophy and the Modern Mission of Philosophy." [希腊哲学的本源性使命及哲学的现代任务 *Xila zhexue de benyuan xing shiming ji zhexue de xiandai renwu*]. *Journal of Hanzhong Normal University, Social Sciences* [汉中师范学院学报, 社会科学] 1. Available at http://rdbk1.ynlib.cn:6251/qw/Paper/156584.

Peng, K. and R. E. Nisbett. (1999). "Culture, dialectics, and reasoning about contradiction." *American Psychologist* 54: 741–54.

Perelomov, L. S. (1977). "Mao, The Legalists, and the Confucianists." *Chinese Studies in History* 11: 64–95.

Perris, A. (1983). "Music as Propaganda: Art at the Command of Doctrine in the People's Republic of China." *Ethnomusicology* 27: 1–28.

Pines, Yuri. (2000). "'The One That Pervades the All' in Ancient Chinese Political thought: The Origins of 'The Great Unity' Paradigm." *T'oung Pao* 86: 280–324.

Pollock, Sheldon. (2010). "Comparison without Hegemony." In *The Benefit of Broad Horizons.* 185–204. Leiden: Brill.

Popper, Karl. (1971). *The Open Society and its Enemies.* Fifth revised edition. Princeton, NJ: Princeton University Press.

Pormann, Peter E. (2013). "Classical Scholarship and Arab Modernity." In *Modernity's Classics: Ruptures and Reconfigurations.* Edited by Humphreys and Wagner. 123–41. Heidelberg: Springer Nature.

Qiang Zha (2005). "Reading Xi's Modern Twist on Plato's 'The Republic.'" *Inside Higher Ed* March 9, 2005.

Qing Lianbin (青連斌). (2006). "Classification: Sociological Research and Definition." [階層: 社會學的研究與界說 *Jieceng: Shehuixue de yanjiu yu jieshuo*]. *Study Times* [學習時報], February 13.

Qiu Yue. (2004). "The Construction and Criticism of Plato's *Kallipolis*," *Journal of Anhui Police Vocational College* 1.

Ranieri, P. (2016). "Standing the Test of Time: Liberal Education in a Jesuit Tradition." *Traditions of Eloquence: The Jesuits and Modern Rhetorical Studies*. Edited by Cinthia Gannett, and John Brereton. 263–74. New York, NY: Fordham University Press.

Rawls, John. (1999). *Political Liberalism*. New York, NY: Columbia University Press.

Redding, Gordon. (2002). "The Capitalist Business System of China and its Rationale." *Asia Pacific Journal of Management* 19: 221–49.

Reding, Jean-Paul. (2004). *Comparative Essays in Early Greek and Chinese Rational Thinking*. New York, NY: Routledge.

Ren Xiao 任晓. (2004). "What is Rationalism?" [何谓理性主义? *Hewei lixing zhuyi?*]. *Chinese Journal of European Studies* [欧洲研究] 2: 148–52.

Renger, Almut-Barbara and Xin Fan, eds. (2018). *Receptions of Greek and Roman Antiquity in East Asia*. Leiden: Brill.

Ri Zhi 日知, ed. (1989). *The Study of the History of Ancient City-States*. [古代城邦史研究 *Gudai chengbangshi yanjiu*]. Beijing: People's Publishing House.

Ricci, Matteo. (1942–1949). "Storia dell'Introduzione del Cristianesimo in Cina." In *Documento originali concernenti Matteo Ricci e la storia delle prime relazioni tra l'Europa e la Cina, 1579–1615*. Edited by Pasquale M. D'Elia. Vol. 1, 36. Roma: La Libreria dello Stato. 3 vols.

———. (1985). *The True Meaning of the Lord of Heaven (T'ien-chu Shih-i)*. Translated by Douglas Lancashire, Peter Hu Kuochen, and Edward J. Malatesta. St. Louis, MO: Institute of Jesuit Sources.

Roland, Nadège. (2018). "Examining China's 'Community of Common Destiny.'" *Power 3.0*, January 23, 2018. Available at https://www.power3point0.org/2018/01/23/examining-chinas-community-of-destiny/.

Rong Guangyi 荣光怡. (2013). "The Enlightenment of Plato's Thoughts on Justice in the Construction of a Harmonious Society in my Country." [柏拉图的正义思想对我国构建和谐社会的启示 *Bolatu de hengyi sixiang dui woguo goujian hexie shehui de qishi*]. *Journal of Inner Mongolia University for Nationalities (Social Science Edition)* [内蒙古民族大学学报（社会科学版）] 1.

Rošker, Jana. (2013). "The Concept of Harmony in Contemporary P. R. China and in Modern Confucianism." *Asian Studies* 1: 3–20.

Rowett, Catherine. (2016). "Why the Philosopher Kings Will Believe the Noble Lie." *Oxford Studies in Ancient Philosophy* 50: 67–100.

Samons, Loren J. (2004). *What's Wrong with Democracy? From Athenian Practice to American Worship.* Berkeley, CA: University of California Press.

Sasaki, Takeshi. (2012). "Plato and Politeia in Twentieth-Century Politics." *Études platoniciennes* 9: 147–160.

Saussy, Haun. (2010). "Contestatory Classics in 1920s China." In *Classics and National Cultures.* Edited by Susan A. Stephens and Phiroze Vasunia. 258–267. New York, NY: Oxford University Press.

Schechter, Darrow. (2010). *The Critique of Instrumental Reason from Weber to Habermas.* New York, NY: Continuum.

Schluchter, Wolfgang. (1981). *The Rise of Western Rationalism: Max Weber's Developmental History.* Berkeley, CA: University of California Press.

Schmidt, J. (2000). "What Enlightenment Project?" *Political Theory* 28: 734–757.

Schneider, Axel. (2010). "The One and the Many: A Classicist Reading of China's Tradition and Its Role in the Modern World; An Attempt on Modern Chinese Conservatism." *Procedia: Social and Behavioral Sciences* 2: 7218–43.

Schwarcz, Vera. (1986). *The Chinese Enlightenment: Intellectuals and the Legacy of the May Fourth Movement of 1919.* Berkeley, CA: University of California Press.

Selby-Bigge, L. E., ed. (1962). *Inquiries Concerning Human Understanding and concerning the Principles of Morals.* Oxford, UK: Oxford University Press.

Semedo, Alvarez. (1996). [orig. 1667]. *Histoire universelle du grand royaume de la Chine.* Paris: Kiné.

Sen, Amartya. (2000). "East and West: The Reach of Reason." *New York Review of Books* 47: 33–38.

Seo, J. Mira. (2019). "Classics for All: Future Antiquity from a Global Perspective." *American Journal of Philology* 140: 699–715.

Shankman, Steven and Stephen Durrant. (2003). *The Siren and the Sage: Knowledge and Wisdom in Ancient Greece and China.* Eugene, OR: Wipf and Stock.

Sharpe, Matthew. (2013). "The Poetic Presentation of Philosophy: Leo Strauss on Plato's 'Symposium.'" *Poetics Today* 34: 563–60.

Shaw, Carl K.Y. (2017). "Towards a Radical Critique of Liberalism: Carl Schmitt and Leo Strauss in Contemporary Chinese Discourses." In *Carl Schmitt and Leo Strauss in the Chinese-Speaking World.* Edited by Marchal and Shaw. 37–57. Lanham, MD: Lexington Books.

Shen Sungchiao (2006). "Discourse on *guomin* ('the citizen') in late Qing China, 1895–1911." Translated by Hsiao Wen Chien. *Inter-Asia Cultural Studies* 7: 2–23.

Shen Sungchiao and Chien Y.S. Sechin (2006). "Turning Slaves into Citizens: Discourses of *Guomin* and the Construction of Chinese National Identity in the Late Qing Period." In *The Dignity of Nations: Equality, Competition, and Honor in East*

Asian Nationalism. Edited by John Fitzgerald and Sechin Y.S. Chien. 49–69. Hong Kong: Hong Kong University Press.

Shi Bin 石斌. (2002). "The Moral Appeal of Amoral Political Theories: The Paradox of Realist Perspectives on International Ethics." [非道德"政治论的道德诉求—— 现实主义国际关系伦理思想浅析 *"Fei daode" zhengzhi lun de daode suqiu-xianshi zhuyi guoji guanxi lunli sixiang qian xi*]. *Europe* [欧洲] 1: 1–11.

Shi Yihua 石义华and Lai Yonghai 赖永海. (2002). "Fracture and Integration of the Relationship between Instrumental Rationality and Value Rationality." [工具理性与价值理性关系的断裂与整合*Gongju lixing yu jiazhi lixing guanxi de duanlie yu zhenghe*]. *Journal of State Normal University, Philosophy and Social Sciences Edition* [徐州师范大学学报, 哲学社会科学版] 4: 100–103.

Shui Yidi 水亦棣. (2004). "Politics and Philosophy: Two Interpretations of Leo Strauss by Gan Yang and Liu Xiaofeng." [政治与哲学—— 甘阳和刘小枫对斯特劳斯的两种解读 *Zhengzhi yu zhexue——Gan Yang he Liu Xiaofeng dui si te lao si de liang zhong jiedu*]. *Open Times* [開放時代] 3.

Shun, Kwong-loi and David B. Wong, eds. (2004a). *Confucian Ethics: A Comparative Study of Self, Autonomy, and Community*. Cambridge, UK: Cambridge University Press.

Shun, Kwong-loi. (2004b). "Conception of the person in early Confucian thought." In *Confucian Ethics: A Comparative Study of Self, Autonomy, and Community*. Edited by Kwong-loi Shun and David B. Wong, 183–199. Cambridge, UK: Cambridge University Press.

Sima Qian. (1969). "*Qin Shihuang enji*." ("Annals of the Qin Shihuang"). In his *Shiji*. 245. Hong Kong: Zonghua shuju.

Smith, Steven B. (2006). *Reading Leo Strauss: Politics, Philosophy, Judaism*. Chicago, IL: University of Chicago Press.

Soles, David. (1995). "Confucius and The Role of Reason." *Journal of Chinese Philosophy* 22: 249–261.

Song Fugang 宋富钢. (1988). "Change in the Republic's Three Hereditary Classes and Its Historical Basis." [理想国三等级的世袭变异及其历史基础*Lixiang guo san dengji de shixi bianyi ji qi lishi jichu*]. *Academic Journal of Zhongzhou* [中州学刊] 1: 41–44.

Spalatin, Christofer A. (1975). "Matteo Ricci's Use of Epictetus's *Enchiridion*." *Gregorianum* 56: 551–7.

Spence, Jonathan D. (1969). *To Change China: Western Advisers in China 1620–1960*. Boston, MA: Penguin.

———. (1985). *The Memory Palace of Matteo Ricci*. New York, NY: Penguin Books.

———. (1991). *The Search for Modern China*. New York, NY: Norton.

Sprenger, Arnold. (1991). "A New Vision for China: The Case of Liu Xiaofeng." *Interreligio* 19: 2–10. Originally published in *China Heute* 9, no. 6 (1990): 157–71.

Standaert, Nicolas, ed. (2001). *Handbook of Christianity in China.* Volume 1. 635–1800. Leiden: Brill.

———. (2003). "The Transmission of Renaissance Culture in Seventeenth-Century China." *Renaissance Studies* 17: 367–91.

Standaert, Nicolas and Adrian Dudink, eds. (2002). *Chinese Christian texts from the Roman Archives of the Society of Jesus* [耶穌會羅馬檔案館明清天主教文獻 *Yesu hui luoma dang'an guan ming qing tianzhujiao wenxian*]. Taipei: Taipei Ricci Institute.

Statman, Alexander. (2019). "The First Global Turn: Chinese Contributions to Enlightenment World History." *Journal of World History* 30: 363–92.

Strauss, Leo. (1941). "Persecution and the Art of Writing." *Social Research* 8: 488–504.

———. (1952). *Persecution and the Art of Writing.* Chicago, IL: The University of Chicago Press.

———. (1964). *The City and Man.* Chicago, IL: The University of Chicago Press.

Sturniolo, Anthony C. (2016). "Influences of Western Philosophy and Educational Thought in China and their Effects on the New Culture Movement." Master's thesis, State University of New York College at Buffalo.

Su Xiaokang 苏晓康 and Wang Luxiang 王鲁湘. (1991). *Deathsong of the River: A Reader's Guide to the Chinese TV Series Heshang.* Translated by Richard Bodman and Pin Pin Wan. Ithaca, NY: Cornell East Asia Series.

Su Yu 蘇輿, ed. (1970 [1898]). *Selected Writings on Protecting the Doctrine* [翼教丛编 *Yijiao congbian*]. Taipei: Tailin Quaofen Publishing House.

Sun, Anna. (2013). *Confucianism as a World Religion: Contested Histories and Contemporary Realities.* Princeton, NJ: Princeton University Press.

Sun Ruoqian 孙若茜. (2018). "We Must Still Reflect on the 80s. The 30th Anniversary of the Editorial Board of 'Culture: China and the World.'" [依然要思考80年代—"文化: 中国与世界"编委会30周 年 *Yiran yao sikao 80 niandai—"wenhua: Zhongguo yu shijie" bian wei hui 30 zhounian*]. Available at http://ny.zdline.cn/h5/article/detail.do?artId=13596.

Suskind, Ron. (2004). "Faith, Certainty and the Presidency of George W. Bush." *The New York Times Magazine* October 17, 2004.

Syea, E. (2016). "Nietzsche on Greek and Indian philosophy." In *Universe and Inner Self in Early Indian and Early Greek Thought.* Edited by R. Seaford. 265–278. Edinburgh: Edinburgh University Press.

Tang Shiqi 唐士其. (2011). "The Middle Way and Power: China's Traditional Wisdom and Strauss's Classical Rationalism." [中道与权量— 中国传统智慧与施

特劳斯眼中的古典理性主义 *Zhongdao yu quanliang—zhongguo chuantong zhihui yu shitelaosi yanzhong de gudian lixing zhuyi*]. *International Politics Research* [国际政治研究] 48(2): 101–19.

Tang Xiaobing. (1996). *Global Space and the Nationalist Discourse of Modernity: The historical thinking of Liang Qichao.* Stanford, CA: Stanford University Press.

Tang Yijie 汤一介. (2015). *Confucianism, Buddhism, Daoism, Christianity and Chinese Culture.* China Academic Library. Springer: Heidelberg.

Taylor, Charles. (1995). "Two Theories of Modernity." *The Hastings Center Report* 25: 24–33.

Taylor, Martha C. (2010). *Thucydides, Pericles, and the Idea of Athens in the Peloponnesian War.* Cambridge, UK: Cambridge University Press.

Teon, Aris. (2016). "Mao Zedong, Legalism and Confucianism: Similarities and Differences." *The Greater China Journal* 5. Available at https://china-journal.org /2016/05/16/mao-zedong-legalism-confucianism-similarities-differences/.

Tu Wei-ming 杜维明. (1991). "The Enlightenment Mentality and the Chinese Intellectual Dilemma." In *Perspectives on Modern China: Four Anniversaries.* Edited by Kenneth Lieberthal et al. 103–118. Armonk, NY: M.E. Sharpe, Inc.

———. (2000). "Multiple modernities: A Preliminary Inquiry into the Implications of East Asian Modernity." In *Culture Matters: How Values Shape Human Progress.* Edited by Lawrence E. Harrison and Samuel P. Huntington. 256–66. New York, NY: Basic Books.

———. (2003). "Beyond the Enlightenment Mentality." In *Liberating faith: Religious Voices for Justice, Peace, and Ecological Wisdom.* Edited by Roger S. Gottlieb. 163–76. Lanham, MD: Rowman & Littlefield Publishers.

———. (2010). *The Global Significance of Concrete Humanity: Essays on the Confucian Discourse in Cultural China.* Delhi: Munshiram Manoharlal Pub Pvt.

Turner, Bryan. (2002). "The problem of cultural relativism for the sociology of human rights: Weber, Schmitt, and Strauss." *Journal of Human Rights* 1: 587–605.

Turner, Stephen. (2008). "Blind Spot? Weber's Concept of Expertise and the Perplexing Case of China." In *Max Weber Matters: Interweaving Past and Present.* Edited by Fanon Howell, Marisol L. Menendez, and David Chalcraft. 121–134. Burlington, VT: Ashgate.

Van Norden, Bryan W. and Kwan Im Thong Hood Cho. (2019). "Why the U.S. Needs to Understand Chinese Philosophy." *The Conversation* July 20, 2019. Available at https://www.usnews.com/ . . . 07 . . . /why-the-us-needs-to-understand-chinese -philosophy.

Venturi SJ, and Pietro Tacchi. (1911–1913 [1584]). "Letter to Giambattista Roman, Treasurer of the government in the Philippines, Zhaoqing, September 13, 1584." In *Opere Storiche del P. Matteo Ricci S.I. Comitato per ler onoranze nazionali con prolegomena.* Vol. 1: 45. Macerata: Giorgetti. 2 Vols.

Vittinghoff, Natascha. (2002). "Unity vs. Uniformity: Liang Qichao and the Invention of a 'New Journalism' for China." *Late Imperial China* 23: 91–143.

Wagner, Rudolf G. (2013). "A Classic Paving the Way to Modernity: The Ritual of Zhou in the Chinese Reform Debate Since the Taiping Civil War." In *Modernity's Classics: Ruptures and Reconfigurations.* Edited by Sarah C. Humphreys and Rudolph G. Wagner. 77–99. Heidelberg: Springer Nature.

Waley, A., trans. (1979). *Confucius: The Analects.* London, UK: Everyman.

Walker, D. P. (1972). *The Ancient Theology. Studies in Christian Platonism from the Fifteenth to the Eighteenth Century.* Ithaca, NY: Cornell University Press.

Wang Bei 王蓓. (2003). "The Ideological Focus of the Ideal State." [《理想国》的 思想聚焦 Lixiangguo de sixiang jujiao]. *Journal of Shanxi Normal University (Philosophy and Social Sciences)* [陕西师范大学学报（哲学社会科学版）]. 3.

Wang Bibo 王碧波. (2011). "A Comparative Study of the Theories of Harmonious Society between Plato and Confucius." [柏拉图与孔子和谐社会理论比较研 究 Bolatu yu kongzi hexie shehui lilun bijiao yanjiu]. Master's thesis, Sichuan University of Foreign Languages.

Wang Cenggu 仝增嘏, ed. (1983). *A History of Western Philosophy.* Shanghai: Shanghai People's Press.

Wang Chao 王超. (2014). "Educational Love: A Noble 'Lie' about Teachers' Love." [教育爱：师爱中的高贵"谎言"Jiaoyu ai: Shi ai zhong de gaogui "huangyang"]. *University Education* [大学教育科学] 4: 64–9.

Wang Guoyou 王国有. (2006). "Western Rationalism and Its Modern Destiny." [西方理性主义及其现代命运 Xifang lixing zhuyi ji qi xiandai mingyun]. *Jianghai Academic Journal* [江海学刊] 4: 55–60.

Wang Hai 王海. (1999). "Gu Zhun: Greek City-States and the Origin of Its Democracy." *Perspectives* 1(3).

Wang Huaiyu 王懷聿. (2009). "The Way of Heart: Mencius' Understanding of Justice." *Philosophy East and West* 59: 317–63.

Wang Hui 汪晖. (1989). "Prophesy and History: the 'May Fourth' Enlightenment Movement in Modern Chinese History." [预言与危机(上篇)— 中国现代历史 中的"五四"启蒙运动 Yuyan yu lishi: Zhongguo xiandai lishizhong de 'Wusi' qimenyundong]. *Literary Review* [文学评论] 3: 17–25.

———. (2001). "On Scientism and Social Theory in Modern Chinese Thought." In *Voicing Concerns: Contemporary Chinese Critical Inquiry.* Edited by Gloria Davies. 135–156. Lanham, MD: Rowman & Littlefield Publishers.

Wang Huiran 王慧然. (2010). "Rationalism and Western Modernity Crisis." [理性 主义与西方现代性危机 Lixing zhuyi yu xifang xiandai xing weiji]. *Academic Exchange* [学术交流] 6: 21–4.

Wang Jing 王瑾. (1996). *High Culture Fever: Politics, Aesthetics, and Ideology in Deng's China.* Berkeley, CA: University of California Press.

———. (2016). "The Polis and Its Guardians: A Reading of *Republic* II.347a–376c."
[柏拉图笔下的城邦與護衛者—《王制》第二卷374a–376c發微 *Bolatu bixia
de chengbang yu huwei zhe—«wangzhi» di er juan 374a–376c fawei*]. *The Chinese
Journal of Classical Studies* [古典研究] 26: 1–14.

Wang Junlin 王钧林. (1982). "On Aristotle's View of Country from 'The Politics.'"
[从《政治学》看亚里士多德的国家观 *Cong "zhengzhixue" kan yalishiduo de de
guojia guan*]. *Qilu Journal* [齐鲁学刊] 5: 55–60.

Wang, Kai 王 楷. (2015). "On the Dimension of Self-cultivation of Li in Xuncian
Philosophy." *KronoScope* 15: 93–117.

Wang Li 王利. (2009). "Strauss's Inspiration" [施特劳斯的启示 *Shitelaosi de qishi*].
Dushu [读书] October 10, 2009. 41–5.

Wang Qiaoling. (2000). "The Comparison of Moral Metaphysics between Kant and
Confucius." *New Theory of Tianfu* 4.

Wang Tao 王涛. (2012a). "Why is China interested in Strauss?" [中国为什么对列
奥·施特劳斯感兴趣? *Zhongguo weisheme dui lieao shitelaosi gan xingqu*]. *Social
Outlook* [社会观察] 8: 78–80.

———. (2012b). "Leo Strauss in China." *Claremont Review of Books* May 2, 2012. 12
(2): 80–82.

Wang Wenwu 王文武. (2009). "The Progressive Significance of Social Stratification
in Chongqing." [重慶社會分層的進步意義 *Chongqing shehui fenceng de jinbu
yiyi*]. *Guiyang Daily* [貴陽日報]. December 11, 2009.

Wang Xuan, Kasper Juffermans, and Caixia Du. (2016). "Harmony as Language
Policy in China: An Internet Perspective." *Language Policy* 15. Available at https://
link.springer.com/article/10.1007/s10993-015-9374-y.

Wang Xu 王旭. (2016). "An Interpretation of Aristotle's Theory of Government."
[解读亚里士多德的政体论 *Jiedu yalishiduo de de zhengti lun*]. *China University Humanities and Social Sciences Communication Network* [中國高校人文社
會科學傳播網]. 1–10. Available at https://www.sinoss.net/show.php
?contentid=73974.

Wang Yang 王揚. (2014). "The Harmonia of Plato's *Republic*." [柏拉圖 "理想國" 中
的和諧 *Bolatu "lixiang guo" zhong de hexie*]. *The Chinese Journal of Classical Studies* [古典研究] 1: 50–68.

Wang Yong. (2012). "An Interpretation of Plato's Theory of the Harmonious Society."
[柏拉图的和谐社会思想诠释 *Bolatu de hexie shehui sixiang quanshi*]. *Journal of
Tibet Nationalities Institute: Philosophy and Social Sciences Edition* [西藏民族学
院学报：哲学社会科学版] 10. Available at https://taoshumi.com/subject/D0
/2012/506998.html.

Wang Yuanming 王元明. (2009). "The Basis of Chinese and Western Political Theory in Human Nature." [中西政治学说的人性论基础 *Zhongxi zhengzhi xueshuo*

de renxinglun jichu]. *Journal of Tianjin Normal University, Social Science Edition* [天津师范大学学报] 3: 8–13.

Wardy, R. (2000). *Aristotle in China: Language, Categories and Translation.* Cambridge, UK: Cambridge University Press.

Wawrytko, S. (1982). "Confucius and Kant: The Ethics of Respect." *Philosophy East and West* 32: 237–57.

Webel, Charles P. (2014). *The Politics of Rationality: Reason through Occidental History.* New York, NY: Routledge.

Weber, Max. (1951). *The Religion of China: Confucianism and Taoism.* New York, NY: Free Press.

———. (1958). *The Protestant Ethic and the Spirit of Capitalism.* Translated by Talcott Parsons. New York, NY: Charles Scribner's Sons.

———. (1961). *General Economic History.* Translated by F. H. Knight. London: Collier Books.

———. (1978). *Economy and Society: An Outline of Interpretive Sociology.* Edited by Guenther Roth and Claus Wittich. Berkeley, CA: University of California Press.

———. (2004). *The Vocation Lectures.* Edited by David Owen and Tracy B. Strong. Translated by Rodney Livingstone. Indianapolis, IN: Hackett Books.

Wen Tao. (2006). "The Harmonious Society of Justice and the City State—On the Harmonious Society of Plato's 'Utopia.'" [正义城邦和谐社会— 论柏拉图《理想国》的和谐社会 *Zhengyi chengbang hexie shehui—lun Bolatu "lixiang guo" de hexie shehui*]. *Journal of Jiangnan University, Humanities and Social Sciences Edition* [江南大学学报（人文社会科学版)] 1.

Weng, Leihua. (2010). "Plato in Modern China: A Study of Contemporary Chinese Platonists." PhD Dissertation, University of South Carolina.

———. (2015a). "The Straussian Reception of Plato and Nationalism in China." *The Comparatist* 39: 313–34.

———. (2015b). "Re-locating Plato: A Chinese Translation and Interpretation of Plato's Symposium." *Intertexts* 19: 67–82.

Whimster, Sam and Scott Lash, eds. (2006). *Max Weber, Rationality and Modernity.* London, UK: Routledge.

Whitehead, A. N. (1979). *Process and Reality: An Essay in Cosmology.* New York, NY: Free Press.

Wilson, Bryan R., ed. (1970). *Rationality. Key Concepts in the Social Sciences.* Oxford, UK: Blackwell.

Wong, David. (2019). "Comparative Philosophy: Chinese and Western." *The Stanford Encyclopedia of Philosophy.* Edited by Edward N. Zalta. Available at https://plato .stanford.edu/archives/win2019/entries/comparphil-chiwes/.

Wu Enyu 吴恩裕. (1979). "On Political Thought of Plato and Aristotle." [论柏拉图和亚里士多德的政治思想 *Lun bolatu he yalishiduo de de zhengzhi sixiang*]. *Philosophical Research* [哲学研究] 3: 35–44.

Wu Gaojun 吴高君. (2003). "Economic Research of Ancient Greek City-States." [古希腊城邦经济研究 *Gu xila chengbang jingji yanjiu*]. *The Northern Forum* [北方论丛] 2: 34–37.

———. (2014). *The Great Dragon Fantasy: A Lacanian Analysis of Contemporary Chinese Thought*. Singapore: World Scientific Publishing Company.

Wu Huiyi. (2017). *Traduire la Chine au XVIIIe siècle: Les jésuites traducteurs de textes chinois et le renouvellement des connaissances européennes sur la Chine (1687–ca. 1740)*. Paris: Honoré Champion.

Wu Jia 吴佳. (2013). "Research on Instrumental Rationality and Value Rationality in Ideological and Political Education." [思想政治教育中的工具理性和价值理性研究 *Sixiang zhengzhi jiaoyu zhong de gongju lixing he jiazhi lixing yanjiu*]. Master's Thesis, Nanjing Forestry University.

Wu Junbin 伍俊斌. (2007). "On the basic theory of civil society construction." [公民社会建构的基础理论研究 *Gongmin shehui jiangou de jichu lilun yanjiu*]. Dissertation. Party School of the CPC Central Committee [中共中央党校].

Wu Qingping. (2020). "Doubts about He Xin's Critique of Ancient Greek History." http://webcache.googleusercontent.com/search?q=cache:3eKZPH75wSQJ:www.bbglobe.com/Article/Default.aspx?aid%3D111426&hl=en&gl=au&strip=1&vwsrc=0. Based on a snapshot of the page as it appeared on 2 Aug 2020 11:29:19 GMT but has since disappeared.

Wu Shuchen 武树臣. (1985). "On Aristotle's Concept of Rule of Law." [亚里士多德法治思想探索 *Yalishiduo de fazhi sixiang tansuo*]. *Law Studies* [法学] 5: 43–5.

Wu Xiuyi 吴修艺. (1988). *China's Cultural Fever.* [中国文化热 *Zhongguo wenhua re*]. Shanghai: Shanghai People's Press.

Wu Yuqin 吴于廑. (1963). "On the Two 'Objective Historians in the West.'" [论西方古今两个"客观"史学家 *Lun xifang gujin liang ge "keguan" shixue jia*]. *Jianghan Journal* [江汉学报] 6: 30–9.

Wu Zhiqiang 吴志强. (1991). "River Elegy, Student Movements, and Cultural Changes." [河殇, 學潮, 文化變遷 *Heshang, xuechao, wenhua bianqian*]. *China Spring* [中國之春] 98 (July): 63–5.

Xia Xingyou 夏兴有. (2018). "The Cultural Genes of Chinese Roads." [中国道路的文化基因 *Zhongguo daolu de wenhua jiyin*]. *Guangming Daily* [光明日报] September 17, 2018.

Xia, Florence C. (2002). *Sojourners in a Strange Land: Jesuits and Their Scientific Missions in Late Imperial China*. Chicago, IL: The University of Chicago Press.

Xiao Fan 萧凡. (1980). "Is Plato the 'First Communist Theorist?'" [柏拉图是'第一个 共产主义理论家'吗? *Bolatu shi 'di yi ge gongchan zhuyi lilun jia ma?*]. *Jinan Journal Philosophy and Social Sciences Edition* [暨南学报, 哲学社会科学版] 4: 71–4.

Xiao, Xiaosui 萧小穗. (2005). "Intellectual Communication East and West: A Historical and Rhetorical Approach." *Intercultural Communication Studies* 15: 41–52.

Xiao, Yang. 萧陽. (2002). "Liang Qichao's Political and Social Philosophy." In *Contemporary Chinese Philosophy*. Edited by Chun-Ying Chen and Nicholas Bunnin. 17–39. Oxford, UK: Wiley-Blackwell.

Xie Huiyuan 谢惠媛. (2014). "The Moral Rationality and Validity of Political Behavior—Based on the Comparison of Plato and Machiavelli Thoughts." [政治行 为的道德合理性与有效性— 基于柏拉图与马基雅维里思想的比较 *Zhengzhi xingwei de daode heli xing yu youxiao xing—jiyu bolatu yu majiya wei li sixiang de bijiao*]. *Gansu Social Sciences* [甘肃社会科学] 5: 49–52.

Xin Fan. (2018). "Imagining Classical Antiquity in Twentieth-Century China." In *Receptions of Greek and Roman Antiquity in East Asia*. Edited by Almut-Barbara Renger and Xin Fan. 202–18. Leiden: Brill.

Xu Datong 徐大同. (1981). "My Humble Opinions on the Research Objects of Political Science—An Investigation of the History of Research Objects." [关于政 治学研究对象的浅见— 政治学研究对象的史的考察 *Guanyu zhengzhi xue yan jiu duixiang de qianjian——zhengzhi xue yan jiu duixiang de shi de kaocha*]. *Journal of Tianjin Normal University* [天津师院学报] 6: 39–42.

Xu Guiquan 徐贵权. (2003). "On Value Rationality." [论价值理性 *Lun jiazhi lixing*]. *Journal of Nanjing Normal University, Social Science Edition*. [南京师大学报, 社 会科学版] 5: 10–14.

Xu Jian 徐戬. (2010). "The Noble Competition." [高贵的竞赛 *Gaogui de jingsai*]. In *The Quarrel between the Ancients and the Moderns and the Self-consciousness of Civilization: Strauss in the Context of China* [古今之争与文明自觉: 中国语境中 的施特劳斯 *Gujin zhizheng yu wenming zijue: Zhongguo yu jingzhong de shitelaosi*]. Edited by Xu Jian. 1–33. Shanghai: East China Normal University Press.

Xu Jilin 许纪霖. (2000). "The Fate of an Enlightenment—Twenty Years in the Chinese Intellectual Sphere (1978–98)." Translated by Geremie R. Barme with Gloria Davies. *East Asian History* 20: 169–86.

Xu Songyan 徐松岩. (1998). "There is No 'Industrial and Commercial City State' in the Ancient World." [古代世界不存在 '工商业城邦' *Gudai shijie bu cunzai 'gongshangye chengbang'*]. *Journal of Chongqing Normal University, Philosophy and Social Sciences Edition* [重庆师范大学学报(哲学社会科学版)] 1: 103–6.

Xu Tianshi 徐天使. (2010). "The Problem of the Noble Lie in the Ideal State." [理想 国中的谎言问题 *Lixiang guo zhong de huangyan wenti*]. *Knowledge Economy* [知识经济] 12: 175–176.

Xu Xiaoxu 徐晓旭. (2004). "The Concept of 'Nation' in Ancient Greece." [古希腊人的"民族"概念 Gu xila ren de "minzu" gainian]. Journal of World Peoples Studies [世界民族] 2: 35–40.

Xu Yu 徐瑜 and Qian Zaixiang 钱在祥. (1981). "Aristotle's Writings in China." [亚里士多德的著作在中 Yalishiduo de de zhuzuo zai zhongguo]. Journal of Sichuan Society for Library Science [四川图书馆学报] 1: 51–54.

Xu, Ben. (2001). "Postmodern-Postcolonial Criticism and Pro-Democracy Enlightenment." Modern China 27: 117–47.

Xu, Keqian. (2006). "Early Confucian Principles: The Potential Theoretic Foundation of Democracy in Modern China." Asian Philosophy 16: 135–48.

Xuyang Jingjing. (2013). "Confucius Goes Green." Global Times, Dec. 12, 2013. Available athttps://www.pressreader.com/china/global-times/20131212/281517928930544.

Yang Guorong. (2019). "The Idea of Reason and Rationality in Chinese Philosophy." In his Philosophical Horizons: Metaphysical Investigation in Chinese Philosophy. 178–96. Brill: Leiden.

Yang Jun 杨军 and Zuo Jianhui 左建辉. (2007). "The Development Vein of Western Rationalism." [西方理性主义的发展脉络 Xifang lixing zhuyi de fa zhan mailuo]. Journal of Baoding Teachers College [保定师范专科学校学报] 20: 8–11.

Yang Rui 杨锐, Xie Meng 谢梦, and Wen Wen 文雯. (2019). "Pilgrimage to the West: Modern Transformations of Chinese Intellectual formation in Social Sciences." Higher Education 77: 815–29.

Yang Xiao. (2002). "Liang Qichao's Political and Social Philosophy." In Contemporary Chinese Philosophy. Edited by Chung-Ying Chen and Nicholas Bunnin. 17–39. Oxford, UK: Blackwell.

Yang Xiaolin. (2001). "The Ideal State, the Great World and the Well-off Society—On the Political Ideals of Plato and Confucius." [理想国、大同世界和小康社会— 论柏拉图和孔子的政治理想 Lixiang guo, datong shijie he xiaokang shehui—lun bolatu he kongzi de zhengzhi lixiang]. Journal of Guangxi University for Nationalities (Philosophy and Social Sciences) [广西民族大学学报 (哲学社会科学版)]. 12.

Yang, Mayfair Meihui. (2002). "The Resilience of Guanxi and Its New Deployments: A Critique of Some New Guanxi Scholarship." The China Quarterly 170: 459–76.

Yang, S. and B. Stening. (2013). "Mao Meets the Market." Management International Review 53: 419–48.

Yang, Sheng-keng 杨深坑. (1989). "Tao, Logos, and Communicative Rationality in the Educational Process." Bulletin of Graduate Institute of Education, Taiwan Normal University 31: 315–37.

Yi Ning 易宁 and Li Yongming 李永明. (2005). "Thucydides's Theory of Human Nature and his Outlook on History." [修昔底德的人性说及其历史观 *Xiuxidide de renxing shuo ji qi lishi guan*]. *Journal of Beijing Normal University, Social Sciences* [北京师范大学学报, 社会科学版] 6: 79–86.

Yong Huang. (2011). "Can Virtue Be Taught and How? Confucius on the Paradox of Moral Education." *Journal of Moral Education* 40: 141–59.

Yu Jiyian and Nicholas Bunnin. (2001). "Saving the Phenomena: An Aristotelian Method in Comparative Philosophy." In *Two Roads to Wisdom? Chinese and Analytic Philosophical Traditions*. Edited by Bo Mou. 293–312. Chicago, IL: Open Court.

Yu Jiyuan 余纪元. (1998). "Virtue: Confucius and Aristotle." *Philosophy East and West* 48: 323–47.

———. (2004). "The Chinese Encounter with Greek Philosophy." In *Greek Philosophy in the New Millennium*. Edited by Livio Rossetti. 187–198. Sankt Augustin, Germany: Academia Verlag.

———. (2005). "The Beginning of Ethics: Confucius and Socrates." *Asian Philosophy* 15: 173–89.

———. (2014). "Feng Youlan and Greek Philosophy." *Journal of Chinese Philosophy* 41: 55–73.

Yu Liu. (2014). "Adapting Catholicism to Confucianism: Matteo Ricci's Tianzhu Shiyi." *The European Legacy* 19: 43–59.

Yu, Shirley Ze. (2019). "In Africa, the Beijing Consensus is Pushing Confucius over Plato." *LSE* September 18, 2019. Available at https://blogs.lse.ac.uk/africaatlse /2019/09/18/africa-beijing-consensus-confucius-plato-education/.

Yu Ying. (2015). "Classical Studies is Not the Way Liu Xiaofeng and his Associates Do It." [古典学 不是刘小枫他们搞的那套 *Gudianxue bushi Liu Xiaofeng tamen gaode natao*]. *Critical News* [古典学], February 7, 2015.

Zarrow, Peter G. (1997). "Liang Qichao and the Notion of Civil Society in Republican China." In *Imagining the People: Chinese Intellectuals and the Concept of Citizenship, 1890–1920*. Edited by Joshua Fogel and Peter G. Zarrow. 232–57. New York, NY: M.E. Sharpe, Inc.

Zeng Bing 曾冰. (2007). "Summary of Western Rationalism." [西方理性主义述评 *Xifang lixing zhuyi shuping*]. *Journal of the Postgraduates of Zhongnan University of Economics and Law* [中南财经政法大学研究生学报] 6: 156–60.

Zeng Zhaoming 曾昭明. (2016). "Fukuyama on Trump—The 'Chinese Moment' after the 'End of History?'" [曾昭明专欄: 福山論川普—「歷史終結」後的「中國時刻」? *Fushan lun chuan pu—'lishi zhongjie' hou de 'zhongguo shike'*?] November 20, 2016. Available at https://www.upmedia.mg/news_info.php?SerialNo =7576.

Zhang Bobo 张波波. (2016). "The Socratic Elenchus." [蘇格拉底式辯駁 *sugeladi shibian bofa*]. *Chinese Journal of Classical Studies* [古典研究] 28:1–21.

Zhang Desheng 张德胜, Jin Yaoji 金耀基, and Chen Haiwen 陈海文. (2001). "On the Golden Mean: The Reason of Instrumental Reason, Value Reason and Communication Reason." [论中庸理性: 工具理性、价值理性和沟通理性之 *Lun zhongyong lixing: Gongju lixing, jiazhi lixing he goutong lixing zhi*]. *Social Science Research* [社会学研] 2: 33–48.

Zhang Foquan 张佛泉. (1971). "The Formation of Liang Qichao's Concept of State." [梁啟超國家觀念之形成 *Liang qichao guojia guannian zhi xingcheng*]. *Journal of Politics* [政治學報] 1: 1–66.

Zhang Guangzhi 张广智. (1982). "On Thucydides's Naive Materialism." [试论修昔底德朴素唯物主义的历史观 *Shilun xiuxidide pusu weiwu zhuyi de lishi guan*]. *Fudan Journal, Social Sciences Edition* [复旦学报, 社会科学版] 4: 108–12.

Zhang Hui 张辉. (2003). "Introduction to the Chinese Translation." [中译本前言 *Zhong yiben qianyi*]. In Plato's *Symposium* [柏拉图会议*Bólātú huìyì*]. Translated by Liu Xiaofeng. 1–15. Beijing: Huaxia Publishing House.

Zhang Jian 张建. (2007). "From Inside Harmony of Mind to Harmony of Outside World—a Key to Plato's *Republic*." [从心灵内部的和谐到外部世界的和谐—把打开柏拉图《理想国》*Cong xinling neibu de hexie dao waibu shijie de hexie—yi ba dakāii Bolatu 'lixiang guo' de yaoshi*]. *Journal of Kunming University* [昆明大学学报] 3.

Zhang Liang 张亮. (2001). *The Tiananmen Papers*. Edited by Andrew J. Nathan and Perry Link. New York, NY: Public Affairs.

Zhang Lili 张立立. (2013). "To Whom Does the 'Noble Lie' Lie?" [向谁而说的'高贵的谎言' *Xiang shei er shuo de 'gaogui de huangyan'*]. *World Philosophy* [世界哲学] 1: 60–8.

Zhang Longxi 張隆溪. (1992). *The Tao and the Logos: Literary Hermeneutics, East and West*. Durham: Duke University Press.

———. (1998). *Mighty Opposites: From Dichotomies to Differences in the Comparative Study of China*. Stanford, CA: Stanford University Press.

———. (2015). "Meaning, Reception, and the Use of Classics: Theoretical Considerations in a Chinese Context." *Intertexts* 19: 5–21.

Zhang Ming. (2011). "A Reflection on the Crisis of Modern Liberal Democracy from the Perspective of Leo Strauss's Concept of Regime." [从施特劳斯政体观反思现代自由民主制的危机 *Cong shitelaosi zhengti guan fansi xiandai ziyou minzhuzhide weiji*]. *Journal of Huazhong University of Science and Industry, Social Science Edition* [华中科技大学学, 社会科学版] 1: 40–7.

Zhang Shuang 张爽. (2009). *Study on the Background of Modern Chinese Intellectuals*. [现代化背景下的中国知识分子研究 *Xiandaihua beijing xia de zhongguo zhishi fenzi yanjiu*]. Harbin: Heilongjiang University Press.

Zhang Wentao 张文涛. (2010). "Strauss, Classics, and the Chinese Problem." [施特劳斯、古典学与中国问题 Shitelaosi, gujianxue yu zhongguo wenti]. In *The Controversy between Ancient and Modern and Civilization Consciousness: Strauss in the Chinese Context.* Edited by Xu Jian. [古今之争与文明自觉: 中国语境中的施特劳斯]上海: 华东师范大学出版社 Gujin zhizheng yu wenming zijue: Zhongguo yu jingzhong de Shitelaosi]. 233–63. Shanghai: East China Normal University Press.

Zhang Xiaomei 张小妹. (2009). "Justice and Harmony: The Inspirational Significance of Plato's Theory of Justice." [正义与和谐—柏拉图正义理论的启示意义 Zhèngyì yǔ héxié—Bólātú zhèngyì lǐlùn de qǐshì yìyì] *Journal of Hunan Institute of Humanities, Science and Social Science Edition* [湖南人文科技学院学报] 1.

Zhang Xudong. (1997). *Chinese Modernism in the Era of Reforms. Cultural Fever, Avant-garde Fiction, and the New Chinese Cinema.* Durham, NC: Duke University Press.

———. (1998). "Nationalism, Mass Culture, and Intellectual Strategies in Post-Tiananmen China." *Social Text* 55: 109–40.

———. (2010). "Strauss in China: A Summary of Research and Controversy." [施特劳斯在中国: 施特劳斯研究和论争综述 Shitelaosi zai zhongguo: Shitelaosi yanjiu he lunzheng zongshu]. In *The Controversy between Ancient and Modern and Civilization Consciousness: Strauss in the Chinese Context* [古今之争与文明自觉: 中国语境中的施特劳斯]上海: 华东师范大学出版社 Gujin zhizheng yu wenmin gzijue: Zhongguo yu jingzhong de Shitelaosi]. Edited by Xu Jian. 120–29. Shanghai: East China Normal University Press.

Zhang Yiwu 正文快照. (1996). "Humanistic Spirit: The Last Mythology." [人文精神: 最后的神话 Rénwén jīngshén: Zuìhòu de shénhuà]. In *In Search of the Human Spirit* [人文精神寻思录 Renwen jingshen xunsilu]. Edited by Wang Xiaoming 王晓明. 137–41. Beijing: Wenhui Publishing House.

Zhang Zhongming 章忠民. (2000). "The Advancing and Deduction of the Rational Concept of Ancient Greece." [古希腊哲学中理性观念的提出及其演绎 Gu xila zhexue zhong lixing guannian de tichu ji qi yanyi]. *Journal of Fujian Teachers University, Philosophy and Social Sciences Edition* [福建师范大学学报: 哲学社会科学版] 4: 32–9.

Zhao Fujie 赵馥洁. (2001). "On the Unity of Value Rationality and Instrumental Rationality in Chinese Philosophy." [论中国哲学中价值理性与工具理性的统合意识 Lun zhongguo zhexue zhong jiazhi lixing yu gongju lixing de tonghe yishi]. *Journal of the Humanities* [人文杂志] 4: 41–7.

Zhao Suisheng 赵穗生. (1997). "Chinese Intellectuals' Quest for National Greatness and Nationalistic Writing in the 1990s." *The China Quarterly* 152: 725–45.

Zheng Qi. (2013). "Carl Schmitt, Leo Strauss, and the Issue of Political Legitimacy in China." *American Foreign Policy Interests* 35: 254–64.

Zheng Xiaowu and Zheng Jianping 曾小五、曾建平. (2010). "A Comparison of Confucius's and Plato's Conceptions of a Harmonious Society." [孔子和柏拉图关于和谐社会构想的比较 Kongzi he bolatu guanu hexie shehui gouxiang de bijiao]. *Guangming Daily* [光明日报]. February 23, 2010.

Zhou Lian 周濂. (2009). "The Most Fashionable and the Most Relevant: A Review of Contemporary Chinese Political Philosophy." *Diogenes* 56: 128–37.

Zhou Yiqun 周轶群. (2017). "Greek Antiquity, Chinese Modernity, and the Changing World Order." In *Chinese Visions of World Order: Tianxia, Culture, and World Politics*. Edited by Ban Wang. 106–28. Durham, NC: Duke University Press.

———. (2022). "Which Tradition, Whose Authority? Quests and Tensions in Contemporary Chinese Reception of Greek Antiquity." Forthcoming in *KNOW*.

Zhu Hanguo 朱汉国. (1999). "Inventing New Paradigms: Characteristics and Implications of Intellectual Transformations During the May Fourth Movement." [创建新范式: 五四时期学术转型的特征及意义 Chuangjian xin fanshi: Wusi shiqi xueshu zhuanxing de tezheng ji yiyi]. *Journal of Beijing Normal University, Social Sciences Edition* [北京师范大学学报, 社会科学版] 152: 50–7.

Zong Chenghe 宗成河. (2002). "Comments on Liu Xiaofeng's interpretation of Nietzsche." [评刘小枫的尼采解读 Ping Liu Xiaofeng de nicai jiedu]. *Zhejiang Academic Journal* [浙江学刊] 5: 134–44.

Zuckert, Catherine and Michael Zuckert. (2006). *The Truth about Leo Strauss: Political Philosophy and American Democracy*. Chicago, IL: University of Chicago Press.

Zuo Jingquan 左景权. (1987). "Discussion of the Translation of Greek Classics." [漫谈希腊古典名著的翻译 Mantan xila gudian mingzhu de fanyi]. *Social Science Front* [社会科学战线] 1: 224–32.

INDEX

New Youth (Xin qingnian). See Chen
   Duxiu
Newton, Isaac, 112
Ni Peimin, 119
Nie Minli, 15, 81, 144–45
Nietzsche, Friedrich, 132
Nisbett, R. E., 121
Noble Lie, 12–13, 87–98, 135, 141, 158,
   171–72, 176; in American politics, 99,
   172; harmony as, 102–3. See also
   Kallipolis
nomos, 139, 152
Nuremburg trials, 114

Olympic Games, 54, 116
On Grouping (Shuo Qun). See Liang
   Qichao
On the New Citizen (Xinmin Shuo).
   See Liang Qichao
On the Origin of China's Weakness
   (Zhongguo jiruo suyuan lun). See
   Liang Qichao
One Belt, One Road, 183
Opium Wars, 10, 17, 29, 46
opposites, 121–22

Palmer, James, 183
Pan Wei, 50, 56, 70–72, 92
Pan Yue, 56, 73–76
Paul of Tarsus, 78
Pericles, 55, 58
philosopher-king, Platonic, 27, 86–92,
   102, 142–43, 164, 171
philosophy, as a western term, 191n9
Piraeus, bought by Chinese, 183
Plato, 98, 117, 176–79; among the Jesuits,
   27–28; Gorgias, 152; legacy of, 83;
   Laws, 152; musical harmony in,
   151–53, 226n32; notion of the Forms
   in; Phaedo, 152; on rationality, 114–15;

Republic, 11, 83–84, 98–100, 103,
   135–37, 142, 151–52, 154, 170–71, 176,
   178; Symposium, 136. See also justice
polis, 32, 43–44, 56, 80, 101; in the
   ancient east, 66–67, 75
Popper, Karl, 89–90
Pu-yi, 30, 197n51

Qiang Lianbin, 95
Qiang Zha, 102
Qing dynasty, fall of, 2, 11
Qiushi, 63–65
quarrel between the ancients and the
   moderns, 133

rationality: analogical, 120–21; instru-
   mental, 13, 105–9, 216n 115–17; 216n47;
   Enlightenment, 37, 106, 110–13;
   Platonic, 86–87, 117, 124, unConfucian,
   120–2; value, 105. See also logic
rationalization, 213n11
Rawls, John, 2, 132
reception, as use or abuse, 189n3
ren, 118–19, 160, 166–67, 171, 177
Ricci, Matteo, 17, 19–28; "Twenty-Five
   Paragraphs" of, 21–22
Rites Controversy, 195n11
River Elegy, 42–47, 49
Rong Guangyi, 154
Rousseau, 2, 30; understanding of
   democracy, 200n88
Rowett, Catherine, 91

Sappho, 178
Schall von Bell, Johann Adam, 18
Schmitt, Carl, 131
Semedo, Alvarez, 19
Seneca, Lucius Annaeus, 196n25
Shakespeare, 73
Shen Hong, 146

A NOTE ON THE TYPE

This book has been composed in Arno, an Old-style serif typeface in the classic Venetian tradition, designed by Robert Slimbach at Adobe.